Disruptive In

Disruptive Inclusion

*Why and How Christian Adult
Learning is for Everyone*

Jen Smith

scm press

© Jen Smith 2024

Published in 2024 by SCM Press
Editorial office
3rd Floor, Invicta House,
110 Golden Lane,
London EC1Y 0TG, UK

www.scmpress.co.uk

SCM Press is an imprint of Hymns Ancient & Modern Ltd
(a registered charity)

Hymns Ancient & Modern® is a registered trademark of
Hymns Ancient & Modern Ltd
13A Hellesdon Park Road, Norwich,
Norfolk NR6 5DR, UK

British Library Cataloguing in Publication data
A catalogue record for this book is available
from the British Library

ISBN 978-0-334-06533-3

Typeset by Regent Typesetting
Printed and bound in Great Britain by
CPI Group (UK) Ltd

Contents

Acknowledgements

It is impossible to identify each time, person, place and event that has influenced this book. Although projects like this are not generally acknowledged as team sports, I am deeply grateful that God has given me the following 'teams' and for the ways (both obvious and hidden) they have loved, challenged and supported me as I have written. 'Thank you' feels deeply insufficient.

Team Gradden/Smith/Occomore. Thank you for being the first ones to teach me that I could achieve anything I put my mind to and daring me to go for it. You make me braver.

Team Manchester. Thank you for helping me realize that challenge and joy are often the same thing. You made me more determined.

Team Samuel. Thank you for not taking no for an answer. Your insistence that I have something to offer makes me dig deep when it gets tough.

Team Pasadena. Thank you for sharpening my focus and deepening my resolve. You made me more appreciative.

Team KST. Thank you for showing me your potential and posing important questions that demand a better response. You make me proud.

Team Trish. Thank you for being so good at what you do. You release me to be the best of who I am.

Team Champagne Mondays. Thank you for helping me practise the extraordinary in the ordinary. You helped bring many of this project's themes to life.

Team Source. Thank you for setting a different kind of table and making a place for me, whether I am OK or not. You make me hopeful.

Team Friday Morning. Thank you for showing me that hope is grounded in commitment and patience. You made me kinder.

Team Queen's. Thank you for showing me new possibilities. You help me imagine better things to come.

Team Hull. Thank you to the wider community of John's colleagues who have encouraged this work – particularly Trevor Cooling and ISREV members, thank you for your generosity of spirit. You made me feel welcome. To Marilyn and the Hull family, thank you for your faith in me. I hope I have captured something of John's spirit, as I have certainly caught a measure of his contagious determination. You have inspired me.

Team Supervision. Thank you for offering great examples of *in-between* teaching and learning. You have demonstrated to me how excellence is often achieved through compromise and making space for the unexpected, not via single-minded self-promotion and interest. You have made me a better writer, and hopefully also a better person.

Team SCM: Thank you for believing that this theme needs a wider airing and that my work might play a role in that. Your diligence and attention to detail has made this better than it ever would have been.

Prologue

This book is about learning: how learning happens and how learning can be more effectively encouraged in a range of settings, particularly in adults and even more particularly (but not exclusively) in adults who identify as Christians. Learning is understood in many ways but it plays an important role, in various forms, in the understanding and practice of Christian faith across the Church. Despite this, many learning resources and guides, designed for (or aimed at) Christians, are created with professional educators and institutions in mind. In the majority of cases, they offer guidance on what should be taught and perhaps who should do the teaching, but they rarely explore the practicalities of how effective Christian adult learning happens (more on exactly what this means soon) or offer advice on how it could be improved. This book is an attempt to address this.

Ideally, I would love to help you wrestle with the issues raised here over coffee and cake and explore their potential consequences for learning and teaching in your contexts. However, I am reliably informed that, despite my prodigious cake-eating ability, this is unrealistic. So, as the next best option, I have made every effort to write this book conversationally, with the aim of facilitating a multi-directional dialogue with ourselves, each other, the Bible, wider Christian tradition, and God. I encourage you, wherever possible, to carefully examine the ideas presented here as one part of a much larger, and ongoing, dialogue. Fully entering into this process will (hopefully) raise a range of questions for you, including but not limited to: what is Christian adult learning? What makes it Christian? Who is included and excluded from conversations about it and about improving it? What questions need to be asked and honestly answered to ensure learning is more accessible for everyone, both in churches and in other settings? If this book helps you to explore some of these issues, or even become aware that they exist, I will consider it successful.

Readers of this book will probably fall into the following categories. You may be a teacher, tutor, preacher, lecturer or another form of educator. The topics discussed here are designed to challenge, inspire and raise a range of questions for all Christian educators, regardless of your subject or setting. Ultimately, however, this book is primarily designed with non-professional Christian learners and educators in mind. By non-professional, I mean that Christian adult learning is not limited to those on formal theology courses or qualified educators. Nor does it only apply to those with official teaching or formational roles in churches. Rather, the ideas discussed in this book aim to enrich conversation, understanding and practice of Christian adult learning in all the ways and places it happens. Of course, Christian adult learning happens in universities and colleges, theological education institutions (TEIs) and in church services, but equally importantly, Christian adults are learning in playgrounds as they wait for their children to come out of school, at the gym and the supermarket, at concerts and on train journeys and around the kitchen table. Whatever your experience of formal education, if you think that becoming a better learner (which is not the same as being clever!) is an important part of following Jesus (or even if, considering this now for the first time, it strikes you that it could play a role) – this book is for you. Finally, if you are not a person of Christian faith, but are interested in investigating the potential connections between Christianity and learning, your voice is particularly needed in this conversation. Regardless of how you participate in this dialogue, I am so glad you are here!

This book has three parts, split into eight chapters, an interlude, an epilogue and a selection of *selahs* (explained below). Part I begins by redirecting the conversation. It asks exactly how Christian adult learning has been understood and then presents a case for what I call a *disruptive-inclusive* approach to Christian adult learning and the essential reasons why I think it is worth exploring. The interlude then offers an extended example from the fourth Gospel of how disruptive inclusion is grounded in the biblical narrative.

Building on this, Part II redefines the task of Christian adult learning by explaining why disruptive inclusion can be considered a Christian approach to learning, specifically drawing on the Bible, the nature and character of God and the identity and character of the Christian Church. Chapter 5 then suggests that the Christian basis for disruptive inclusion cannot be fully expressed by providing new answers to old questions; it requires that we ask different kinds of questions about the aims and functions of Christian adult learning with the help of some key imagery and metaphors. In particular, we will explore how images such as crossing thresholds, pilgrimage, home and playful poetics can help us better imagine the *where* and *why* of disruptive inclusion.

In Part III, the discussion focuses on how a disruptive-inclusive approach reshapes the practicalities of teaching and learning in various settings. Chapters 6, 7 and 8 ask what disruptive-inclusive teaching and learning looks, sounds and feels like in different learning settings and modes. Finally, the epilogue wrestles with how we can continue and expand the conversation even further.

Among the various parts and chapters, you will also discover a selection of asides called *selahs*. Nobody really knows what the word *selah* signifies, but it appears repeatedly and seemingly randomly throughout the Psalms (see, for example: Pss 50.6, 62.4, 84.4, 140.8 and many more). One of the most popular ideas is that *selah* indicates a kind of pause in the music or a contemplative moment for reflection. My favourite suggestion is that it shows the places where the choir and musicians were forced to stop singing and playing because the music leader broke a string![1] I use the term here similarly – the *selahs* are short asides, taking a break from the main flow of

the argument to add something a little different before getting
back to the main point.

Getting the most out of this book

1. As you read, keep in mind that in many places the medium
   may be the message. In other words, disruptive inclusion
   may be modelled or experienced as well as explained! If you
   find that particular chapters or sections go in unexpected
   directions, or some of the ideas jar with your preconceptions
   or raise significant questions for you, try not to just agree or
   disagree with my claims or explanations. Name the potential
   tensions or questions raised for you and remain present to
   them and to God. Notice your responses, note them down
   and return to them later. Keep in mind that identifying
   why you respond in a particular way is generally far more
   important than how you respond.
2. Read with a critical (analytical, not negative) eye and a
   pencil, pen or stylus. Circle key ideas. Note in the margins
   where you have questions or more thinking is needed. Draw
   arrows or stars where you identify connections to your own
   experience or context(s). Note how you would respond or
   questions you would ask if we were discussing over coffee
   and cake. Think about the learners in your classroom, congregation, community or home who are both the most and
   least likely to benefit from the various arguments presented.
3. In this book you will encounter a wide array of voices. This
   is a deliberate choice and an attempt to model how rich
   learning can become when you learn with others. And so
   my heartfelt plea is that you will add your own voice to my
   voice and the many conversation partners I include in this
   book. Read with those who think differently to you. Read
   with those who love exploring new ideas and approaches
   and those who are naturally sceptical of change. By 'others',
   I do not just mean family, friends and wider community, but
   also other writers, commentators, bloggers, podcasters and

speakers. I have avoided cluttering the pages with lots of technical footnotes and instructions. However, at the end of each chapter those who wish to delve deeper will find signposts to both similar and contrasting views. Practise putting diverse voices in dialogue with each other. Ask how others' views both align and conflict with the suggestions presented here. If all else fails, get in touch with me; maybe we can put together a plan for improving Christian adult learning in your context(s) over coffee and cake after all!

4. If nothing else, allow the words of these chapters to wash over you as an encouragement from a fellow learner-pilgrim, and a provocation that Christian adult learning settings across the world need thinkers, pray-ers, do-ers and learners just like you! My prayer is that your journey into disruptive-inclusive Christian adult learning is as life-giving as mine has been so far.

Jen Smith, summer 2023, Derby, UK

Notes

1 This is how Old Testament scholar John Goldingay describes *selah*: 'Rise (*selâ*). Dictionaries usually connect the word *selâ* with the root *sālal*, 'rise'. It comes at the end of lines in psalms without any consistent patterning. While it sometimes comes at the end of sections (Ps. 66), it often comes in the middle of a section or in the middle of a sentence (Pss. 67; 68). It may be a liturgical or musical direction ('raise the voice'?), but we do not know. I understand that David Allan Hubbard advocated the theory that it was what David said when he broke a string, which is the most illuminating theory because there is no logic about when you break a string, and there is no logic about the occurrence of *selâ*'. John Goldingay, *Psalms: 1–41* (Grand Rapids, MI: Baker Academic, 2006), p. 599.

PART I

Redirecting the Conversation

Before carefully discussing what disruptive-inclusive Christian adult learning is and how it works, it is important to clarify a few key things. Although terms such as *pedagogy* (learning methodology) and even theology may be unfamiliar or intimidating, none of us join this conversation with a blank slate. We are all, consciously or unconsciously, shaped by our educational experiences, whether formal or informal, positive or negative, and I am no different. It would be deeply hypocritical to present this book as an attempt to facilitate honest and vulnerable dialogue about learning without being willing to go first, and so in Chapter 1 I begin by offering some insights into my own learning journey to this point.

If this book is a conversation, the second important thing to clarify is what we are actually talking about. There is nothing more frustrating than getting to the end of a conversation only to discover that you and your partner have been talking about different things the whole time. The aim is not to agree on a single definition of any specific term but to clarify the scope of the discussion. Specifically, I will explain how this book understands and uses the term *Christian adult learning* (and perhaps more crucially, how it does not) and the importance of defining it so carefully.

Third, having drawn some boundaries around our conversation, we then need to begin to sketch an outline of where Christian adult learning finds itself in the first decades of the twenty-first century. Where are we and how did we get here? And finally, before presenting and explaining a disruptive-inclusive approach to Christian adult learning in detail, I offer an invitation to think critically about how *you* approach the topic. What has influenced your thinking in this area up to now? How do your background, past experiences and current context(s) shape your participation in our discussion?

Having created space in Chapter 1 to explore some of the significant factors influencing how both you and I understand Christian adult learning, and clarified the focus and boundaries of the specific approach proposed here, Chapter 2 gives an overview of disruptive-inclusive Christian adult learning. It also begins to explain how disruptive inclusion contrasts with existing approaches and techniques and the potential benefits it offers. Why is a different approach needed? Is tweaking existing understanding and practice not possible? Following this, the interlude considers the theme of Christian adult learning through the lens of a specific biblical passage. It demonstrates what can be discovered about being Christian adult learners from Jesus' claim to offer access to life in all its fullness (John 10.10).

I

Me, You and Christian
Adult Learning

In the early 2000s I trained as a classroom teacher. During my training, I took part in a speed networking activity that aimed to match trainees with professional coaches in a very short timeframe. Each time a bell was rung, everyone in the room had to find a new conversation partner and offer an elevator-pitch style of self-introduction, before moving on and repeating the process. Honestly, I find making snap judgements in pressurized situations very stressful, but I found this an unexpectedly valuable exercise. Specifically, it revealed how I see myself and what I perceive as the most defining elements of my character and worldview, even if I find it impossible to articulate them clearly when under pressure. In this spirit, I begin here by sharing the three things about me that I think give the most helpful sense of who I am and why effective Christian adult learning is so important to me, and lay some foundations for later chapters.

First, my default position assumes that there is something to learn from every situation and person, unless proven otherwise. I have found this particularly true of things, people, and situations that, at first, seem unrelatable or difficult to understand. I try to fight the instinct to run away and hang around long enough to get the most out of any opportunities that may arise. This pattern has been reinforced in a variety of settings, but perhaps most prominently in the range of previously unfamiliar Christian denominations in which it has been my privilege to worship as an adult. I grew up worshipping in independent, free church communities, but during my undergraduate studies

I worshipped in an Anglican setting. Then, during my time as a postgraduate in the USA, I participated in a Presbyterian worshipping community, and I now practise faith in an independent house church setting. I am also extremely honoured to have studied and worked alongside Christians from a wide range of traditions, from Coptic Orthodox to Pentecostals and almost everything in between. The more of the breadth of the Church I experience, the deeper my conviction that questions of faith and belief cannot be navigated well without allowing ourselves to be constantly reshaped by others' questions; these present us with diverse ideas that would be impossible to imagine, never mind navigate and respond to, on our own.

Second, I both envy and pity those who easily compartmentalize their lives. As will become increasingly clear, creating separate, non-overlapping modes or sectors of life does not come easily to me. In fact, my path has been defined by the search for links or overlap between ideas (and even whole arenas of life) that many consider conflicting, or at least to have nothing in common. The best example of this is between faith and professional arenas. After completing an undergraduate degree in modern foreign languages, I trained as a school teacher (and continue to find teaching in live settings a deeply life-giving activity). However, in the early years of classroom teaching I struggled to understand the relationship between my identity as a teacher and a person of Christian faith. As I investigated further, I discovered that there were only very few voices attempting to develop the discussion at these intersections. Eventually, it became clear that I would not be able to fully express my identity as an educator (or even begin teasing out what this might mean), without some help in navigating the intersection between education and Christian theology. From then on, the journey to my current position as a theology tutor in higher education has involved the repeated crossing of supposed boundaries (more on this later), creating opportunities for traditionally separated ideas not only to exist together but actively to inform each other.

Third, those who have been taught by me, heard me preach

or joined me in watching *Only Connect*[1] know that I greatly prize good questions, because I believe they have far more theological and pedagogical value than acceptable answers. Whether in friend, sister, aunty, teacher or colleague mode, I am always wondering how to improve the quality of the questions I pose in order to create more and richer spaces for better answers to percolate, be brought into the open and eventually evolve into even better questions. For example, the round of *Only Connect* in which contestants must sort 16 clues into four groups of four (made more difficult by the fact that multiple clues fit into several categories) inspires much richer team conversation, much deeper lateral thinking and potentially a much more satisfying outcome than discovering whether a *Mastermind* contestant can remember how many top 40 singles Elvis had in his lifetime! This is not to suggest that certain types of question are always more appropriate than others, but that as a Christian educator one of my foundational convictions is that the best service I have to offer the Church (and Christian learning more broadly) is to pose carefully considered (and increasingly richer) questions – of God, of each other, of the Bible – *and* to respond to others' questions in ways that encourage the same.

Having outlined three patterns of behaviour that I believe best offer a window onto my character, I find that, just as with the speed networking activity, distilling my personality into a set number of themes seems deeply dissatisfying. To ease this sense a little and add a further level of texture to the backdrop of disruptive inclusion, I conclude this introduction by sharing a deeply influential experience that not only gives a sense of my own learning journey to this point but also begins to introduce some of the key principles of disruptive inclusion to be unpacked in later chapters.

It was in about week three of the ten-week course that a shy young woman close to the front of the tiered lecture theatre gathered herself to ask our tutor a question. Although I no longer remember my fellow student's name nor exactly what she asked, many years on I remain deeply grateful that she summoned the courage to speak out, because her interaction with our tutor has had a significant influence on my efforts to suggest and model something better. The response the tutor offered was delivered in such an abrupt and dismissive tone that it was clear to the whole class that she considered the question so ridiculous as to make it unworthy of any further focus. It was as if the educator's entire manner was aimed at exposing the student's lack of knowledge and skill.

As I left the classroom reeling from what I had witnessed, I felt both defensive on behalf of my classmate but also genuinely puzzled by what the tutor may have been trying to do. By the time the initial shock had settled, I had convinced myself that the tutor must have some (hidden) grand plan and so I set out to discover it! In a one-to-one meeting, I tried hard to give her the benefit of the doubt. I really did expect an *ah-ha* moment as she explained how this was all part of a well-considered and biblically-inspired scheme to create an effective classroom environment and ultimately help students in their learning. As I pushed harder and harder for an explanation, the tutor calmly put down the pen she had been tossing between her fingers, deliberately made unbroken eye contact with me, and with more than a hint of pride said, 'Jen, what you need to understand is this: I drop students in deep water. Inevitably, some drown.' As our conversation ended, I fought desperately to keep my face from displaying the exasperation I felt at her audacity. On my walk home I recorded the exact phrases she had used into my phone, knowing that I would need evidence if I was going to believe in the months and years to come that this really happened.

Unsurprisingly, in the weeks following this incident few others voiced questions in class sessions. For me, this fuelled a thought experiment about the relationship between Christian faith and the nature of learning that has not lost momentum since. Why is there such a disconnect (even for the seemingly well-informed and well-trained) between the content and method of Christian adult learning? The tutor in the above example was clearly very knowledgeable on the topic and, as

I discovered, also able to clearly articulate an understanding of her role as a Christian educator. So why did she not see the obvious disconnect that was clear to most of the rest of the room? The conflict I observed in her approach was not that Christians should simply be *nicer* (although, honestly, that too), but that she repeatedly drew our attention to the almost bottomless perseverance of the God of the Bible with bumbling and bemoaning humanity while simultaneously modelling a *sink or swim* approach to learning.

At the end of the module, students were asked to write a brief reflection on what they had learned during the course. Although my views on Christian adult learning have developed significantly since then, the final paragraph of my offering could have been written for this book. It raises (albeit in seed form) many of the key ideas that have come to define the posture to Christian adult learning that I now refer to as disruptive inclusion.

I have learned that it's not just OK to not know an answer or even be able to hazard a guess in the right direction – it's absolutely necessary in life to stumble through the darkness on occasion, if only as a reminder that we're not the ones in control. I want to be the kind of teacher who constantly points to the stars while simultaneously acknowledging that sometimes the stars might be too much to try for today. Some days, the best learning we can do is to hold on tight, pray like never before, keep our eyes fixed for promises appearing on the horizon and dare to believe that God is as good as God claims to be.

What is Christian adult learning? Context and posture

Having offered a sense of how I approach Christian adult learning and a few hints why, the next task is to invite you to do the same. If you have had negative experiences in formal learning environments (whether school, university or church settings), you are not excluded from this conversation, in fact quite the opposite. Whether you loved school so much that you voluntarily continued into higher education, or you could not get out of school quickly enough and now avoid anything vaguely resembling a classroom, the key issue is not whether you consider yourself academically successful, but that each of us seriously explores how experiences in formal education influence our understanding of, and attitude to, learning more generally. The easiest way to do this is to ask: What ideas, settings and emotions do you associate with learning? Do you understand why? Are your responses based in past or present experiences? Do any of your answers change if you replace *learning* with *Christian learning*? Do learning and Christian learning mean the same to you? Most importantly, do you think your answers to these questions shape your expectations of how others help you learn and/or influence how you support others in their learning? As is almost always true, our answers to these kinds of questions are constantly shifting and I would recommend that you note your responses at this point and return to them as you progress through the book. Later, if you notice that your answers change or you become less convinced of your initial responses but do not yet know what to replace them with, do not be concerned – this is entirely to be expected.

If your response to the above questions is, 'But I am not really sure what you mean by *Christian adult learning*', fear not, you are in good company. The use of terminology at the intersection of Christian faith and learning is very confusing. For example, for those who borrowed this book from a theological library, the other books on the same shelf have titles including (but not limited to): religious education, Christian teaching, Sunday school, pedagogy, practical enrichment, growth, faith development, lifelong-learning, training, spiritual formation and discipleship.[2] Similarly, an online search for the phrase Christian adult learning gives few exact matches and the algorithms include what they consider multiple similar terms to those found on the physical, library shelf. Throughout this book I purposely only refer to learning (and on a few occasions teaching and learning) and far more commonly use the phrase Christian adult learning to describe its key ideas. Before going any further it is important to carefully explain why.

Ultimately, there is little agreement within academic scholarship about whether religious education, Christian learning, training, discipleship, faith development, discipleship, pedagogy, or various combinations of the terms, are just ways of expressing the same underlying concept or whether they refer to different ideas altogether, and if so, how? This lack of clarity is both an underlying cause and a symptom of the difficulties of progress in this area. How can we work out if we agree or disagree on how to move forward if we are not even sure we are talking about the same thing? Since the early decades of the twentieth century multiple conversations have been simultaneously (and even interchangeably) progressing. However, overall these have not given rise to any clear ways forward.[3] Throughout this book I almost always refer to its main subject as Christian adult learning in an attempt not to add further confusion, but the significance of this phrase goes beyond an attempt at simplicity and clarity.

First, my use of Christian adult learning is designed to clearly signal what this book is not about. Although there are undoubtedly some areas of overlap, the following chapters do not directly address religious education in schools, nor how educational institutions with a Christian ethos can integrate Christian values and beliefs. Neither do I discuss the content of adult education programmes in churches or theological training establishments. If your interest is in any of these areas, many excellent volumes already exist.[4] My use of Christian adult learning is not limited to formal educational opportunities but refers to a way of life in which Christian adults locate and embrace opportunities for learning in both seemingly mundane routine and pivotally significant life events, whether we are aware and able to articulate them or not. As a 2020 study found: 'We learn all the time. We learn without knowing that we are learning. We even learn as we breathe, simply and progressively.'[5] Therefore, rather than formal educational settings (usually classrooms) being understood as the ultimate (or even only) locations for learning, I suggest that they are better imagined as laboratories or rehearsal studios where learning is practised with the aim of being better prepared to fully participate in the range of learning opportunities on offer in everyday life. Rather than everyday life being the support act for the main learning event that happens elsewhere, more formal learning settings provide opportunities for *dry runs* of the kinds of learning scenarios that cannot be otherwise prepared for.

Another key thing to note about my understanding of the phrase Christian adult learning is how the words relate to each other. This requires a brief (and don't worry, simple) excursion into English grammar. In the most basic terms, adjectives describe things. For example: 'a big red bus'. In this phrase, big and red describe what the object is like. Therefore big and red are adjectives (or, you could say, they function adjectivally). Easy so far. But what about the phrase 'a slow train'? This is not quite so straightforward because there are a few options. It could work similarly to the bus example, with slow describing an inherent and unchanging characteristic of the train. Slow is what the train is like and therefore it functions adjectivally. If we take it this way, the phrase means that the train is not just moving slowly – it is slow by nature and is never anything but slow. However, what if, in the above example, the word slow only describes the train's movement at a particular time and place? The phrase then suggests that the train can (and does) move quickly at other times but is just going slowly at one specific moment. In this sense, the word slow functions as an adverb – describing how a specific action is done, not the nature of an object per se. This same choice between adjective and adverb exists in the phrase Christian adult learning. Christian can function adjectivally to describe what adult learning is. Alternatively, it could be taken as an adverb, describing the way in which adult learning is done. If you are not a word lover this may seem like a finicky distinction, but it makes a huge difference. We will explore this more in Chapter 3, but for now the important thing to note is that when I refer to *Christian adult learning*, I am using *Christian* adverbially, that is, a Christian way in which adult learning can be done, rather than a selection of statements about what should be taught and learned in order for learning to be recognized as Christian.

One final point about the phrase Christian adult learning. If you search for it online, in the first few pages of results you will probably find several references to Professor John Hull's 1985 book, *What Prevents Christian Adults from Learning?* Although Hull does not use the phrase Christian adult learning as consistently as I do (in fact, he joins many others in relatively inconsistent use of terminology), it is important to recognize that his work, and the above book in particular, has had a profound influence on my thinking and that my approach to Christian adult learning consciously builds on and develops many of his arguments.[6] Hull's influence continues to shape my thinking and provides much of the underpinning structure for what I refer to as a disruptive-inclusive approach to Christian adult learning. (Having clarified exactly how I understand the phrase, for ease all references to Christian adult learning will appear as CAL from this point on.)

Connection over retention?

Among all Hull's views on CAL, one fundamental concept has shaped my thinking more than any other. Because learning happens in all of life (and not just in formal learning settings), its success cannot be measured in terms of information retained or associated exam results or assignment grades. In its place, Hull suggests a different indicator of CAL progress: the quality of connected engagement between self, others, the wider learning environment and God. He explains that when learning becomes about levels of connectedness rather than levels of attainment, the fundamental aim of CAL is being 'more aware ... more coherent, more integrated, more supple, readier for further change and better related to the reality which faith confronts today.'[7]

This challenges some widely-held contemporary views about how learning works. Hull argues that CAL cannot be reduced to the possession of particular information or even the mastery of certain skills. In fact, its defining feature is not information per se, nor even application of knowledge and skills, but the adoption of a specific attitude or posture to the entire learning process (that is, all of life!) that enables its different components to interact. Returning to my favourite topic of cake, if we imagine learning as a sponge cake, then information is flour, eggs, sugar and butter. You cannot make a cake without them, but neither does the finished product magically appear simply by storing the ingredients in your kitchen. Learning is the result of the interaction of a particular set of components in a particular way, combined in specific conditions. Ingredients are only as good as the approach the baker takes to using them. For many of us, imagining learning in this way is challenging because we have been formed in and by educational systems that are only minimally interested in the skill with which particular ingredients are combined and whose central focus is limited to whether or not particular ingredients are present. Few contemporary educationalists disagree with the claim that information retention and regurgitation cannot be the principal basis of learning. However, the practice of many of the same practitioners would suggest the exact opposite. Ultimately, many contemporary learning systems and practices communicate loudly that *what* learners know rather than *how* they know it, or their ability to creatively contextualize their learning, is what is really important.

Alternative approaches to learning do exist, with the later decades of the twentieth century seeing experimentation in various directions.[8] However, for the most part, the vast majority of Christian adult learners have been formed and conditioned in educational structures in which the learning currency (what is deemed most valuable and can be exchanged for progress and status) or pivotal measuring stick remains the retention and accurate recall of knowledge. In the light of this, Hull's alternative suggestion, that learning is ultimately concerned with increasing ability to make connections, stands in stark contrast. At the heart of CAL, he suggests, is the task of growing awareness of what is unknown as well as what is known; of recognizing and analysing existing connections and exploring options for development. In this way, effective learning is not a straightforward, linear process from ignorance to understanding. Instead, it makes space for things, people and ways of thinking that had previously been considered useless or even dangerous. Even if the early parts of this process lead to more questions and confusion, each stage plays an important role in allowing learners to reroute old pathways and explore new territory.

Paying even closer attention to Hull's words, the key idea he proposes is that effective learners are not those who have already changed and are considered to have arrived at a place of new, superior knowledge. Effective learners are not necessarily changed but readier for further change. This concept of growing in the skill of being on the move, and letting go of ever fully arriving at a permanent learning destination, is at the heart of disruptive inclusion (more on this in Chapter 5). For Hull, CAL is not the successful completion of a course you have signed up to, nor the podcast you have been listening to, nor the certificate you receive for passing an exam or reaching any kind of desired end goal. Marking and celebrating progress is important, but disruptive-inclusive CAL is defined by the posture adopted by learners as they navigate a given situation or scenario. This shifts the conversation about CAL from a discussion of what it is to how it works.[9]

The various consequences of connected CAL are unpacked throughout this book, but before closer analysis of disruptive inclusion, here are a few general consequences of connected CAL to whet your appetite and set the scene for our ongoing conversation. First and foremost, it levels the CAL playing field in a much-needed way. Although worked out in different ways, regardless of age, academic ability, (dis)ability, educational opportunity or proficiency level everyone can connect with self, God and the wider world. CAL is an invitation to humility, vulnerability and embracing tension, not a test of intelligence. So this makes CAL about practising locating and embracing learning opportunities as they present themselves – almost everywhere! This is not to underestimate the extent of the challenge that different forms of connectedness provide for some learners (particularly those with autism and other sensory and socially-impacting conditions), but connectedness can be expressed in many ways, meaning that all can meaningfully participate. From those with significant physical or mental disabilities that limit verbal communication and comprehension to world-leading academics (and recognizing that some learners are in both those categories!), no one is excluded from the responsibility and privilege of reaching in some respect for deeper, wider or more nuanced connectedness.

There are also consequences for educators. Where learning is about developing in awareness and ability to connect, rather than collecting, sorting and recalling information, effective educators are not all-knowing oracles but lead learners who model and support other learners in adopting particular techniques and postures. These example learners equip others to recognize opportunities and actively engage in them more quickly, rather than instructing or aiding their navigation towards the 'correct' answer (more about being right and wrong in Chapter 3). One of the biggest differences that this creates is that, in comparison to the traditional function of educators as guiding learners towards clarity by protecting them from potential conflicts and confusion, this approach requires actively introducing learners to potential obstacles and then skilling them in their effective navigation.

Finally, I appreciate that defining CAL as an attitude or posture may raise the concern that almost anything might be included in it. My response to such fears is twofold. First, yes, it opens up the possibilities of what kinds of adult learning might be considered to be Christian, but second, it does not necessarily follow that the integrity or authority of Christianity and its fundamental message is compromised (whatever you consider this to be). If Christians are called to live after God's example and bear witness to God's ways in all areas of life, then there must be more (and therefore also fewer) *Christian* ways of doing everything, from organic chemistry to internet coding and knitting to plumbing, that are not only defined by underpinning beliefs and convictions but go beyond the content of teaching and learning to how ideas and actions are taught and learned and towards what end. The material involved in CAL is not unimportant. Particularly where we have direct guidance and therefore (at least some) clarity on how God would have us act in the world, the content of learning has a critical role to play, even if interpreting the information we do have is far less straightforward than many claim. However, what do we do in the many cases where either specific guidance is not given or there is freedom in interpreting or applying guidance? In other words, what if CAL not only functions in providing answers on how to live but also guides us in how to proceed when it does not? Rather than either manufacturing answers where they do not exist or throwing our hands up in despair, I am deeply convicted that the most effective and substantial way of approaching CAL is to find a posture (you may prefer the language of a frame of mind, an outlook, a demeanour or an approach) that can be adopted in all circumstances and is modelled on Scripture, evokes the character and nature of the Christian God and leverages the assets of Christian community – I call my contribution to this disruptive inclusion.

Questions/activities

- Write your own 2-minute elevator-pitch style of introduction focusing on the things you think most shape your views on and experiences of learning.
- What are some of the psychological obstacles associated with the terms *learning* or *education* for you? How do they shape your attitudes and engagement in learning in ongoing ways?

- Which teacher/tutor/educator has had the biggest influence on you up to this point in your life? Why? What was/is it about their approach that most impacted you?
- What language do you use in your church/denomination/ community for what I refer to as CAL? What does this reveal about your underpinning views?
- When you describe something as Christian, do you understand its *Christian-ness* adjectivally or adverbially? That is, do you think it is Christian because of what it is/does, or because of how it goes about its actions? What difference does this make?
- How do you respond to Hull's suggestion that the aim of CAL is to be 'more aware ... more coherent, more integrated, more supple, readier for further change and better related to the reality which faith confronts today'? Can you identify the reason(s) for your responses?

Notes

1 *Only Connect* is a BBC quiz show in which contestants are given a range of clues and must find ideas that connect them. An example of a question is: 1. Table, 2. Trap, 3. Exam, 4. Alarm. Answer: things that are set. A full database of the show's questions can be found here: https://ocdb.cc/ (accessed 31.07.2023).

2 This is probably shelf mark 377 (Dewey decimal system) or BV.1499 (Library of Congress).

3 This is the first of multiple places where a fuller discussion can be found in my doctoral thesis: https://research.vu.nl/en/publications/ what-prevents-christian-adults-from-learning-in-fresh-perspective.

4 For example: Trevor Cooling, *A Christian Vision for State Education: Reflections on the theology of education* (London: SPCK, 1994); Johannes M. Luetz and Beth Green (eds), *Innovating Christian Education Research: Multidisciplinary perspectives* (Singapore: Springer, 2021); and Perry Shaw, *Transforming Theological Education: A practical handbook for integrative learning* (Carlisle, UK: Langham Global Library, 2014).

5 Éamonn Dunne and Aidan Seery (eds), *Pedagogics of Unlearning* (Baltimore, MD: Project Muse, 2016), p. 15. This study explores how

old skills, habits and patterns may need to be undone before new ones can be adopted.

6 Hull spent most of his professional career as Professor of Religious Education at the University of Birmingham, writing, researching and teaching about the connections between self, faith and learning, but spent (what he referred to as) his retirement years as Professor of Practical Theology at the Queen's Foundation for Ecumenical Theological Education, also in Birmingham. For more on Hull's background see: Dennis Bates, Gloria Durka and Friedrich Schweitzer (eds), *Education, Religion and Society: Essays in honour of John M. Hull* (London: Routledge, 2006).

7 John M. Hull, *What Prevents Christian Adults from Learning?* (London: SCM Press, 1985), p. 82.

8 Among the most popular is Montessori learning, named after Italian educator Maria Montessori, with its emphasis on learners leading their own hands-on experiences. Project Based Learning also embeds different parts of the traditional curriculum into multi-task, real-world projects.

9 These ideas are not unique to me or Hull. Hull's focus on prioritizing growth in quality and scope of relatedness via embracing challenge is shared by many. Peter Jarvis explains: 'Through the process of maturation human beings have a variety of experiences some of which might integrate creatively with the previous biography but sometimes a process of restructuring occurs'; Peter Jarvis, 'Learning as a religious phenomenon' in P. Jarvis and N. Walters (eds), *Adult Education and Theological Interpretations* (Malabar, FL: Krieger Pub. Co., 1993), p. 10. Jack Mezirow envisages Christian maturity as a 'development process of movement through the adult years toward meaning-perspectives that are progressively more inclusive, discriminating, and more integrative of experience'; Jack D. Mezirow, 'Perspective transformation', *Studies in Adult Education* 9:2 (1977), pp. 153–64, p. 159.

2

From Here to Somewhere Else: Why and How?

There is a scene in one of my favourite films, *Back to the Future Part II*, where the main characters (Doc and Marty) have just returned from time-travelling into the future (2015!) to their native 1985 only to discover that they have caused some major changes to the only reality they had previously known. Marty suggests that they should return to the future (hence the film's title) to stop a disastrous chain of events from happening. However, Doc explains that if they go straight back to the future from the version of 1985 in which they find themselves, this will not have the desired effect because 'If we travel into the future from *this* point in time, it will be the future of *this* reality.'[1] And so Doc suggests that the only realistic hope they have of changing the future is to go *back* in time and fix the issue at the source and, predictably, various shenanigans ensue.

While I appreciate that we do not have Doc and Marty's ability to move backwards and forwards in time (and acknowledging, but also lovingly ignoring, the film's enormous plot holes), Doc's advice is helpful to our discussion about CAL as a reminder of the strength of the connections between the past, present and future. Forward progress cannot avoid being influenced by our current position and state, which are in turn a product of the past! Without assessing the key traits of where and how CAL presently finds itself, we are far less likely to be able to navigate a way forward that retains the good and exposes and improves on the not so good. Therefore, before moving on to how CAL might be improved, it is important to outline briefly some of what I believe to be the defining characteristics of early twenty-first-century CAL theory and practice.

What's the problem with here?

As already established, there is no consensus on exactly how to understand or explain the relationship between Christian faith and adult learning. Those interested in religious education in schools have formed their own disciplines and sub-disciplines (although these are far from settled), but the ideas and processes influencing what I refer to as CAL, as practised in classrooms, churches and a range of other settings, have not attracted the same level of interest (or at least co-ordinated and structured discussion).[2] This makes it much more difficult to identify and track any developments in CAL theory and practice; and given the diversity that exists among the learners and learning settings it represents, broad generalizations are unhelpful. However, we do have to begin somewhere. Therefore, even if only to offer further insight into how my experiences and perceptions have given rise to disruptive inclusion, I therefore offer here three observations of patterns that influence how Christian adults learn in the early twenty-first century.

First, if I were to ask a group of adult learners in any of the settings where I currently teach, 'What are you learning at the moment?', almost certainly their answers would relate to the content of the subject matter or the new skill in question: 'I am studying French history', 'I am learning pottery' or 'I am studying the history of the Church'. On the other hand, a response such as 'I am learning how to be a better learner through embodied imagination' would at best seem vague and at worst a little pompous. Despite some recent developments encouraging learners to take ownership and monitor their own progress, a common pattern that shapes much current CAL understanding and practice is that learners are rarely encouraged to consider themselves as active participants in their own learning, or even to think carefully about how their learning occurs.

Bizarrely, even in teacher training settings, as well as faith-based learning scenarios, I find that how learning happens is generally not thought of as the substance of learning. Unless they went to a particularly progressive school, have a particular kind of educationalist in their life or are just naturally interested in how things work, few people explore beyond the idea that learning is about finding answers to questions, discovering and retaining knowledge that may be tested at various points. Behind the scenes, teachers and educators are perhaps expected to think about the best ways that learning happens but learners are not expected to be involved in, or even aware of, the discussions.

Linked to this, educational structures (my primary experience is in the UK and the USA) are generally governed by an endless quest for superior teaching and learning methods, meaning that only very rarely are new and existing techniques employed in parallel. A good demonstration of this is a technique called differentiation. When I trained to become a classroom teacher in the early 2000s, we were taught that differentiation was a non-negotiable cornerstone of good classroom practice. Its aim was to create multiple access points into the learning content, so that all learners could engage with as few obstacles as possible. This mostly took the form of creating different levels of worksheets for those with lower literacy skills or more complex activities for those who would find the initial tasks straightforward to complete. Differentiating every lesson was extremely challenging (arguably impossible), but it was considered so fundamental that we had little choice but to try our best. However, nearly 20 years on, differentiation has fallen out of favour and all but disappeared from the latest training materials, replaced by concepts such as adaptive teaching and mastery.[3]

I raise this issue not because I have particularly strong opinions on differentiation or any of the methods that have since been introduced in its place, but because educators are so busy trying to incorporate the newest suggested techniques that there is little room to analyse the value of either the incoming or outgoing approaches! For example, teachers were not invited to question how and why differentiation might be more or less effective, either when it was being hailed as the foundation of good practice or even now that it has been relegated and replaced by other priorities. Over time, this means that many learners and educators are caught on a conveyor belt of reactively experiencing or delivering whatever educational method or idea is currently popular, with little opportunity to stop and reflect. Or the opposite response is perhaps even more prevalent: the disillusionment and pressure of constantly implementing change means that some just stick to what they have always done. I am not suggesting that educators should stop innovating, nor that ineffective methods should not be allowed to drop away, but that a 'one in, one out' or 'either/or' approach to learning methodology will never allow for the rich pedagogical improvements that are so needed.

Third and finally, over the last generation there has been a growing importance placed on adult learners' perceptions of their own experience and progress. In most cases this is linked to how the relationship between learners and educational institutions is increasingly becoming that of customer and service provider, meaning that learner satisfaction is an increasingly important factor. In school settings this is sometimes known as pupil voice; in further and higher education settings it takes the form of internal and external feedback forms and/or staff–student consultative committees. In all educational settings, ensuring positive learner experiences is top of the agenda. Overall, I think this is a positive move if it encourages educators to design courses, modules and sessions with learners in mind (this may sound obvious, but is not always the case). However, putting such a strong focus on how students feel about their learning can be problematic. This is because many learners associate positive, effective learning experiences with familiarity, comfort and encouragement, which in turn may not always be conducive to effective learning processes.

In other words, the best kinds of learning may occur when learners are either unaware of it or would not recognize their experiences as positive. In fact, as a 2019 study at Harvard University demonstrates well, in some cases 'actual learning and feeling of learning [are] strongly anticorrelated.'[4]

In one part of this Harvard study, a class was split into smaller groups for the final sessions of a course. One group was assigned a tutor who used highly active and interactive learning strategies. The other group were given 'highly polished' but passive lectures (that is, the students just listened). At the end both groups were asked about their experiences. The students who received the 'highly polished' lectures expressed a much more positive response than those who had the more interactive experience. However, when the two groups were tested on the concepts introduced in the sessions (admittedly, largely based on information understanding and recall), the learners in the interactive group performed far more highly. The study summarized:

> The effort involved in active learning can be misinterpreted as a sign of poor learning ... On the other hand, a superstar lecturer can explain things in such a way as to make students feel like they are learning more than they actually are.[5]

Therefore, although learners' feelings about their learning experiences are far from unimportant, for multiple reasons learners' expectations that good learning should feel positive, comforting or even encouraging means that, by definition, they often interpret difficult, demanding or disruptive learning experiences as bad learning or poor learning progress. However, the most basic conclusion of the Harvard study is that effective learning rarely feels good. In fact it suggests that the best kinds of learning may need to feel a little uncomfortable or destabilizing to be effective. Or, at the very least, it highlights the need to be aware that learners' impressions of the process are not the most accurate barometer of whether (and what) effective learning progress is actually happening.

Although easier to track and demonstrate in education more broadly, I have observed the influence of all these patterns in theological education institutions and church learning settings. I have rarely found opportunities for Christian adult learners (or educators!) to think critically about the relationship between faith convictions and learning participation. Among the many post-church conversations about whether I agree with a preacher's interpretation of a passage or the theological significance of certain prayers or hymns used in a service, I have yet to participate in a conversation about the appropriateness of the learning methods used (except when I initiated it). Although maybe not discussed in the same technical terms, CAL is also strongly influenced by the quest for the best approach to teaching and learning in theological and church settings. Many conversations concerning theological training and church teaching and preaching centre on simple binary choices: More or less content? Wide and shallow or narrow and deep? Information or skills-focused? Expositional address or simple thematic message? Accessible homily or rigorous exegetical analysis?

But perhaps the strongest influence is the call for CAL to be a positive experience: there is a deepening expectation that CAL should be fun (or at least not boring or off-putting)! As far back as the 1980s, Hull recognized how often Christian learning spaces, rather than being places defined by learning challenge and progress, had become 'learning havens',[6] that is, protecting people from, and providing some form of antidote to, the problematic and provocative learning patterns provided in the world beyond the Church. In learning havens, success is defined by how comforted and approved learners feel in their existing beliefs. Increasingly, in some parts of both the Church and theological education institutions, there is a serious financial incentive to keep learners happy. If learners do not *enjoy* (or at least feel as if they are benefitting from) their learning experience, they may take their fees (or tithes) elsewhere. However, if learning experiences only ever affirm and consolidate, is learning progress really happening?

Is a paradigm shift really necessary?

Returning to *Back to the Future*, clearly the writers wanted to give their characters just enough scientific-sounding dialogue to make it seem as if they know what they are talking about, without confusing the audience with too many technical terms. At one point, Doc explains that if time travellers were to meet either the older or younger versions of themselves, it might result in 'a time paradox, the results of which could cause a chain reaction that would unravel the very fabric of the space time continuum.'[7] I am reliably informed that in the world beyond Hollywood film scripts the space time continuum actually relates to gravity and not time. However, the idea of *paradox* is extremely helpful for our purposes, when used to describe the interaction of two (usually contradictory) ideas or qualities. For example, an object that appears static but is in fact always moving; or maybe someone who is simultaneously fully divine and fully human! A paradox is something that goes against existing and generally accepted rules but remains real and/or possible. Doc and Marty had to avoid paradox at all costs because they believed that if their older and younger selves crossed paths it would have permanent, transformative effects. I would encourage the opposite approach – that the paradoxical is an important component of the way forward for CAL because creating a permanent state of transformation is what we desperately want!

However, it strikes me that many aspects of the contemporary experience of Christian adult learners are focused on avoiding paradox. Whether by limiting learners to the *what* and keeping them away from the *how/why* of learning, continually striving for the single best approach to teaching and learning, or prioritizing positive feelings about learning above all else, conflict and disruptions are to be avoided at all costs. But what if Christian adult learners were encouraged to ask what, why and how questions of their learning progress and learn to live well within the tensions that this will probably create? What if educators abandoned the idea that there is a single, superior teaching and learning technique that will remove all the barriers to participation and began to explore combining multiple old and new ways of learning? What if we accepted that, just as in life more broadly, it is often the more challenging and discombobulating experiences that support effective learning and that therefore *feeling* negatively about learning is not necessarily a sign that something is ineffective? What if we allowed ourselves to imagine that the tensions created by holding some of these potentially paradoxical ideas and approaches together might result in highly effective learning environments?

If the path forward for CAL includes purposefully embracing the paradoxical, it cannot be achieved by just a few tweaks to current thinking and practice. It will require a paradigm shift – a complete reimagining of what we are trying to achieve and how. Doc and Marty's recurring problem (the final *Back to the Future* reference, I promise!) was trying to navigate life in the future according to old rules, and vice versa. For example, they discover that early 1950s teenagers have no framework for understanding or responding to rock and roll and that cars with combustion engines cannot be refuelled in the Old West. In short, obvious as it may sound, if your context is changed or disrupted in some fundamental way(s) ploughing on as if nothing has happened is rarely an effective strategy. Most recently, we need look no further than the example of the Covid-19 pandemic. This not only offered the world a new problem to solve but called into question the very definition of a problem. It raised questions about how truly global problems are solved; how human life can continue with diseases that cannot be fully eradicated; and how national governments respond in times of crisis. In several ways, the pandemic posed the ultimate paradigm shift in living memory, demonstrating how applying only existing knowledge, skills and experience to new challenges is sometimes insufficient.

Therefore, before closely analysing how disruptive-inclusive CAL works, it is important to clarify that it is not just a tweak to existing approaches. It works in conjunction with existing methods but calls for a reconfiguration of how every element of teaching and learning is designed and practised. Disruptive inclusion suggests that we both imagine and do CAL differently than before. It is not a missing piece that can be slotted into an existing puzzle but asks whether we might have misunderstood the type of puzzle we were facing all along. Disruptive inclusion requires learners to become active participants in their own learning progress: it invites both educators and learners to explore how learning happens as well as what they are learning. Also, by definition, a disruptive-inclusive approach to CAL requires embracing the tension created when multiple (potentially conflicting) concepts or approaches sit together and are encouraged to dialogue with each other. The aim of disruptive inclusion, therefore, is not to replace existing teaching and learning methods but to sharpen and redirect their emphasis.

I would encourage you not to think of disruptive inclusion as a new key that opens doors that other keys cannot. Rather, it presents a way of effectively employing keys already in our possession and inspiring the creation of new ones, not only to open gates and doors we are currently facing but also any future entrances we may encounter. It suggests that the best way forward for both learners and educators is not to continue to search for the single correct learning method but to practise adopting a particular learning *posture* that enables more effective progress in multiple situations and learning modes. Disruptive inclusion asks 'What if people, places and concepts that are currently excluded from learning could be repurposed to support CAL progress?'

The mechanics of disruptive inclusion

As we dig deeper into disruptive inclusion, the temptation may be to ask 'What is it?' However, because it is not a *method* per se (or, at least, not the kind with a checklist to work through) but instead a posture or attitude, the best way to explore disruptive inclusion is not to search for an ultimate, fixed definition but to ask how it functions. What exactly are the proverbial cogs in the disruptive-inclusive machine? What are its necessary components and what form does disruptive-inclusive learning progress take? With the help of some key ideas from Hull's *What Prevents Christian Adults from Learning?*, we will explore how disruptive inclusion works, particularly focusing on the roles of *bafflement, optimum distance* and *multiplicity of vision.*

As is (hopefully) becoming clear, but is worth repeating, one of the most important things to recognize about disruptive inclusion is that its defining factor is not what might be traditionally referred to as *learning content*. In fact, if disruptive-inclusive learning could be said to have any specific substance, it would be defined as anything learners experience as challenging, unforeseen or unpredictable. In Hull's words, effective learning happens 'when the structures of life are upset; when the crises of life come upon us.'[8] When such upsets occur, in whatever form, disruptive inclusion suggests that the best way to learn is to embrace the tension and confusion that often accompanies them: 'learning breakthrough happens when someone dares to include something they had formerly considered unable to find God in or through.'[9] However, disruptive inclusion is not an exercise in self-punishment or defeatism, but making space for disruption in learning can give access to increased freedom, self-knowledge and a sense of wider connectedness. Adopting a disruptive-inclusive posture creates the opportunity for what may have, at first, presented as a learning obstacle to become co-opted or reclaimed as an opportunity for dynamic and transformative progress.

The core concept of disruptive inclusion is not new. Many scholars (most notably in education, theology and psychology) have drawn attention to the pedagogical importance of unforeseen challenges or situations in which learners 'have reached the limit of our ability to understand, to analyse, to clarify and interpret.'[10] When existing knowledge, skills and other resources are unable to support learners in navigating their present reality, it leads to 'the dismantling of time-honoured certainties, where comfort, equilibrium, coherence and predictability for one's life disappear.'[11] In the simplest terms, learners are *baffled*.[12] Learners can respond to bafflement in a variety of ways. First, they can attempt to avoid disruption and return to a more familiar or comfortable space (all references to learning *places* or *spaces* can equally apply to physical or metaphorical locations). Or they may choose to ignore or refuse to accept disruption and attempt to continue as before. Alternatively, learners can choose to acknowledge and actively engage with the source of bafflement – making space for both the simultaneous discomfort and freedom that come with being unequipped or unsure how to respond. This final option is the first step towards disruptive inclusion – making it possible for challenging and unpredictable circumstances to act as a springboard for new and more aware thinking and action in multiple and irreversible ways. In short, including disruptions creates the potential for learners to navigate larger, richer and more connected learning spaces.

Few of us struggle to imagine a baffling situation. A personal or professional curve ball is thrown in your direction. Redundancy. Illness. A job opportunity that has significant personal and professional implications. A global pandemic that disproportionately kills the most vulnerable in society and results in restrictions on everyday life. You feel out of your depth. You realize that you do not have the resources, skills or understanding to problem solve your way through. There is no clear plan for progress. In disruptive-inclusive terms, this is not a position of weakness. Disruptive-inclusive CAL suggests that being equipped to deal with every situation that may arise is not possible; more than this, it is not even desirable. The critical factor is not trying to force the correct scenario for learning to occur but adopting the kind of posture that creates the opportunities for effective learning to happen wherever and however learners find themselves.

When unforeseen circumstances arise, disruptive-inclusive learners resist the temptation to simply ignore the disruption and hope it just goes away. Neither do they attempt to put as much distance (metaphorical or otherwise) as possible between themselves and the presenting disruption. Nor do they downplay the challenges and pretend that existing resources and skills are sufficient after all. Instead, they consciously recognize the information, skills and resources to which they do have access and those currently beyond their reach. They consciously recognize their present capacity and limitations and allow the presenting disruptions to pose important questions and create the opportunities for new or reordered connections between self, God, others and wider reality.

Breaking it down further, an effective disruptive-inclusive learning posture has two simultaneous and paradoxical elements. First, learners embrace the unknown or unfamiliar idea, person or territory that exposes the insufficiency and/or inappropriateness of existing skills and knowledge. This brings with it a sense of vulnerability but also a sense of adventure and freedom. Freedom is possible because while learners are being oriented outwards and challenged to make space for the new, unknown or not easily navigable, learners are also drawn into a renewed sense of connectedness that grows into a new (but not necessarily familiar) sense of home and belonging (more on this in Chapter 5).

Before going any further, it is important to clarify a few things that disruptive inclusion does *not* involve. First, the creation of opportunities for Christian adult learners to increasingly *include* disruptions is not another way to suggest that learners simply find ways to change their mind, care less, or more easily accept previously unknown or disagreeable ideas. Including disruption requires learners to make critical space in their worldview, not agree where they previously disagreed. The word *critical* is key to this claim: let me explain how with another food example.

Some years ago, inspired by a trip to Thailand, my housemate and I began experimenting with the use of ginger. As good disruptive-inclusive learners, despite the challenges it posed to our cooking style, we chose not to ignore, downplay or reject the potential role of ginger in a range of recipes. However, after extensive experimentation of including ginger in our cuisine, it came to play very different roles in our palates and menus. My housemate came to the opinion that, after God, ginger is one of the things that best holds the world together! As a result, she continues to put ginger in almost everything from biscuits to smoothies, cakes and cocktails to curries and stews. I, on the other hand, take a very different view. As it stands, I believe that for ginger to make its optimal contribution in the world, its use should be limited to refreshingly light, zingy (usually Thai) curries.

However, we both continue to take a *critical* stance to ginger, meaning that despite our disagreement on the appropriate extent of its role, we both continue to make space for the other's view. I am still open to new suggestions and experimentations, but apart from this I also concede that ginger plays a (near) life-defining role for my friend (and many others). Even though I maintain that ginger biscuits should be banned, their influence on my friend's worldview does not go away just because I reject them! Even if I were to exclude ginger entirely from my diet, it would still need to be included in my worldview because its wider influence is unaffected by my opinion on it. Equally, my friend recognizes that she cannot assume that everyone shares her view that ginger can solve almost all the world's problems! The inclusion of disruptions in learning is not a process of fully aligning with conflicting or competing views but (at the very least) suspending the assumption that my current, personal position is the only valid perspective from which reality can be usefully understood.

Second, disruptive inclusion is not about persevering through temporarily unpleasant conditions to arrive at a cosier, more comfortable destination. Rather, disruptive inclusion does not just propose an alternative learning destination, it de-emphasizes the concept of permanent arrival altogether. Disruptive inclusion suggests that making learning progress requires that we take our current location seriously, but also that success may be as much about *how* learners find themselves in the present moment rather than necessarily *where* they find themselves or even where they are headed. This can be difficult to imagine because success is usually defined as the crossing of particular attainment markers or finish lines. Disruptive inclusion changes the focus from *getting there* (wherever 'there' may be) to *being here* and encouraging learners to develop awareness of potential connections in and to the reality in which they currently find themselves. The irony is that removing the idea of an ultimate destination seems to help learners get to places they could never otherwise have reached.

To understand fully how bafflement functions in disruptive inclusion, we must zoom in a little closer still. Imagine the levels of disruption experienced during a baffling life experience as a line on a graph (the actual process is very rarely linear, but this works as a helpful starting point). As a learner embraces unforeseen and potentially chaotic circumstances, the line on the imaginary graph ascends. As the learner begins to find coping mechanisms and/or ways of including the disruptive circumstances in their worldview, the initial panic and potential paralysis begin to recede and the line on the graph flattens out and then slowly arcs downwards. This point, just after learners have experienced the peak of the disruption, is so pivotal to the whole learning process that Hull gave it a name: 'optimum distance'.[13] It is so potentially influential because learners find themselves in an in-between place,[14] where decreasing levels of disruption and simultaneously increasing opportunities for inclusion (acceptance, leaning in, making peace, being able to recognize the potential opportunities or simply locating something/someone in a worldview) meet, creating the ideal conditions for the exploration of new insights and the forging of new connections. Hull explains optimum distance in visual terms:

> If a picture is too far away, you can't see the details, but if it is too close then, once again, the details are lost. There is an optimum distance for clarity of definition, and this seems to apply not only to our sight, but to our beliefs as well.[15]

Optimum distance provides the ideal position from which learners will still experience sufficient disruption so as not to take their new situation for granted, but will also have access to just enough connection to the past for fresh insights and connections between self, others, God, the created world to begin to be imagined. *Optimum distance* provides the ideal learning conditions of safe but not comfortable.

There is one final aspect of the disruptive-inclusive learning process to consider. The effectiveness of bafflement and optimum distance are due to their ability to provide access to in-between learning spaces where learners simultaneously find themselves in multiple camps and can begin to practise what Hull refers to as 'multiplicity of vision'.[16] This was not just an abstract idea for Hull, but an expression of his own experience of physical sight loss. Its pivotal concept is that as learners enter optimum distance, they gain access to multiple and simultaneous modes of perception and processing. This allows for metaphorical boundaries to be crossed and makes it possible for learners to practise observing and analysing reality from multiple positions. *Multiplicity of vision* is not just concerned with arriving at a particular view and then permanently settling there. In fact, as we have already considered, it is far less about learning how to arrive at any particular destination than it is about practising being deeply (but also nimbly) present in the here and now!

Therefore the whole idea of disruptive inclusion is that in the process of repeatedly moving in and out of optimum distance learners become more adept at holding different worlds of meaning together and engaging from multiple and different positions. Once learners stop critically engaging and begin to take their present reality for granted, they need to move back into optimum distance and begin the process of being disrupted again. This is not a step backwards but the path of genuine progress, because each time learners enter optimum distance they take with them all the knowledge, skills and experiences they have encountered since last there. In this way learning becomes a process in which the metaphorical lines separating comfort from tension are repeatedly redrawn. Over time, as learners practise embracing the disruption of the unknown, previously intimidating and baffling spaces and scenarios become included and learners are drawn further and further beyond their original boundaries of comfort and familiarity.

Selah 1: Disruptive inclusion and neurodiversity: finding the sweet spot

The most common question asked of me when I introduce disruptive inclusion is, 'What about learners who cannot cope with existing levels of disruption in their lives, or those who have particular reasons for trying to avoid or limit disruption?' This is an important question to address before progressing further, particularly in relation to those whose learning is influenced by dyslexia, dyspraxia, ASD, ADD or ADHD (the acronyms stand for: Autistic Spectrum Disorder, Attention Deficit Disorder or Attention Deficit Hyperactivity Disorder).[17]

The core principle of disruptive inclusion is not to increase the quantity of disruption in learning as much as possible but to identify the most favourable combinations and connections for optimum distance to be entered. In simple terms, disruptive-inclusive CAL is about finding a learning sweet spot, rather than turning up the disruptive dial as far as possible. Learning goes far beyond brain chemistry, but it is interesting that some recent developments in the area of neuroscience align with the idea of a learning sweet spot, suggesting that there is a specific point at which levels of challenge and student interest combine to produce peak brain responses.[18] A 2019 study went so far as to quantify the 'edge of our competence – not so hard that we are discouraged, but not so easy that we get bored'[19] and concluded that the 'engagement peak' in human learning occurs at about 85 per cent. In other words, in terms of brain chemistry, peak learning progress is not demonstrated when learners can solve all the problems presented, but rather at a point where the optimum response is not offered approximately 15 per cent of the time. This means that the best learners do not get everything right!

A similar strand of neuroscientific research that seeks to measure the optimal responses in learning of the prefrontal cortex (a part of the brain associated with personality, decision making and other complex processes) resonates strongly with the central theme of disruptive inclusion. In its analysis of how 'humans and other animals adjust their learning strategies nearly optimally depending on the level of uncertainty or the volatility of their environment',[20] this research discovered that specific learning tasks were completed more successfully when administered in changing and unpredictable, rather than consistent, conditions. When problems, their outcomes and rewards were presented to learners in an irregular way, the brains of those tested were over time more successfully able to navigate a range of increasingly complex problems.

In several significant ways I am not claiming that these studies speak directly to the core questions raised in this project about CAL. This is for several reasons. First, because the research is not focused on adult human learners. Second, because the research was conducted in individual, test conditions, with learners out of their normal environments. Finally, and more significantly, the research only defines learning success as the ability to find the single correct response to objective problems, that is, it only takes into account accuracy or 'error rates', not quality or posture of response.[21] However, regardless of this, these studies are useful reminders that the goal of disruptive inclusion is to find a pedagogical sweet spot, where learners are best positioned to navigate potential obstacles rather than eliminate or avoid them. And further, that scientific evidence increasingly suggests that if optimum learning conditions exist, they probably include some form of insurmountable problem (at least, at first) and an unpredictable/disruptive setting.

Applying this to the relationship between disruptive inclusion and neurodiversity, it suggests that neurodiverse learners' sweet spots will be, exactly as the title suggests, diverse! Therefore it means that no teacher or learner (whether they self-identify as neurodiverse or not) should expect their optimum distance to be the same as others'. All learners make a range of complex decisions that influence their navigation of various learning settings, but as we all experience learning environments and conditions differently the decisions made will be at different levels and for different reasons. Neurodiverse learners may be particularly sensitive to disruptive circumstances/ relational connections or find them particularly challenging, but in disruptive-inclusive terms, this does not put them at a disadvantage, nor does it suggest that neurodiverse learners must endure extremely stressful or disproportionately demanding conditions to be successful. In fact, quite the opposite.

As will be fully explained in the final section of this chapter, those who intuitively respond in ways that are not generally supported or accommodated by mainstream education systems or methods are not inferior learners. They may have disengaged from (or at the very least, not reached their potential in) institutional learning, exhausted by the obstacles put in their way by inflexible institutional structures. However, at the same time many neurodiverse learners become extremely skilled at finding alternative ways to meaningfully engage in learning that plays to their own strengths.

Either way, disruptive inclusion provides opportunities for neurodiverse learners to thrive by suggesting that those who are experienced in responding to disruption (in whatever ways and at whatever levels) are actually the most advanced at finding learning sweet spots: circumstances have often forced them to be deeply aware of their own learning processes. While I appreciate that the terms neurodiverse and neurotypical are genuine attempts at moving away from the language of a spectrum in which those with specific learning needs are considered further away from a generic 'normal', I am not convinced that it is helpful to categorize any learner as neurotypical. Does the comparison between diverse and typical not just reinforce the idea that some people learn as they are supposed to while others present as outliers or atypical examples? I think it would be to all learners' benefit if those who have found creative ways to thrive in systems that generally misunderstand their learning needs were considered models of how disruptive circumstances can be embraced as the raw ingredients of effective learning progress.

First steps into disruptive inclusion: blurring the lines between inside and outside, light and dark, sight and blindness

As promised, this book is not just about disruptive inclusion but also models what the process can feel like. If, at this stage, the concepts of bafflement, optimum distance and multiplicity of vision have left you ... well, baffled, do not be concerned, it is all part of the process! One of the major challenges with not only replacing one idea with another but also completely shifting the basis on which an entire concept is imagined is that some of the boundary lines between longstanding existing categories are moved and perhaps even scrapped altogether. For most readers of this book, disruptive inclusion challenges the assumption that learning is a process of moving from ignorance or confusion to clarity by suggesting the opposite idea: that not resolving things (at least not instantly) might actually be the most valuable part of learning. However, including disruption in learning is not just for its own sake or to try something new. As we have just considered, sometimes when you stand too close to something it can obscure rather than improve your view. Therefore, to help us move beyond the peak of disruption into optimum distance, this section takes a few steps back from the detailed analysis of disruptive inclusion we have just considered and offers a few extended metaphors to help us take in disruptive inclusion from several angles. Specifically, we will ask: How is it possible/what does it mean for learners to be in two places at once or move repeatedly between several realities? And what potential impact does it have?

Our first image is from church architecture. If you enter an old church building you may immediately find yourself in what is traditionally referred to as the narthex. In contemporary terms, the narthex is probably best described as a kind of lobby area; the entrance hall where people dry themselves off from the rain or prepare themselves to go back out into the elements. Professor of religious education Bert Roebben describes how, as well as its practical function of allowing entrance and exit, a church's narthex has a symbolic role in representing the place of crossover between the church and the wider community – a meeting point for those on their way in and out, a kind of 'buffer zone between the outside world and the inner sacred space ... both a pedagogical and theological place of confrontation.'[22] In centuries past, many historic churches were not just places of worship for the local population but also functioned as milestones for pilgrims. Roebben reflects on how, for the pilgrim, a church's narthex functioned as a 'both-and' place: a source of comfort and challenge addressing both physical and spiritual needs. 'Craving for water and coolness on their journey', pilgrims step over the church's threshold and 'are confronted with something completely different from what they had expected and hoped for in the narthex of the church building.'[23] Roebben fleshes out what he means with an example from the Madeleine church in Vézelay, France:

On their journey through the Burgundian hills, along one of the four central axes of the French route to Santiago de Compostella, pilgrims turn into two-legged shambling creatures craving refreshment. Is there anybody who can quench their thirst and offer them a cooling breeze? Something extraordinary happens when entering the narthex: their entreaty for refreshment is answered with beautiful sculptures of the Christian salvation history. The triumphing Christ wants to offer them 'inspired water', something completely different to what they expected and hoped for. But at the same time a sigh of recognition resounds in their souls. They let go of their overarching search for salvation and let themselves be found (in this case by Christ). The quest receives new meaning, the longing is rearranged, questions that have been asked along the way are not solved but rephrased. Life receives new meaning: a new sense (pedagogically) and a new direction (theologically).[24]

Imagining a narthex as a learning space can help illustrate how optimum distance works in disruptive-inclusive learning. In a church's narthex, a pilgrim is, in effect, in two places at once. They are not yet fully in the holy sanctuary, but they are in church. They come with a specific view of their own needs and how they might be met, but in the in-between space of the narthex these are 'not solved but rephrased'. As they pass through the narthex, they realize that although they may have primarily entered for physical rest and refreshment, they find something else that they (perhaps) did not even know they needed. The narthex nourishes and provides some relief but also raises questions, demands attention. It can be passed through frequently, but it is not a place where anyone remains for extended periods of time. As many have observed, and as will be further explored in Chapter 5, pilgrimage and journeying more broadly are key themes in understanding how Christian faith relates to learning, particularly to the concepts of being *in-between* and crossing thresholds. Roebben concludes that there is a mysterious quality to a narthex that makes it an insightful image for Christian learning. It is 'about being at a threshold, neither here nor there, crossing into an unknown space of perplexing and often transformative energy.'[25]

On a similar theme, Hull explored the concept of crossing between what he referred to as the 'known and unknown learning worlds' located either side of his front door.[26] Just as doors have two sides, he observed, they also have two functions: they divide *outside* from *inside* but they also connect the two. Particularly for blind people, they welcome into warm, familiar and controlled environments but also usher out into dangerous, unfamiliar and thoroughly uncontrollable spaces. Despite its unpredictability and the associated loss of control, Hull was compelled to venture beyond his front door. However, he knew that he must also take advantage of the familiarity of inside, enabling him to relax and achieve a level of independence. Therefore the pattern of repeatedly going in and out became for Hull a foundational learning discipline (explored in much more detail in the upcoming interlude), with his doorstep not just representing the fixed boundary line between the two realities but the distinction between the confidence of home and difficulties of the unknown beginning to blur over time. He eventually became so practised at passing between the two that, just by bringing the existence of his home environment to mind, he could partially recreate its conditions wherever he was. He found that just by knowing that protected, predictable and familiar conditions existed somewhere, he was able to draw on some of the confidence and rest they brought even when not physically there. Hull reached a point at which feeling 'at home' became more of a state of mind than a physical location (more on this in Chapter 5).

Another theme Hull repeatedly used to explain how different learning realities exist alongside each other, and even overlap, was his experience of light and darkness. Towards the end of his life Hull reflected on how he had changed since his initial years of physical blindness:

> The feelings of panic have long since subsided. My blind skin … has got thicker. I have become less aware of the darkness. As the light has faded and the memory of the light has faded, then the awareness of the darkness has also faded. So, I don't feel as if I'm in the dark. Ah, I don't go round thinking I'm blind. I just live my life and I, I love it.[27]

The first stage Hull refers to is 'the fading of the light'. Little by little he explains how he lost access to the only world he had ever known – a visual one. Stage two he calls 'the fading of the memory of the light'. Here Hull could no longer physically see anything but was yet to become accustomed to living in darkness. He speaks of himself as caught between worlds – trapped in an in-between space where his sighted memories and imagination were still vivid enough for him to retain what he called 'shadowy but mobile visual memories',[28] but where he was simultaneously forced to 'reassemble' himself as a blind person in a blind world.[29] He explained stage three as growth in awareness of the darkness, when visual memories were no longer accessible and the strangeness of the 'new' place in which he found himself came to the fore. This stage might be understood as the other side of the coin to stage two. The peak of disruption had passed and the principal task had become developing awareness of, and comfort in, new surroundings. Finally, stage four was 'fading in awareness of darkness'. Ultimately, every disruptive learning event or arc lands in a place where what used to be scary, unknown and all-consuming becomes a new kind of normal, a sort of home ground that raises few questions any more. So it was true for Hull that in relation to his blindness – from the trauma and questioning of the early days – he eventually arrived at a point where his wife Marilyn recalled him joking about how blindness had become just a hobby to him![30]

Progress through stages two and three aligns with optimum distance: the point of maximum disruption has passed and begins to recede just a little.[31] Scholars in a range of academic disciplines refer to a similar theory called the Goldilocks principle, in which there is just enough access to the familiarity of what used to be but, equally and simultaneously, competing realities are no longer entirely overwhelming or paralysing, making it possible to (at least) recognize both, or maybe even draw connections between the two.[32] Hull also described this ability to pass between (or participate in an inner dialogue between) multiple different realities or worldviews as becoming a *trans-world interpreter*,[33] helping others to interpret the spaces they do not or dare not access for themselves.

But finally, for Hull, it is not that CAL is about simply swapping one reality for another; it is an entire shift in learners' perceptions of the value of where they have been, where they are and where they may progress on to. In Hull's diaries from the early years of his blindness, he tells a story that eventually provided the title for the published collection of entries:

Touching the Rock.[34] The entry for 22 August 1986 (during the first few years of complete physical blindness) describes a deeply formative event on the island of Iona. Deep in the developing awareness of darkness, confusion, frustration and associated isolation, and without sighted help to navigate in a new place, Hull became disoriented and was forced to use his sense of physical touch to find his way around the Abbey, finally happening upon what turned out to be the main altar.

Despite the clear trauma of this event, Hull reflected on it in the following way: 'There is something urgent and intense about trying to touch a rock when you are being swept away, but from that safer place it is possible to survey the experience from a wider perspective.'[35] If you quickly skim this comment, you might be tempted to think that the safer place he refers to is a later, less vulnerable and broader space from where he had once again found his bearings and could look back with hindsight on the difficulties of this event. But if you read closely, the place Hull refers to *is* the vulnerable, disruptive experience he has at the altar and not another, later or reoriented position. Hull had come to understand that the moment when he felt most exposed and disrupted was the place from which he could most clearly and effectively perceive reality. Hull's disruptive-inclusive learning experience had not merely taken him on an adventure and then returned him to its starting point; it had forced him to reassess how everything holds together and relates to each other, culminating in the statement: 'I have learned that darkness and light are both alike to God.'[36] Hull had not just swapped one reality for another but learned to reassess the value of the entire process. From somewhere that must be quickly escaped from, the murky, difficult-to-define, dangerous, *in-between* spaces became for Hull a source of life. Places that he considered safe, not because they offered comfort and security but the exact opposite.

Selah 2: Harmonious or dissonant learning?

If you had to describe what good, effective learning sounded like in musical terms, what kind of a sound would come to mind? Would it be a well-trained orchestra, or a group of children with recorders, all just making whatever noise they can ... all at once? Or perhaps it would be a string quartet playing Beethoven or Freddie Mercury in full flow with Queen? Whatever kinds of instruments, voices or types of music you imagine, more than likely you will be thinking of music that creates harmonious rather than dissonant sound. In general, most music sounds pleasant because it takes the form of what music theorists refer to as vertical harmony. It works by stacking combinations of sounds on top of each other according to the rules of Western musical composition. These notes are either played or sung simultaneously, resulting in a single, simple, harmonious sound (think a strummed guitar chord or barbershop choir). The opposite of this would be if each member of a barbershop choir sang in a different key and with different timings, creating musical dissonance. Paul Ingram has described the experience of dissonance as 'an impression of inescapable noise or acute disorder ... a sense of intolerable wrongness.'[37] In the 1950s, psychologist Leon Festinger created a theory called cognitive dissonance, in which he claims that, at the most basic level, humans prefer balance and consistency in every area of life.[38] Therefore when inconsistencies or tensions arise, humans' most natural response is either to eliminate or repair the inconsistencies.

However, returning to music theory, more recently a third option has come to prominence somewhere in between vertical harmony and dissonance: horizontal harmony. At its most basic level, horizontal harmony ignores some of the rules that normally govern what sounds pleasant. For example, it allows notes to be played/sung together that would normally be deemed to clash, and it also allows multiple, independent melodies to be played or sung at the same time. It makes new suggestions about the kinds of notes that create suspense and tension and the kinds of sounds that suggest rest or resolution to the listener. Horizontal harmonies (also referred to as counterpoint harmony or polyphony) even sometimes go so far as to include implied harmonic incompatibilities (that is, according to the rules of music, notes that should not sound good together!).

This creates innumerably more harmonic possibilities than in vertical harmony, meaning that for those more familiar with music according to the rules of standard Western composition (that is most of us!), listening to jazz or other uses of horizontal harmonies can be much more demanding but also much more rewarding. Horizontal harmonies reshape listeners' expectations at every turn, but also provide access to new musical possibilities. Fundamentally, horizontal harmony proposes that when several semi-independent tunes are played or sung in parallel something new emerges from their combination. We will revisit the role of emergence in CAL in Chapter 4, but here it is enough to get a general sense of how new, emerging realities arise as learners dare to play multiple tunes at once! Vietnamese-born Roman Catholic theologian Peter Phan applies this concept to second-generation Asian Americans:

> Being neither this nor that allows one to be both this and that. Belonging to both worlds ... persons have the opportunity to fuse them together and out of their respective resources, fashion a new, different world, so that persons at the margins stand not only between these worlds and cultures but also beyond them. Thus, being betwixt and between can bring about personal and social transformation and enrichment.[39]

Phan understands that those who live in the betwixt and between (borrowing French philosopher Albert Camus's famous book title) do not just straddle their particular realities but also live beyond them by daring to refuse the suggestion that they do not belong together. If disruptive inclusion were musical it would be a horizontal harmony, in which the co-existence of concepts that, some suggest, should not result in a good outcome gives rise to new possibilities in unorthodox ways that defy present conventions.

The crux: why bother?

Throughout this chapter I have been careful not to play down the extent of the paradigm shift presented by disruptive inclusion in relation to most current CAL thinking and practice. It is not just another method that seeks to relegate existing approaches, nor does it suggest that we just do the complete opposite of what we have been doing up to this point. Neither can disruptive inclusion be put into practice by completing a checklist. As I have demonstrated through the use of various metaphors, adopting a disruptive-inclusive approach to CAL requires embracing several paradoxical ideas in working towards different kinds of aims and objectives. So the final question to address before exploring the basis for and implications of this proposed shift is: What is at stake? Or more bluntly: Why bother?

If we are to invest significant time and effort in reimagining CAL – how it works and what it aims to achieve – then there really must be some potentially significant reasons why we might want to undertake such a challenging path. Later chapters will unpack many of the potential practical implications of adopting a disruptive-inclusive approach in various teaching and learning settings, but before we get there, one key, underlying reason encapsulates my answer to the question: Why bother? CAL has a diversity and inclusion problem and all current efforts to address it fail to scratch the surface, never mind offer hope for lasting and ongoing change.

In a 2020 interview with *Christianity Today*, former Archbishop of Canterbury Rowan Williams explained his view that the core task of Christian learning is, 'In some ways, to be taken back to that moment of bewilderment about the newness or the distinctiveness or the strangeness of being in this new Christian framework.'[40] He continues that part of this process is for learners to gain a 'new set of relationships ... a new set of perspectives. You see differently, you sense differently, you relate differently.' In summary, he argues that 'theological education is familiarising yourself with how people have found their way around that landscape with the perspectives they've occupied and then learning to pitch your own tent, as one might say, in that territory.'[41] In line with disruptive inclusion, this understanding of CAL imagines a new centre for the entire process, focused around the repeated revisiting of (rather than graduating from) surprise, disruption and *strangeness*. In effect, Williams argues that getting good at pitching a tent (thankfully not literally!) is a (or perhaps the) central mechanism for CAL and that many current learning frameworks and establishments do not encourage this nor celebrate the expert tent-pitchers in our communities.

This language of centre, who gets to be there and why, is also addressed by the queer Asian American feminist scholar June Hee Yoon. Writing about the challenges of finding home, Yoon compares the experiences of those 'assigned the center and ... relegated to the periphery in the system',[42] reflecting on how such categories are defined by those traditionally located at the centre, meaning that many of those who are 'silenced and pushed to the periphery' must find 'true belongingness' in an imagined community.[43] From a Korean American perspective, Yoon observes the number of groups who are deemed not to fit at the centre: 'those at the periphery include women, people of a different religious affiliation, people of a different racial and ethnic group, people of a different nationality, people who are mentally or physically challenged, and people who are not socio-culturally established.'[44]

In a significant way Yoon and Williams both highlight how, rather than celebrating and learning from the long-time nomads, desert wanderers and tent pitchers who have been forced to reimagine home on the peripheries, educational systems generally encourage Christian adult learners to aspire to fulfil the roles of estate owners and home-dwellers – but the route to this goal is only open to some! According to both scholars, exemplar learners are those most practised in navigating bewilderment and strangeness: existing on the edges, perceiving and connecting to the world in new ways and learning from those who have inhabited similar territory in the past. Those who have been living out in the metaphorical theological wilderness, at the wrong end of the 'asymmetry of power', and whose lives are lived in territory 'full of tension, fractures and resistance',[45] are not just those who *should* be at the centre, they are central to CAL processes. The problem persists because many of us with unacknowledged or under-acknowledged privilege think that we are at the centre and are unwilling to cede power or status.

Without apology, if disruptive inclusion can go even the tiniest way to beginning to expose and redress some of the ways in which exemplary, authoritative CAL is thought to be centred around (or, even in some cases, exclusive to) white, straight, English-speaking, middle-aged men who are located in the global North, then I will be satisfied. For too long, not only educational institutions and systems, but the very conceptions and practices of CAL, have purported to be interested in diversity and inclusion while simultaneously stacking the odds against those who have been, and continue to be, pushed to the edges.

Ask yourself honestly, who are the expert tent pitchers in your community/ies? Who are most experienced at living with and in disruption? Almost guaranteed, it is far more likely to be a physically disabled single mum of African heritage or an asylum seeker than it is to be someone like me! Yes, learners who belong to one or more disadvantaged or excluded groups have a natural learning 'advantage' (I use this word ironically, aware that it is easy to describe discrimination as advantage when it is about someone else) because they have been forced to move on and repitch their tent on numerous occasions. They have lived far more in *in-between* spaces than those of us with enough privilege to be able to somehow sidestep or buy our way out of the borderlands into generally recognized and endorsed categories. Let me state this as plainly as possible.

The reason there are not more Black and ethnic minority, queer, disabled, neurodiverse and other traditionally discriminated voices in CAL (whether as teachers, preachers, scholars, writers or learners) is not due to a lack of interest or any sense of inbuilt inferiority. In fact, in both cases, quite the opposite. The reason why academic scholarship, formal theological training institutions and many churches do not represent a wide range of voices is because it suits many of us to maintain ways of understanding and practising CAL that keep certain categories of people out. This is why I am convinced that real improvements cannot be made to the structures, theory and practice of CAL without a complete rethink.

Disruptive inclusion does not need to downplay difference in order to promote genuine inclusivity. Although the exact nature of the disruptive learning challenge will differ from person to person, no one is exempt. Every learner and learning community is presented with the challenge of embracing and finding value in what they cannot know or do, as much as in what they can; in embracing that which is beyond their present reach as much as the substance of their current location. Everything is flipped on its head. As Rob Bell said in 2005, it is time to recognize that brick walls can, in fact, be trampolines.[46] For those learners whose voices have traditionally been perceived as more valuable than others, disruption may require taking a listening posture, finding ways to maintain personal integrity while privileging others' underrepresented views. For those learners who belong to groups constantly pushed to the peripheries of learning, a core challenge will be taking up places in the centre with confidence and trust. How can Christian adult learners build broader and deeper community with diverse others? I firmly believe that reframing CAL around including disruption has the potential to create learning spaces and structures that can facilitate genuine and sustained inclusion of all.[47]

Questions/activities

- Before reading this chapter, how would you have understood CAL? Where do these views come from?
- Do you recognize any of the patterns of 'being here': not being encouraged to think about how learning happens, educational methodology constantly moving on to the 'next big thing' and the push towards positive learning experiences? What influence do these have?
- Explain bafflement, optimum distance and multiplicity of vision in simple terms. What are they and how do they work in CAL?
- What areas of your own learning journey have brought the most disruption? Why?
- Who are the model disruptive-inclusive learners in your communities? What have they been through/what do they do that qualifies them?
- Note your feelings at this point. What are your primary questions? Why?

Notes

1 Robert Zemeckis (dir.), *Back to the Future Part II* (USA: Universal Pictures, 1989).

2 As explained more fully in my thesis.

3 See Roy Blatchford, 'Differentiation is out. Mastery is the new classroom buzzword', *The Guardian* (1 October 2015), available at: https://www.theguardian.com/teacher-network/2015/oct/01/mastery-differentiation-new-classroom-buzzword (accessed 31.07.2023).

4 Louis Deslauriers, Logan S. McCarty, Kelly Miller, Kristina Callaghan and Greg Kestin, 'Measuring actual learning versus feeling of learning in response to being actively engaged in the classroom', *Proceedings of the National Academy of Sciences*, 116:39 (2019), pp. 19251–7. Available at: https://www.pnas.org/doi/10.1073/pnas.1821936116.

5 See Peter Reuell, 'Lessons in learning', *The Harvard Gazette* (4 September 2019), available at: https://news.harvard.edu/gazette/story/2019/09/study-shows-that-students-learn-more-when-taking-part-in-classrooms-that-employ-active-learning-strategies/ (accessed 31.07.2023).

6 John M. Hull, *What Prevents Christian Adults from Learning?* (London: SCM Press, 1985), p. 35.

7 Zemeckis, *Back to the Future Part II.*

8 John M. Hull, *The Learning Church* (Methodist Church: North West and Mann Learning and Development Network, 2015), https://youtu.be/Y_SC-3ppC40 (accessed 31.07.2023).

9 Hull, *What Prevents*, p. 18.

10 Hull, *What Prevents*, p. 57.

11 Daniel Fleming and Peter Mudge, 'Leaving home: A pedagogy for theological education' in L. Ball and J. Harrison (eds), *Learning and Teaching Theology: Some ways ahead* (Eugene, OR: Wipf & Stock, 2015), p. 74.

12 Hull, *What Prevents*, pp. 57–9. Hull defines bafflement as awareness of the differences between lived reality and expectations of how things ought to be. Inversely, he understands confusion as a lack of awareness, understanding or the ability to articulate.

13 Hull, *What Prevents*, p. 54.

14 *Optimum distance* is similar in some respects to Lev Vygotsky's *Zone of Proximal Distance (ZPD)*. For more, see Harry Daniels, Michael Cole and James V. Wertsch, *The Cambridge Companion to Vygotsky* (Cambridge: Cambridge University Press, 2007).

15 Hull, *What Prevents*, p. 54.

16 Hull, *What Prevents*, p. 75.

17 The British Dyslexia Association and the Department for Education have produced a helpful introduction to neurodiversity: https://cdn.bdadyslexia.org.uk/uploads/documents/Dyslexia/A_Guide_to_SpLD_2nd_ed.pdf?v=1554931179 (accessed 31.07.23).

18 Robert C. Wilson, Amitai Shenhav, Mark Straccia and Jonathan D. Cohen, 'The Eighty Five Percent Rule for optimal learning', *Nature Communications*, 10:4646 (2019).

19 Wilson, et al., 'The Eighty Five Percent Rule', p. 2.

20 Bart Massi, Christopher H. Donahue and Daeyeol Lee, 'Volatility facilitates value updating in the prefrontal cortex, *Neuron*, 99:3 (2018), pp. 598–608, p. 598.

21 Wilson, et al., 'The Eighty Five Percent Rule', p. 2.

22 Bert Roebben, 'Narthical religious learning: redefining religious education in terms of pilgrimage', *British Journal of Religious Education*, 31:1 (2009), pp. 17–27, p. 23.

23 Roebben, 'Narthical religious learning', p. 23.

24 Roebben, 'Narthical religious learning', pp. 23–34.

25 Timothy Carson, Rosy Fairhurst, Nigel Rooms and Lisa R. Withrow (eds), *Crossing thresholds: A practical theology of liminality* (Cambridge: The Lutterworth Press, 2021), p. 67.

26 John M. Hull, *In the Beginning There was Darkness* (London: SCM Press, 2001), p. 140.

27 See Peter Middleton and James Spinney, 'Notes on Blindness', *The New York Times* (16 January 2014), available at: https://www.nytimes.com/interactive/2014/01/16/opinion/16OpDoc-NotesOnBlindness.html (accessed 31.07.2023).

28 John M. Hull, *Notes on Blindness: A journey through the dark* (London: Profile Books, 2017), p. 200.

29 John M. Hull, 'Blindness and memory: being reborn into a different world', *Memory Marathon: The Space Arts*, 12–14 October 2012, available here: https://www.serpentinegalleries.org/whats-on/memory-marathon/ (accessed 31.07.2023).

30 Hull, *Notes on Blindness*, p. 199.

31 Hull, *What Prevents*, p. 54.

32 Celeste Kidd, Steven T. Piantadosi and Richard N. Aslin, 'The Goldilocks effect in infant auditory attention', *Child Development*, 85:5 (2014), pp. 1795–804.

33 John M. Hull, 'Teaching as a trans-world activity', *Support for Learning*, 19:3 (2004), pp. 103–6, p. 105.

34 John M. Hull, *Touching the Rock: An experience of blindness.* SPCK Classics (London: SPCK, 2013). A new edition of this book was published and renamed *Notes on Blindness* to coincide with the release of the film with the same name.

35 John M. Hull, *On Sight and Insight: A journey into the world of blindness* (Oxford: Oneworld, 2001), p. 232.

36 Hull, *Touching the Rock*, p. xx.

37 Paul Ingram, *Theological Reflections at the Boundaries* (Eugene, OR: Cascade Books, 2012), p. 4.

38 Leon Festinger, *A Theory of Cognitive Dissonance* (Evanston, IL: Row, Peterson and co., 1957).

39 Peter C. Phan, 'Betwixt and between: doing theology with memory and imagination' in P. C. Phan and J. Y. Lee (eds), *Journeys at the Margin: Toward an autobiographical theology in American-Asian perspective* (Collegeville, MI: Liturgical Press, 1999), pp. 113–34, p. 113. Carlton Turner also recognizes the challenges created in postcolonial Bahamian culture of Christians struggling to understand their place in both the Church and wider socio-cultural spheres of life: a situation Turner describes as resulting in 'Bahamians fully inhabit[ing] both spaces'. Carlton Turner, *Overcoming Self-Negation* (Eugene, OR: Pickwick Publications, 2020), p. 28.

40 Benjamin Wayman, 'Rowan Williams: Theological education is for everyone', *Christianity Today* (19 August 2020), available at: https://www.christianitytoday.com/ct/2020/august-web-only/rowan-williams-theological-education-for-everyone.html (accessed 31.07.2023).

41 Wayman, 'Rowan Williams'.

42 June Hee Yoon, 'Finding home from the in-between space for a queer Asian American Christian woman' in P. L. Kwok (ed.), *Asian and Asian American Women in Theology and Religion: Embodying knowledge* (Cham: Springer, 2020), pp. 59–71, p. 67.

43 Yoon, 'Finding home', p. 66.

44 Yoon, 'Finding home', p. 66.

45 Kwok Pui-Lan, *Postcolonial Imagination and Feminist Theology* (Louisville, KY: Westminster John Knox Press, 2005), p. 43.

46 Rob Bell, *Velvet Elvis: Repainting the Christian Faith* (Grand Rapids, MI: Zondervan, 2005), chapter 1.

47 The arts are often best placed to help us imagine new futures. The best expression I have recently encountered of the kind of diversity and inclusion I am attempting to express here is the 2022 song by Spencer LaJoye, 'Plowshare Prayer'. Available here: https://youtu.be/MhOZv5i7CHY.

Interlude: Learning In and From the Bible

The words *learn* or *learning* appear approximately 100 times in most English versions of the Bible, but they rarely refer to learning in a formal sense. The disciples are not sent on a classroom-based training course. The focus of the Apostle Paul's letters is not on sharing the information gathered during his university studies (although he was undoubtedly proud of his commitment to and prowess in religious training); Abraham and Moses did not have to demonstrate their academic qualifications before following the God who called them. However, the question of how humans develop in and from life's ongoing experiences (or struggle to) is never far from many of the biblical authors' interests. From Samson, Jonah and Ruth to Nicodemus, Mary and Martha, not to mention Jesus' disciples and the Jewish religious leaders, one of the key themes running throughout both biblical testaments is whether (and how) individuals and groups have learned from the past; whether they are able to respond to God and neighbour in the present and are prepared to continue developing in the future.

When it comes to learning *from* the Bible, a common claim is that it should be thought of as a kind of instruction manual for life or even a textbook of Christian discipleship. I understand that these ideas are meant to highlight the Bible's relevance to contemporary life, but am concerned that they are more misleading than helpful. None of the biblical texts are presented to readers in the form of a to-do list for all situations; for the most part the Christian holy scriptures are in narrative form. Stories about individuals and groups attempting (and mostly failing) to follow a mysterious God and a wandering rabbi who claims to represent God on earth. We will return specifically to the relationship between story and disruptive inclusion in Chapter 7, but for now it is enough to say that, by design, story requires interpretation – it only works when there is collaboration between a storyteller who delivers a narrative and a listener/reader who receives it. While there is not enough space to fully explore the relationship between biblical interpretation and learning, there is one key connection that cannot be ignored.[1]

Almost all those who recognize the Bible as Christian Scripture hope to learn from it (or maybe from God through it). In other words, there is an almost universal expectation that Christians ought to be students of the Bible. Most believe that the Bible's primary teaching function comes from its message: its content is useful for guiding, equipping and encouraging. While I do not dispute that the substance of the biblical texts is an essential source of Christian learning, I am deeply convicted that the biblical narrative does not just tell Christians what to learn but offers guidance on how learning happens. Therefore this interlude is an exercise in engaging with the biblical text in this way. It demonstrates what kind of answers a particular biblical text can give when we ask not only, 'What does the Bible teach us?' but also, 'How can the Bible guide and shape our understanding of becoming better learners?'

Most will read this interlude as part of the wider book in which it appears, building on the discussions already begun. However, I have also designed it to stand alone so that it can be used by individuals and groups as a way into the topic of Christian adult learning (CAL) that does not require having already read the whole book. Think of the relationship between this section and the rest of the book as like eating ice cream at the beach or in the intermission at the theatre. I am told that it is possible to go to the beach without eating ice cream, but I can only imagine that the experience is significantly worse for it! Similarly, this interlude is designed to enrich and develop the wider conversation concerning CAL, but it can equally be enjoyed on its own and/or out of the generally accepted order (again, not unlike ice cream). Later chapters will explore various ways in which including disruption can be said to constitute a biblical approach to Christian learning, but this interlude provides a worked example of how the understanding and practice of CAL can be both informed by, and modelled on, the biblical narrative. In other words, as well as discussing the potential relationship between the Bible and disruptive-inclusive CAL, this section invites you to experience it.

Rereading John 10 through the lens of learning

Even if you are very familiar with John 10.1–18, I strongly suggest that you take a careful look at the passage in several versions and keep it open as you read on. It may also be interesting to note down your answer to the following question before you begin and revisit your answer at the end: 'What does it mean for Christians to access life in all its fullness and how do they do it?'

The fourth Gospel (so as not to confuse multiple books and people called John) is the source of many bumper-sticker Bible verses. For God so loved the world, no one comes to the Father except through me, I am the resurrection and the life: all from the fourth Gospel. Among the most quoted is John 10.10, where Jesus' claim to be the good shepherd allows him to provide access to life in all its fullness. 'The thief comes only to steal and kill and destroy. I came that they may have life, and have it abundantly.' However, as is common with a bumper-sticker approach, John 10.10 has become disconnected from the wider passage in which it appears. Specifically (and hopefully not too controversially) I would argue that separating John 10.10 from John 10.9 makes it more difficult to understand either verse. John 10.9 declares Jesus to be a gate (or in some English versions, a door) that makes three things possible for the sheep: to enter the sheepfold and be saved, to go in and out, and to find pasture.[2] Although the exact relationship between these key ideas and fullness of life is not clearly spelled out (that is, there is no 'so', 'therefore' or 'thus' in between verses 9 and 10), it seems reasonable to suggest that they are connected. Before delving into the potential details of that connection, however, it is important to recognize that the entire chapter is built around the idea that whatever is possible for the sheep is due to Jesus' roles as both shepherd and gate, and so we must carefully consider this first.

A key difference between John 10 and other parts of the fourth Gospel where Jesus makes 'I am ...' statements is that whereas the other instances use just one image or set of images, ('I am .... the bread of life, or the resurrection and the life, or the true vine', etc.), John 10 contains several different, overlapping metaphors. Some prominent twentieth-century biblical scholars found this deeply problematic and pointed out that it makes no sense for Jesus to be both the shepherd who enters via the gate (v.2) *and* the gate itself (v.9). For example, biblical scholar C. H. Dodd dramatically declared that John 10 should be thought of as 'the wreckage of two parables fused into one'.[3] However, rather than seeing the intertwined imagery of shepherd and gate as problematic or a puzzle to be solved, I am far more inclined towards an approach like that of John Ashton, who imagines the passage as 'an intricate mosaic .... two statements that are not contradictory but mutually illuminating.'[4] Therefore my approach to John 10 does not aim to fix what is wrong with it but instead to explore the issues raised by its use of shepherd and gate images side by side.

I have heard multiple sermons on this passage that offer a neat response to how Jesus functions as both good shepherd and gate for the sheep. As the good shepherd, Jesus provides safety from danger in the sheepfold to those who request access and enter via the gate (usually the sheepfold is presumed to represent the Church, although I think this reading is problematic in several ways).[5] The pivotal point in many readings of John 10 is that Jesus' protection is provided in a very specific way. In the ancient world, shepherds generally moved around with their sheep, meaning that permanent, physical sheepfolds or gates were often not available. In many cases, sheepfolds might be 'nothing more than a rough circle of rocks piled into a wall with a small open space to enter.'[6] In these cases, shepherds used their own bodies as physical barriers between the sheep and the dangers outside. So in John 10 Jesus' body provides security for the sheep inside the sheepfold, functioning as an entrance for those who accept his help and a barrier for those who do not. This is what Jesus is referring to (John 10.11–15) when he says that the Good Shepherd lays his life down for the sheep, simultaneously functioning as shepherd and gate.

I am not an expert in ancient shepherding techniques, nor do I have any reason to doubt that shepherds used their own bodies as protective shields when other barriers were unavailable. But a careful reading of John 10 raises some significant questions about relying too heavily on the above interpretation. First, although John 10.9 begins by explaining that sheep are saved by entering the sheepfold, the sheep's movement does not end there. The sheep's first entrance into the sheepfold begins a cycle of repeated leaving and re-entering via the gate in the pursuit of pasture. There is no suggestion that sheep welcomed in via the gate are then permanently kept inside. Second (and crucially), if the primary aim of the shepherd's body or a physical gate is to keep sheep permanently inside and their enemies permanently outside, the story Jesus tells in John 10 reveals this as a highly ineffective technique! From the chapter's opening verse, some thieves and bandits are revealed as already in the sheepfold, having found alternative ways in that avoid the gate: the sheep's enemies are everywhere.

Freedom of movement, not current location

So if Jesus' sheep do not permanently remain in the sheepfold and the sheep's enemies are found on both sides of the gate, what makes Jesus a good shepherd and an effective gate? What benefits does using the gate to enter the sheepfold offer?

The first key to answering these questions is to recognize that neither the sheep nor the enemies in John 10 can be identified based on location. Being inside the sheepfold is not a marker of the salvation and guidance offered by the shepherd; and equally, neither are those on the outside necessarily excluded. The defining factor in whether sheep belong to the shepherd or not is how entrance and exit are achieved. Those who have climbed into the sheepfold and purposely avoided the gate do not belong to the shepherd; those who have entered the sheepfold via Jesus and exited again (multiple times) continue to belong to Jesus, even when they go far from the sheepfold in search of pasture. The measure of who belongs to Jesus and orients their life around him is signalled by the ability to move freely between the terrain that lies within the gate and the terrain beyond the gate.

This means that distinguishing between those who rely on Jesus' salvation and ongoing guidance and those who do not listen to the shepherd's voice and forge their own path, is not always as obvious as it may seem. This is reinforced by the two words used to describe those who climb into the sheepfold. At first the words do not seem particularly noteworthy: they describe those who take what is not theirs without permission or authority (the Greek terms are usually translated into English as bandit/thief and robber). However, when we discover that these two words only appear in one other place each in the entire fourth Gospel, might these specific choices convey more than the obvious?

The two Greek terms appear in different places to describe individuals with very different roles in Jesus' story. One appears in John 12.6, revealing Judas as having stolen from the disciples' common purse. The disciple who betrays Jesus is the ultimate trusted insider who seems to be on the right path, but whose actions betray his true motivation to benefit himself. The other term describes Barabbas, the revolutionary for whose freedom the crowd cries in John 18.40. There is some disagreement among English translations over how to represent the word used to describe Barabbas. Some opt for robber or bandit, but taking into account the parallel stories from the other biblical Gospels, it is likely that Barabbas was not just a petty thief but a violent revolutionary whose actions risked the political and social stability of Jerusalem. Interestingly, however, as the crowd repeatedly shout his name, the literal meaning of their shouts is 'son of the father' or 'son of the rabbi' (*bar* meaning son, *abba* meaning father). Even though, just as today, the meaning of ancient names was not always at the front of people's consciousness (for example, my name means 'the fair one' but I do not assume that everyone who calls my name is consciously complimenting my complexion!), the Gospel writer does make a point of including this revolutionary's name at a part of the story that comes directly after Jesus explains to his disciples (at length) about the importance of the relationship between him and his father (see John 17). Although it is impossible to know whether ancient audiences would have made this connection, it seems to me that the irony between Jesus' true sonship and the crowd's choice of this Barabbas (son of the father) would have been difficult to miss! So, returning to John 10, if the fence jumpers represent the likes of Judas (the insider who is really an outsider), might Barabbas represent the opposite (the outsider who, perhaps unknowingly, points to Jesus' true identity)? Either way, what we can securely say is that although it may seem that John 10's fence jumpers are easily identifiable, if they could look like either Judas or Barabbas, perhaps it is not as easy as we might think to tell who belongs and who does not.

This has a few significant implications, but one of the biggest relates to the function of the shepherd. If the shepherd's role is not just to let the sheep in and keep the enemies out, then what is it? Rather than functioning as a dividing wall separating the sheep from the enemies, what if Jesus' role is the opposite? What if, as the gate, Jesus acts as a point of connection and orientation for those who trust and listen to him, linking the various spaces between which the sheep move and making the enemies' movement more difficult? Only those who are willing to enter and exit via the Jesus gate have 'free and easy interchange between the inside and the outside.'[7] In 1985 Professor John Hull concluded about Jesus' role in John 10: 'This is the work of the good shepherd, who does not close and lock the door, but makes his own mobile, living body the point of entrance and exit.'[8]

Going in and out?

So far we have focused on two key ideas in John 10. First, that Jesus' function in the passage is as both shepherd and gate for the sheep. Second, we have identified that the sheep and the sheep's enemies are on both sides of the gate – it is not accurate to say that the sheep are inside and the enemies are outside. Finally, then, before we ask how any of this relates to learning, there is one final detail from the chapter to closely consider: what does it mean to 'go in and out and find pasture' (10.9b)? If we are to reconnect the idea of the abundant life that Jesus offers in 10.10 and the rest of the passage, then we must ask what it means to go in and out in search of pasture.

There is some discussion among scholars about whether this passage's description of the sheep going in and out of the sheepfold refers to (at least the imagined) physical movement of sheep or whether the phrase is symbolic of something beyond entrance and exit to the sheepfold. For example, biblical scholar Herman Ridderbos identifies a connection between John 10.9 and Moses' deathbed speech where he tells Israel, 'I am 120 years old today. I am no longer able to go out and come in. The LORD has said to me, "You shall not go over this Jordan"' (Deut. 31.2, ESV). Going in and out, Ridderbos argues, is a common Semitic (the family of ancient languages that includes Hebrew and Aramaic) expression for the passage of everyday life.[9] And so, in Deuteronomy, Moses' recognition that he can no longer go in and out is a way of saying that his earthly life is at an end, not necessarily a reference to any specific physical journeying. When Solomon takes his father's throne, 1 Kings 3.7 offers a similar example: 'I am only a little child; I do not know how to go out or come in.' The Psalmist also expresses God's proactive oversight of the passage of human life in similar terms: 'The LORD will keep your going out and your coming in from this time on and for evermore' (Ps. 121.8).

There is no definitive way to prove whether the reference to sheep going in and out in John 10 imagines sheep embarking on specific journeys or refers more generally to the overall progress of life, nor do I think it makes a huge difference either way. The main reason I mention it here is as a good example of how deeply embedded the imagery of John 10 is in the biblical narrative (particularly in the Hebrew Bible). In fact it could even be argued that coming in and going out is a key organizing motif of Israel's life with God. Repeatedly, in the Hebrew scriptures, Israel finds her redemption in the process of being physically led in and out by God. From Abram's departure to an unknown land, safe passage out of Egypt through the Red Sea, crossing of the Jordan into the Promised Land and exile from and eventual return to Jerusalem, the recurring pattern of Israel's witness to God is one of repeatedly leaving and returning.

However, the pattern runs deeper than just a repeated action; it becomes a key identifier of God's nature – God is revealed and known as the one who gathers Israel in and then leads them out. For example, the prophet Micah delivers God's promise to the exiles:

> I will surely gather all of you, O Jacob, I will gather the survivors of Israel; I will set them together like sheep in a fold, like a flock in its pasture; it will resound with people. The one who breaks out will go up before them; they will break through and pass the gate, going out by it. Their king will pass on before them, the LORD at their head. (Micah 2.12-13)

Notice here that God is the primary actor – God leads, gathers, breaks out and moves out before the people. Yes, Israel follows, but God's actions make progress possible.

Returning to John 10, God's proactive guidance is represented by the shepherd's voice. In both Micah and John 10, God is not necessarily physically present with the people/sheep. In Micah, God moves out before the people, showing them the way. Equally in John 10, it is the familiarity and guidance of the shepherd's voice, and not necessarily the shepherd's near physical presence, that provides the needed orientation and guidance. Regardless of whether God's people find themselves in places that are traditionally associated with God's presence (the mountains, the river Jordan, Jerusalem), or not (Egypt, Babylon or the desert), the pattern remains of God continually leading Israel in and out. Wherever they are, they are offered multiple opportunities to listen for God's voice guiding and helping them to navigate new, unexpected and potentially challenging spaces and situations. Hearing God's voice is not an instant fix for their predicament; it does not somehow teleport them to a safer location (Israel were probably in Egypt and the desert for hundreds of years) but they are reoriented and reconnected to God, and to their own identity as witnesses to God, in and through all of their experiences.

Finally, it is important to recognize that, according to John 10.9, the aim of the sheep's going in and out is to locate pasture. This means that, whatever pasture refers to, it is found outside as well as inside the sheepfold! Although John 10.9 is the only place where the term is translated as pasture in the New Testament, the connection between pasture and God's people appears multiple times throughout the Bible. Most commonly, the Psalms express Israel's life with God in terms of being the sheep of God's pasture (see Pss. 74, 79, 95, 100). But upon closer inspection, pasture is not only associated with times of plenty but also goes deeper, pointing to Israel's true identity. For example, Psalm 74.1: 'O God, why do you cast us off for ever? Why does your anger smoke against the sheep of your pasture?' This psalm addresses a moment of crisis in which the people feel abandoned by God and the Psalmist uses the image of pasture to question God: 'Isn't this who we are? ... If we belong to you, then this shouldn't be happening to us? This isn't the way things are supposed to be!'

For Israel, being the sheep of God's pasture is a question of identity and belonging, not just temporary success or crisis. This sense is reinforced in Psalm 100.3: 'Know that the LORD is God. It is God that made us, and we are God's; we are God's people, and the sheep of God's pasture.' Regardless of where they end up, the source, identity and belonging of God's people remains constant and the life they access is based in whose they are, not where they are. As Israel discovered, whether in Jerusalem or Egypt, in the temple courts or sitting on Babylonian riverbanks, God's orienting, guiding and uniting voice offered them access to life in all its fullness, even (perhaps even particularly) when it seemed most unlikely or impossible. The people of God discovered that flourishing occurs in moving according to God's voice, not necessarily in arriving and remaining. Whatever life in all its fullness looks, sounds and feels like, it is not only associated with ease, comfort and familiarity, but also with challenge and navigating the unknown.

What does any of this have to do with CAL?

John 10 is one of many teaching moments in the fourth Gospel. Jesus offers the story of the good shepherd and the gate for the sheep in response to the Pharisees' questions around the healing of the man born blind in chapter 9, where the discussion centres on who really sees (and can therefore lead others) and who cannot. The Pharisees approach the conversation assuming that, compared to the others involved, they are the expert seers and knowers. They are confident that Jesus has broken Jewish law and have already decided who is at fault for the boy's blindness and the proper resolution for the situation. However, as is common in Jesus' encounters with Jewish authorities in the Gospels, by the end of the exchange the authorities' assumptions about the way things work have been undermined and the wider audience is invited to join the Pharisees' ironic question, 'Are we blind too?' (9.40, NASB).[10] So although John 10 is unlike the parable of the Sower and other passages where Jesus follows up with an explanation of how it should be understood and applied, Jesus' explanation of his role as shepherd and gate continues the discussion from John 9 about the Pharisees' misconceptions that they are the examples to follow when it comes to knowing, teaching and leading (made clear by the fact that the idea of who really sees is raised again in 10.21). As is Jesus' custom (which will be further explored in Chapter 3), rather than directly challenging the Pharisees and telling them they have it all wrong, he presents an alternative framework for his audience(s) to wrestle with.

I draw attention to the Jewish authorities here for a specific reason – their function in the community was to be a kind of pipeline through which the life of God could flow to all God's people (and even all the world!). By keeping the Law and modelling to others how to do the same, they were meant to be the ideal conduit of the goodness, abundance and generosity of God, spilling out into the everyday lives of anyone who would follow. This takes us back to our opening question: what can we understand about accessing life in all its fullness through Jesus by considering John 10 through the lens of learning? I hope that by this point you have already formed some ideas of your own, but the many facets of my answer to this question boil down to a single theme: Jesus demonstrates how life in all its fullness is ultimately accessed via connectivity and not separation. It is about getting better at going in and out rather than just finding a protected spot and remaining there.

As shepherd and gate, Jesus enables progress and growth by facilitating free movement and orienting increasingly bold adventure, not by drawing hard lines between in and out and encouraging sheep to remain in one place. In the most basic way, reading John 10 through the lens of learning reimagines the shape of the Christian life from being a series of either-or decisions to being a life spent increasingly in the both-and. Gone is the idea that once they have entered the sheepfold, Christians huddle together in safety waiting for something to happen; this is replaced by the concept that accessing all the life that Jesus offers looks a lot more like navigating the back and forwards of life, practising holding together seemingly conflicting realities and leveraging the uniquely rich learning conditions that are created as they interact.

There are obstacles and potential distractions everywhere to navigate and new pastures to explore. To do this requires developing skills of going in and out. One of the mistakes made by the Jewish authorities was that rather than orienting around, and listening for, God's voice, they had placed themselves as the static and central hub of the community's learning framework. In John 9, they present themselves as the all-knowing teachers, with everything to instruct and nothing to learn. Through the physically blind young man, Jesus offers an alternative and deeply conflicting claim about how teaching and learning really work. It is those who rely on and orient their lives by Jesus the gate who have the free movement and associated confidence necessary to access the fullness of God's life. When challenges invariably arise, Jesus' voice provides a reminder of the comfort and protection available to those who belong to the shepherd, wherever and in whatever situation they are found.

Much more could be said here, but in closing here are a few key ideas to ponder further. First, if we visually represented the movement of the sheep in John 10, going in and out of the gate and following the shepherd's voice, their progress would far more closely resemble a child's first scribbles or an unravelled ball of wool than a straight line. In other words, this passage suggests that CAL (and teaching!) is not a process of simple, uninterrupted progress towards a single ultimate destination, nor is it even concerned with the perseverance to remain. Rather than measuring progress by asking how close learners are to a fixed but probably distant goal, the measure is one of quality of connection or relatedness to a pivot point – Jesus! For the sheep, the value of their adventuring is not primarily about where they go but about how the orienting voice of God allows them to engage meaningfully with their surroundings, wherever the path to pasture takes them.

Second, my reading of John 10 makes some important claims about learner responsibility and agency. If the key skill of progressing in CAL is going in and out, then it is not a process linked only to academic proficiency but a skill that all learners can practise and improve! Access to life in all its fullness is not a binary (either-or) state, but a skill that learners have a responsibility to continually develop by lingering in the *in-between* spaces. It can be helpful to think about this in terms of learning to cross borders or boundaries: the concept that, somehow, the places (both metaphorical and otherwise) where two or more conditions meet give rise to particularly potent opportunities for growth and development.

Al Barrett and Ruth Harley call these spaces *edge-places* and describe them like this:

> Edge-places are not simply the boundary between one habitat and another, lines that you cross from one to the other like national borders. In these ecological borderlands, species from the two neighbouring habitats interact and intermingle, and a greater diversity and density of life is found there than in either of the two distinct habitats within themselves – making them places full of huge potential.[11]

Therefore, as gate for the sheep, Jesus represents a rich place of crossing where multiple habitats intersect. (In learning terms, habitats may represent various subjects or areas of theological conviction, methods, denominational difference, seasons of life, etc.) Thus the core challenge of CAL becomes how to cross well and improve at crossing. This is not to say that such boundaries are always straightforward to cross. As Hull reminds us: 'There are correct and incorrect ways to cross boundaries. When a boundary is crossed incorrectly it becomes a barrier, and the result is confusion, but when a boundary is crossed in the right way, it becomes an open gate.'[12] Chapter 5 develops this idea in much more detail, but ultimately what Hull is arguing here is that no learner is a victim of circumstance. Depending on the posture adopted, every element and stage of life (and particularly the transitions between them) can potentially facilitate or impede CAL. Hull explains this shapeshifting phenomenon as similar to how river rapids are both 'a source of testing and danger ... [and a] source of power',[13] going so far as to argue that even Christian faith itself is capable of 'Holding the believing adult in the stagnation of infancy or adolescence, but it can also become for him a rainbow bridge linking the various stages of his life together in a power and beauty rarely experienced by non-religious people.'[14]

Learning progress is ultimately determined, not by the situation in which learners find themselves or the conditions with which they have to cope, but by the strength of the dynamic partnership between shepherd-gate and sheep. In this partnership learner progress depends on developing knowledge of, and reliance on, the shepherd's guiding voice and following Jesus' example of optimum entrance and exit.

Questions/activities

- How did you respond to the opening question: What does it mean for Christians to access life in all its fullness and how do they do it? Is your response any different now?
- Do you see any conflict in Jesus being both shepherd and gate in John 10?
- Can you empathize with a pattern of life that goes backwards and forwards, in and out of the sheepfold? How does this influence our understanding of the goals of the Christian life?
- If CAL is a process of locating pasture, how can we do this more effectively?
- Take a look at Jesus' other 'I am' statements in the fourth Gospel. Do they include elements of movement, connection and transformation?
- Retell John 10 to a friend/family member without looking at the text (maybe even record yourself). Notice the details that you include and the elements of the story you either forget or de-emphasize. Can you identify any reasons for this? Repeat the exercise a few times.

Notes

1 Some good places for further reading: Dale Martin, *Pedagogy of the Bible: An analysis and proposal* (Louisville, KY: WJK Press, 2008); John Shortt, *Bible-shaped Teaching* (Eugene, OR: Wipf & Stock, 2014); Trevor Cooling, 'Enabling the Bible to control learning' in K. Goodlet and C. Collier (eds), *Teaching Well: Insights for educators in Christian schools* (Barton ACT: Barton Books, 2014), pp. 53–62.

2 While the lack of consensus among English translations of θύρα (door or gate) may seem incidental (CEB, NIV and NRSV opt for gate; NIV, NASB and ESV for door), the choice carries significant interpretational power. Does the Gospel writer envisage Jesus as door or doorway for the sheep? The object filling the space, or the space itself that makes entrance and exit possible?

3 Charles Harold Dodd, *Historical Tradition in the Fourth Gospel* (Cambridge: Cambridge University Press, 1963), p. 363. Among the other prominent examples of this is Rudolf Bultmann, who commented in 1972:

> Thus while vv. 8 and 10 seem to continue the thought of vv. 1–5, vv. 7 and 9 run counter to it, for here the door is not thought of as the way through which the shepherd goes into the sheep, but as the door through which the sheep are led out to pasture and led back again into the fold; and in so far as this section refers to Jesus, the image alters from verse to verse. (Rudolf Bultmann, G. Beasley-Murray et al. (trans.), *The Gospel of John: A commentary* (Oxford: Basil Blackwell, 1971), p. 359).

He concludes that John 10 could not have originally followed John 9 and therefore John 10.19–21 must have been the original conclusion to the story of the man born blind, not the good shepherd discourse. He surmises that the order of John's Gospel chapters 9—10, as it presently stands, is the work of a later redactor.

4 John Ashton, *Studying John: Approaches to the fourth Gospel* (Oxford: Clarendon Press, 1994), p. 129.

5 For more, see: John M. Hull, *What Prevents Christian Adults from Learning?* (London: SCM Press, 1985), p. 130. Equating inside the sheepfold as the Church, in comparison to outside as 'other' to the Christian faith, requires a very loose definition of Church. Equally difficult to maintain is an interpretation in which 'inside' represents the familiar, that is, a learner's own denominational practices and theology, as opposed to unfamiliar branches of the Church, Christian views and practices.

6 See for example, 'What did Jesus mean when he said, "I am the door" (John 10:7)?', *Got Questions?*, https://www.gotquestions.org/I-am-the-door.html (accessed 31.07.2023).

7 Hull, *What Prevents*, p. 67.

8 Hull, *What Prevents*, p. 67.

9 For example, Herman Ridderbos, *The Gospel According to John: A theological commentary* (Grand Rapids, MI: Wm. B. Eerdmans, 2016), p. 358.

10 For more on this, see John M. Hull, *In the Beginning There was Darkness* (London: SCM Press, 2001).

11 Al Barrett and Ruth Harley, *Being Interrupted: Reimagining the Church's mission from the outside, in* (London: SCM Press, 2020), p. 142.

12 John M. Hull, 'First Sunday in Lent: I am the Gate for the Sheep' in P. Clifford (ed.), *Jesus: Hope for Life: The Christian Aid/Hodder Lent book 2002* (London: Hodder & Stoughton, 2001), pp. 9–10, p. 10.

13 Hull, *What Prevents*, p. 185.

14 Hull, *What Prevents*, p. 159.

PART II

Redefining the Task

We have reached the middle phase of our discussion. Having redirected the conversation, before we attempt to reshape practice in Part III, the next goal is to redefine the task of CAL. Imagining the three parts of this book as a movie trilogy: the opening part set the scene, gave a general sense of the plot and some of the key characters in our disruptive-inclusive learning adventure, but now the story needs developing further. As many authors and directors have discovered, the middle part of a trilogy is often the most demanding (but also potentially rewarding) for both creator and audience. The first instalment has all the excitement of introducing new characters and ideas and setting the trajectory; the third provides the opportunity for resolution and a final 'ta-dah' moment; but the middle part of the story often does a lot of the heavy lifting without any of the novelties associated with the opening or closing acts.

According to IMDb (Internet Movie Database) the most popular middle films of trilogies are: *The Dark Knight* (Batman), *The Godfather Part II* and *The Lord of the Rings: The Two Towers* (with an honourable mention for *The Empire Strikes Back*).[1] Although very different, these films have a common function within their respective franchises: they clarify, consolidate *and* complicate. They develop and explain but also further entangle the characters' involvement in the plot and their relationships to one another. In particular, *The Dark Knight* holds a special place in the Batman film genre, not just because of the technologically impressive filming or the adrenaline-fuelled action scenes but the brooding character development of both Batman and his arch nemesis Joker (whose portrayal won Heath Ledger a posthumous Oscar). In summary, a good part II answers questions and poses a whole new set of questions about what the audience thought it knew from part I, with the promise of a pay-off in part III. Although I am not a Hollywood director, my hope is that these central chapters will work similarly to these other examples, in both consolidating the ideas introduced in part I and also posing some new questions raised by disruptive inclusion and its potential implications for the understanding and practice of CAL.

In Chapter 2 I claimed that disruptive inclusion is an approach to CAL that uses the word *Christian* adverbially – that is, what makes it Christian is not necessarily the subject or content of the learning but the approach or posture adopted that influences how learning happens. If this is the case, it raises the question: What is so Christian about including disruption in learning? In Chapters 3 and 4, my responses to this question will explore several major areas of Christian faith: the Bible, the nature and character of God and the embodied witness of the Church and its practices, and outline the potential contributions each makes to the relationship between Christian faith and disruptive learning. Chapter 5 then offers a further response based on my own experiences, drilling down into key ways in which I have discovered the Christian faith as uniquely positioned to facilitate disruptive-inclusive learning opportunities: not only influencing how CAL happens, but also where and why.

Theology practised or practical theology?

As has already been demonstrated, essential to a disruptive-inclusive approach to CAL is the idea of holding seemingly conflicting ideas or realities together. Before we investigate how this is underpinned and modelled by various elements of the Christian faith, it is also important to recognize that this sense of not squarely belonging in any single category is even true of the conversations this book facilitates. To which academic field(s) does disruptive inclusion belong? Where does

CAL methodology fit within the existing framework of theological disciplines and categories? I have two responses to these questions.

Perhaps unsurprisingly, I am not, on the one hand, interested in arguing over the most appropriate boxes or labels for the various elements of our discussion, mostly because even if an appropriate category could be found, disruptive inclusion is interested in forging connections between various topics rather than successfully and conclusively separating them. By definition, I hope that disruptive inclusion would break out of any category into which it was placed.

On the other hand, however, and particularly in relation to learning, terms of reference have an important role in influencing behaviour and expectations both consciously and unconsciously. For example, those invited to a lecture will probably come prepared to be spoken to/at and not anticipate having much opportunity to actively contribute. On the other hand, those invited to an event called a workshop or facilitated conversation would reasonably expect to play a more active part in a shared discussion. English Professor Marilyn Chandler McEntyre comments: 'When a word falls into disuse, the experience goes with it. We are impoverished not only by the loss of a precise descriptor, but by the atrophy and extinction of the very thing it describes.'[2] What we call things matters because words do not just describe what already is but set expectations and act as gateways that allow existing reality to continue and make new realities possible.

Therefore, when I am asked about my research interests, I am loath to say, 'My work is in the area of Christian adult learning,' unless I have lots of time to explain what that means (I suppose, from now on, I can suggest reading this book!). This is because so many people incorrectly assume that my work has nothing to do with them because they are not involved in academic theology or teaching. In its place I tend to say that my interest is in theological pedagogy or theological learning methodology because, even though it may be confusing or intimidatingly technical, at the very least it conveys that my passion combines (or sits at the crossing point of) what many others consider two separate disciplines. In the introduction to *What Prevents Christian Adults from Learning?* Hull sets out his stall as having a similar, proverbial foot in both camps with one short phrase: he introduces his book as an 'essay on Practical Theology'.[3] By the mid 1980s, Practical Theology was a well-established phrase, but as practical theologian Elaine Graham recognizes, it was also undergoing a transition from specialist use towards a far more generalized definition, well-summarized in 2017 as 'ways of thinking that take both practice and theology seriously.'[4]

At the time of writing, the Wikipedia page for Practical Theology begins:

> Practical theology is an academic discipline that examines and reflects on religious practices in order to understand the theology enacted in those practices and in order to consider how theological theory and theological practices can be more fully aligned, changed, or improved.[5]

Interestingly, it does not explain that many practical theologians would disagree with this opening statement, or at the very least recognize it as incomplete. Exactly how the practical and the theological come together in Practical Theology, or even whether the two are ever fully separated in the first place, is deeply contested. The key question remains whether the task of Practical Theology should begin with the lived components of faith and then analyse these according to theoretical, theological principles (as per Wikipedia) or whether it should work the opposite way around, beginning with theoretical concepts and then asking questions of how they translate into embodied practice.

In line with many of the metaphors already mentioned (a church narthex, horizontal harmonies, going in and out in search of pasture, etc.), my understanding of Practical Theology is that it is best able to bring together the practical and the theological when there is movement in multiple directions, that is, practical concerns influence theological concerns and vice versa. Movement in only one direction will never allow thorough investigation of the full practicality of Christian theology nor the full *theologicality* (I know this is not a real word, but I think it should be) of lived Christian practice. For me, the best way to think about how the theoretical and lived elements of Practical Theology come together is as two sides of the same coin, or two routes up the same mountain. Just as the two main routes up Everest (the South Col Route in Nepal or the Northeast Ridge in Tibet, if you are interested) are said to offer very different overall climbing experiences but ultimately both provide access to the same summit, I would argue that for practical theologians who are serious about their craft, there is no option but to become equally familiar with both paths to the top!

Like Hull, I understand CAL as a task of Practical Theology (even if the exact meaning of this is not completely settled). Therefore, disruptive inclusion must be understood and analysed from both angles: as a lived, embodied experience that is analysed through theoretical theological lenses; and vice versa – as a theology of CAL, analysed through the lens of lived practice. Only when both of these are taken seriously is a case for the *Christianness* of any learning methodology possible. We are going to climb the mountain, taking in the challenges and opportunities that present on the way. Twice.

Notes

1 'The Best Second Film in a Trilogy', *IMDB*, 22 May 2014, https://www.imdb.com/list/ls054625069/?sort=user_rating,desc&st_dt=&mode=detail&page=1 (accessed 31.07.23).

2 Marilyn Chandler McEntyre, *Caring for Words in a Culture of Lies* (Cambridge: Wm. B. Eerdmans, 2009), pp. 29–30.

3 John M. Hull, *What Prevents Christian Adults from Learning?* (London: SCM Press, 1985), p. xi.

4 Pete Ward, *Introducing Practical Theology: Mission, ministry, and the life of the Church* (Grand Rapids, MI: Baker Academic, 2017), p. 5.

5 *Practical Theology*, https://en.wikipedia.org/wiki/Practical_theology (accessed 31.07.2023).

3

The Christian Basis for Adult Learning: Theology Practised

To stretch the mountain metaphor just one step further, the base camp of the first route up the mountain is located in the Bible and some of the core theological convictions that have arisen from it. Beginning in the Christian holy scriptures and some of the foundational Christian beliefs about the nature and character of God, we will explore some of the key patterns and themes that emerge about the potential Christianness of adult learning. What can we learn from the form and contents of the Bible and the God it presents about leveraging disruptive circumstances towards transformation and embracing the tensions of in-between places?

Including disruption in learning: beginning with the Bible

For the vast majority of Christians, beginning with the Bible is not a controversial suggestion. In the Free Church setting where I grew up, at the heart of most discussions was the question of what constituted a biblical or unbiblical approach/decision. These terms were used regularly and confidently, played almost like trump cards to bring conversations to a (sometimes, to my mind, premature) end. As I became more practised in reading and interpreting the Bible, I began to see that very often behind the use of the terms biblical and unbiblical was only a verse or two, or even perhaps a well-known adage that did not appear in the Bible at all! In my experience, the bar for calling something biblical or not can be quite low. This is not to say that I think the terms biblical and unbiblical are without value, but that they need redeeming from overly poor and thin use. In terms of biblical interpretation, readers of this book will represent a whole range of values, lenses and techniques used to work out which contemporary questions and ideas are consistent with the biblical narrative(s) or in contradiction of its values and principles. However, one thing that I hope all can agree on is that if such a thing as a biblical approach to life or learning exists, then its hallmarks are richness, nuance, depth and beauty (more on this last one in Chapter 5). Engaging well with the biblical texts is a weighty task (not as in cumbersome, but significant. The French use the word *large*, which includes both a sense of breadth and importance). It must not be taken lightly and requires careful, multi-layered and deeply nuanced exploration.

However, having highlighted the gravity of the task, engaging with the Bible is also, importantly, not exclusively or prohibitively difficult. Since before the biblical texts were even written down, questions of who hears, reads, interprets and passes on their message has been greatly and repeatedly disputed (see most of church history for how these arguments have rumbled on throughout the centuries). The vast majority of Christians now work on the basis that questions relating to the Bible's contents and meaning are (at least to some extent) for the whole learning community! Most Christians agree (at least in principle if not in practice) that everyone can (and should be encouraged to) participate in the story of God presented in the Bible – not because it is easily accessible and understandable to all *nor* because it is endlessly complex – but because it is both at the same time.

Following the famous claim (whose source is disputed but most commonly attributed to either Augustine of Hippo, c.354–430, or Gregory the Great, c.540–604), if you imagine the Bible as a pool of water, it has a shapeshifting quality that makes it suitable for both children to paddle in and elephants to swim in. Anyone who has returned to the same Bible passage on multiple occasions knows that it works in mysterious ways. As Christians learn, grow and experience God in creation, they unavoidably find themselves swimming differently in the biblical texts. The words on the page are unchanged, but whether due to changed perspectives, learned techniques or simply the passage of time, readers' engagement with the Bible naturally evolves. The Holy Spirit's work in the world and in our lives means that, as we grow, so do the biblical texts in our understanding! This way, the biblical narrative has remained constant through the ages but is also constantly, dynamically developing. Contemporary readers cannot be expected to interpret the Bible as ancient audiences did, any more than these could have been expected to interpret according to our contemporary patterns and concerns. For the purposes of our discussion, the most important thing to notice about how the Bible works as a learning tool is that the biblical texts, taken on their own terms, function according to a range of methodological in-betweens. In biblical learning simple meets complex, specific meets universal, then meets now, theory meets practice, death meets life.

Selah 3: Defining the biblical 'in-between'

I am not alone in claiming that the Bible facilitates multiple, crossover conversations or acts as a kind of bridge between otherwise opposite or conflicting ideas. Chapter 5 goes into more detail of how the language of journeying and physical travelling works with disruptive inclusion, but to spark your imagination here are several examples of how different scholars imagine that the Bible functions in moving between, holding together or altogether blurring the lines between seemingly contrasting concepts.

First, practical theologians John Swinton and Harriet Mowat argue that theology cannot be *either* straightforward *or* complex, it must be both. To explain how these seeming opposites work together, they use the term *complexification*. More specifically, they describe how practical theology 'Seeks critically to complexify and explore situations. Complexification is a process that at first glance seems normal and uncomplicated, but through a process of critical reflection at various levels, is in fact revealed to be complex and polyvalent'[1] (polyvalent means holding multiple meanings at once). To understand the Bible as a complexified learning tool does not mean that it requires complicated technical knowledge to read well, but rather that it draws readers into multi-layered, multi-directional discussions that cross boundaries and lead to unexpected (and sometimes challenging) learning territory. Or, as religious educationist and practical theologian Peter Mudge puts it, complexification requires that we abandon 'quick or easy ways of reaching a false synthesis between text and experiences' and recognize 'the complex wrestling that is often involved in theological reflection.'[2] Similarly, systematic theologian Karen Kilby argues that 'clarity and mystery need not be opposed' because 'whatever clarity means in theology, it cannot be the elimination of all elements of mystery and paradox.'[3] Kilby continues that in Christianity the known and the knowable are not the only source of help and refuge, but that perhaps the only thing that is entirely clear in Christianity is that not everything is![4] As I understand it, complexification and Kilby's reimagined definition of Christian clarity are attempts not to make things complicated for their own sake, but to recognize how patterns of Christian thinking, and the Bible as the principal model of this, are simultaneously simple and complex, clear and mysterious, about one thing and many things, all at once.

For Asian feminist theologian Kwok Pui Lan, the Bible fulfils a different in-between function. She explains that:

On the one hand we have to imagine how the biblical tradition – formulated in another time and in another culture – can address our burning questions of today. On the other hand, based on our present circumstances, we have to reimagine what the biblical world was like, thus opening up new horizons hitherto hidden from us.[5]

Simply put, Kwok's idea is that the relationship between reader and biblical text is 'two-way traffic' or what she refers to as a process of 'dialogical imagination' (more on the role of imagination in learning in Chapter 7): neither is accessible to the other without some form of intermediary interpretation.[6] The biblical tradition invites readers to bring their contemporary selves, questions and concerns to the conversation, but it also does the same: nuancing and reframing who readers are becoming and influencing the questions and concerns being brought to it, creating an infinite interpretational spiral. Another feminist theologian, Elisabeth Schüssler Fiorenza, expresses a similar idea in a slightly different way. Her argument is that taking the historical context of the Bible seriously is not to somehow freeze it as a distant, inaccessible relic that contemporary readers must then strain to get back to, but to recognize it as a more supple, guiding framework that reaches out towards us. She says:

> Instead of reducing the historical richness of the Bible to an abstract principle, timeless norm ... which is to be repeated from generation to generation ... reclaim the whole Bible as a formative root-model; that is, as a historical–ecclesial prototype. To read the Bible not as an unchanging archetype but as a structuring prototype is to understand it as an openended paradigm that sets experience in motion and makes transformation possible.[7]

There is a lot in just these few lines, but Schüssler Fiorenza's fundamental point is that because the Bible belongs completely neither to the past nor to the present day, it has facilitated endless and developing conversation between the two for thousands of years and will continue to do so. As a learning tool, the Bible's invitation is for the text and the reader to reach out to each other and meet somewhere, somehow, in the middle. Whatever biblical learning is, both Kwok and Schüssler Fiorenza understand that it takes a both-and rather than an either-or approach.

For some, using words like complexified, conversational and open-ended to describe the Bible rings loud alarm bells because they seem to undermine biblical authority and its basic instructional nature. After all, 'Your word is a lamp to my feet and a light to my path' (Ps. 119.105), right? However, the following, final example of how the Bible functions as an in-between or both-and learning tool demonstrates how a two-way approach to biblical interpretation need not compromise a high view of biblical authority or high levels of interpretational integrity. In the image of jazz we get a glimpse of how, in biblical learning, known and unknown, boundaried and free might not be polar opposites. As the paradoxical words of educationalist and theologian Gloria Durka so incisively express: perhaps the Bible invites learners to participate in the pursuit of 'learned uncertainty'.[8]

In an important sense, jazz and classical musicianship are alike: technical skill cannot be avoided but it is also only the starting point on the path towards exceptional performance. From another perspective, the classical and jazz musical communities play very different roles in the shaping and ongoing development of their crafts. In general, while the world of classical music functions as a guide to the appropriate application of pre-existing rules, the jazz community encourages its players to constantly find new expression by bending and breaking existing rules. Put simply, jazz musicians do not apply themselves to rules and techniques so that they can learn how best to follow them; they learn the rules to find the most creative ways to keep rewriting them! Applying this concept to the Bible, New Testament scholar Dale Martin claims:

> The notion of improvisation better traces that there is no one right interpretation of a text of Scripture, but that does not mean that all interpretations are just as good as all the others … but the results that are genuinely true and Christian will be those that creatively interpret Scripture within the boundaries and expectations of Christianity.[9]

Martin's point is that interpreters of the Bible and players of jazz experience similar conditions. First, they are freely encouraged (in fact required) to bring their own character and experiences to the interpretive process. The aim is never to copy exactly what and how someone else plays. However, neither can a player/reader just completely make it up as they go along. There are boundaries that must be respected, even if they demonstrate respect for the boundaries by testing their limits!

Martin does not, however, explain exactly who decides such 'boundaries and expectations' and on what basis. As part of a much wider argument for an anti-racist approach to Christian education, Liberation theologian and educationalist Anthony Reddie identifies some of the key factors at play. Contemporary musical improvisation, he explains, cannot simply ignore or abandon the past, because true creative expression is always a deep collaboration between past and present. 'Jazz musicians are constantly re-working an established melody in order to create something new and spontaneous for that split moment in time.' He continues:

> Improvisation is never totally created or made up on the spot; one does not create new art in a vacuum. All jazz improvisation is a negotiation between what has been conceived previously and what emerges in that specific moment ... it all comes from someplace, it isn't entirely yours to make it up as you like, you have a responsibility for this stuff.[10]

One of Reddie's core claims is that, at the heart of arguably the most free-form, creative communities in the world, there is a critical balance at work between freedom of self-expression and responsibility to the historical interpretative community in which each new player or reader takes their place. Reddie claims that Black jazz musicians' performances are not simply the playing of a selection of notes, but participation in a process that 'has been an important chronicler of the Black experience'.[11] As such, the musician carries both the privilege and responsibility of representing and celebrating the community's past and present in their performance. When I hear fearful responses to the suggestion that the Bible functions as a dynamic, disruptive, both-and kind of learning resource, I repeatedly return to this image of the jazz musician. As the pianist plays a solo, in one sense there is no set agenda for what they must play, but simultaneously, for their performance to be recognized within the genre, it must take into account a whole range of technical, compositional, cultural and other factors. Fierce, dynamic individuality meets corporate, shared representation. If a jazz pianist decides to ignore the other musicians (both those who have gone before and those currently accompanying them), jazz is unlikely to be the outcome (or perhaps it will be, but not recognized as such for another generation; however, that is a conversation for another day). My suggestion is that when readers approach the Bible their sole aim should not be to 'play' the score correctly or recreate another musician's solo. Rather, perhaps taking biblical interpretation seriously requires us to play from an in-between place? A place that recognizes the historical, creative, interpretive community/ies we participate in and acknowledges that taking up our place in those same communities is defined by the testing of boundaries and the asking of new, emerging questions.

The Bible. Simple or complex? Then or now? Theirs or mine? Mine or ours? Boundaried or free? The short answer? Yes.

Content and form: message and means

Lin-Manuel Miranda first got the idea for a musical based on the life of Alexander Hamilton when he read Ron Chernow's 2004 biography of the founding father. He later explained to Chernow (who became a consultant for the show) that as he read about Hamilton's tumultuous fortunes he found hip-hop songs just jumping off the pages. Miranda found a synergy, a deep sense of shared trajectory in the content of Hamil-

ton's life and the form of hip-hop. Chernow says: 'There is
... like a perfect match between the intensity, the density of
the hip-hop and Lin-Manuel Miranda presents Hamilton as
this very driven character, so the music and the personality
work together perfectly.'[12] In the best forms of art and literature, what the audience understands is not only communicated
through its words but also reinforced through how those
words are delivered.

As we explored in Part I, because so many conversations
about CAL fully separate what is learned and how learning
happens and concentrate almost exclusively on the former, this
pattern naturally extends to the Bible. In practice, this means
that most Christians come to the Bible with questions such
as 'What does this passage teach/inform us about X?' rather
than 'How does this passage teach us how to learn?' Asking
only one of these two types of questions is like only ever reading the script of Hamilton. Or, alternatively, listening to the
musical's score without the lyrics. Either way, the full power,
creativity and genius of what happens when the two combine
is missed. Before considering a few specific ways in which the
substance of the biblical narrative informs our discussion of
disruptive-inclusive CAL, it is worth recognizing that whatever a biblical approach to CAL consists of, it must take into
account how the form of the Bible influences the communication of its content. Any argument that disruptive inclusion is
informed or modelled by the Bible must apply to its means of
communication as well as its message.

As trustees of the Holy Scriptures, the Church has never
taken the position that any single book of the Bible, nor even
(in some cases) any single version of the same story, is capable
of representing the full richness of God's story. Rather, it is
only when taken together that the biblical library (whether this
includes the intertestamental books recognized by the Roman
Catholic Church or not) in all its historical, cultural, linguistic,
ethnic and theological perspectives[13] points towards the truth
of who God is and how humanity is invited to participate.
New Testament scholar Francis Watson argues that, taken as

a collection, the Bible not only facilitates conversations among contemporary readers, and between readers and the biblical texts, but also encourages readers to put the Bible's 'divergent voices' into conversation with each other.[14] Therefore, if the books of the Bible and their associated styles of writing, cultures, languages, settings and authors can be thought of as encouraging a particular kind of learning, then the Bible's in-built diversity demands that any approach must 'accommodate unresolved dissonance' in a dialogue that does not seek to avoid, downplay or harmonize apparent conflict or tension.[15] An example of this is the fact that 1 and 2 Chronicles retell large sections of 1 and 2 Samuel and 1 and 2 Kings from a different historical perspective.

As before, I recognize that defining the Bible according to a sense of unresolved dissonance may be deeply concerning, but as biblical scholar Walter Brueggemann neatly explains, 'The notion of instability is not an enemy ... but, in fact, an honouring of the detail and nuance of the text that dogmatic closure does not easily entertain or allow.'[16] In other words, acknowledging the tension and feeling the potential instability that may arise when the Bible's diverse contributions are put into dialogue is not a move away from its true nature and character, but brings the distinctive characteristics of Christian Scripture into sharper focus. On the one hand, taking the diversity of the Bible seriously means that some form of disorientation and disruption is inevitable. However, on the other hand, learning with and from the diverse dialogue that occurs within the biblical canon also provides learners with a stable and reliable learning community to operate within.

Imagine the books of the Bible represented by 66 individual books, of different styles, weights, materials, thicknesses and heights, on a long shelf. The books are not held in place by bookends but somehow, as they stand on the shelf, they balance without support. Now begin to separate the books and lift a few from the shelf and the books will begin to fall; some just fall over and some fall on the floor. None of the books are alike, but before they were disturbed, their specific configuration, their collective difference somehow allowed them to stand together. Or you might think of how, in a balanced tug-of-war, those holding the rope can lean back with all their weight and not move until someone gets tired or loses their footing. Theologian and biblical scholar Ellen Davis suggests that in participating in the diverse dialogue modelled by the biblical library we become the latest participants in 'the perpetual struggle of the faith community to test different perspectives.'[17] In this perpetual struggle the collective diversity of the biblical witness allows anyone who wishes, to put their whole weight on the rope – to lean into the discussion with all we have. Yes, there will be some to-ing and fro-ing, but the diversity of the biblical community is able to accommodate any questions we may bring to it. The only way we will find ourselves flat on our backs in the mud is if we completely let go of the rope!

A journey from chaos to order?

Before we consider one of the themes from within the biblical narrative that carries a strongly disruptive tone, another often overlooked aspect of the Bible's learning function is variously called biblical metanarrative, wide-angle view, overall trajectory or biblical theology. The basic idea is that if we think of Genesis to Revelation as a dot-to-dot puzzle, joining up the dots reveals an otherwise hidden picture. If you have been reading the Bible for any length of time you will probably be familiar with various frameworks for understanding the overall message of the Bible. These are usually created by splitting its contents into sub-categories or themes and then providing explanations for how the different puzzle pieces fit back together. Some of the most famous ones follow themes such as salvation history, or condense the Bible's message into the book of Romans, or even envisage it as a five-act play.[18] Each of these has an effect similar to wearing a set of differently coloured glasses that make particular shades come to the fore and others recede into the background. Some believe that there is a single, ideal lens through which the Bible should be read, but I have found (at least some) value and limitations in every version of the biblical dot-to-dot that I have come across so far.

As part of our exploration of how the Bible informs and models disruptive inclusion, we will analyse one specific lens, proposed by Hull in 1985, in which he claims that Genesis to Revelation represents a particular kind of CAL journey. In the most basic sense, Hull presents the sweep of the biblical story as one big learning sandwich (or in technical terms, pedagogical inclusio). In this sandwich, the bread represents the similarities of the beginning and end of the journey. At the outset and the conclusion, as the universe is created and drawn back together, its inhabitants exist in total balanced unity and transparent relationship with each other, God and the rest of creation. You may have heard this explained using the Hebrew term *shalom*. Usually, *shalom* is expressed in English as peace, but it is far more than just a generic sense of calmness or the absence of conflict. *Shalom* describes an active, multilevel relationality in which all the diverse components of reality know their specific roles and freely and fully express themselves in a connected way. In terms of the sandwich filling, Hull imagines the journey from the shalom of Eden to the restored shalom of the New Jerusalem not in terms of a straight or even a single, uninterrupted line, but as a messy, broken and decidedly non-shalomic kind of pathway. He describes it as a journey from wholeness through a differentiation (brokenness, confusion, messiness) that eventually enables a new kind of wholeness to emerge.[19] Hull explains this using the image of a mandala (intricate, geometric, often circular patterns commonly used in Eastern religions), suggesting that the biblical learning journey moves from one mandala to another:

> The Garden of Eden is sometimes shown as a mandala ... one must hack one's way through the dangers of consciousness to reach life. At the end of the process, the Heavenly City is also

described as a mandala, one in which the pain of separation of consciousness from unconsciousness is finally overcome. Between the Garden and the City we have Christ himself, the supreme symbol of the self.[20]

Looking closely at this, Hull undermines two commonly held beliefs about CAL. Generally, many Christians understand that the passage of a successful Christian life begins with ignorance and moves towards knowledge and understanding, or begins with simplicity and moves towards complexity. In biblical terms, the description in 1 Corinthians 3.2 of the transition from milk to solid food is commonly quoted as demonstrating the need of Christians to move on beyond the basic to something more substantial.[21] In contrast to this, Hull suggests that the overarching trajectory of the biblical learning journey begins in beautifully balanced complexity, moves through messily disjointed and disordered complexity and back towards a new expression of God's shalomic order. Second, Hull also challenges the idea that the learning pathway between the beginning and end points of Christian learning journeys ought to be straightforward or without major obstacle! In place of this, Hull proposes that learners should expect the journey from one mode of intricate, inter-related complexity to another to be bumpy.

Mandalas are an effective metaphor for Hull due to their high level of detail and the interconnectedness between the various parts of their designs: the gaps, lines and dots work together to create the whole. Interestingly, however, Revelation's vision of Christ's return is not to the garden where it all began. While multiple components of the initial garden are reimagined in the city of God, it is not a journey back to the start but a progression on to a new (and perhaps better) version of the intricate shalom initiated by God in which humanity was unable to fully participate. There are multiple examples of this, but I find most powerful the fact that not only does the east entrance to the garden, which is barred by angels when humans are removed from Eden (Gen. 3.24), multiply in the New Jerusalem, but the new gates and the foundations of the walls in which the gates appear now bear the names of the 12 tribes and the 12 apostles (Rev. 21.12–14). God's people have gone on a journey from being the reason why shalom deteriorates to being the gateway making others' welcome into God's eternal shalom possible. Where the beginning and end of the story are represented by beautifully balanced intricacy and connectedness, everything in between is in direct contrast. Hull's framework suggests that the journey from shalom to shalom is defined by disorder and will not be easy to predict or navigate. In a similar pattern to the previous discussion about the simultaneously disrupting and stabilizing function of the diverse biblical library, Hull suggests that the shalomic bookends of the biblical learning journey are not just there to taunt learners by drawing attention to what is currently inaccessible to them. Hull explains that, at the physical, metaphorical and theological centre of the journey from Eden to the New Jerusalem, we find 'Christ himself'. Like the function of the shepherd's voice in John 10, the beginning and end of the Bible's metaphorical learning journey provide an orienting security that allows learners not to become paralysed by fear or apathy as they struggle through the divided and unpredictable middle stages of the journey. There is also an encouragement for those who do not currently experience mandala-esque, balanced, intricate shalom: their situation is not just OK but actually a sign of progress. After all, the Christ we find at the centre of the story is a suffering saviour, a seemingly defeated and misunderstood messiah who seems to do everything out of order according to prevailing rules, who gives access to fullness of life by embracing death and making wholeness possible via brokenness.

For Hull, the overarching pattern of the biblical narrative points to a journey in which ignorance and knowledge sit side by side. In an idea that is more fully explained in our next chapter, Hull suggests that CAL is not about overcoming the challenges of this present reality or escaping to another one, but about being here in a different way by bravely acknowledging 'the points of inconsistency, of unrelatedness'[22] that define the here and now. His model calls learners to be inspired that present disruptions are an invitation to join with Jesus (in some small way) in the re-organizing of creation into a pattern that allows everything to ideally flourish and relate, even when (perhaps particularly when) it least seems like it!

Getting lost where bewilderment meets curiosity

Having considered the disruptive tendencies of the form of the Bible's message and its overarching journey from Genesis to Revelation, we finally address its message in a more direct way. The next section will pay close attention to Jesus' role, but there are also multiple other ways in which the Bible's content embraces patterns of disruption. Take, for instance, the repeated pattern of Exodus and return in the Hebrew Bible. For God's people, the various lands they inhabited were not just incidental but deeply connected to their sense of identity as belonging to God. Both physically and metaphorically, Israel repeatedly loses their way. But as Hull says: 'To lose oneself, to become lost, is not a matter of *finding* oneself in unfamiliar surroundings. It is to become detached from that supreme centre of value from which one derives all sense of worth.'[23] Therefore the fact that so much of the biblical narrative is about people who lose their way means that their loss is not just for contemporary readers to note (and potentially judge/criticize), but an invitation to participate in that same loss. This is why Hull claims that so many people experience the Bible as 'an insult to pride'[24] because the biblical narrative is 'An account not merely of the losses that people have experienced, but of humanity experiencing loss of itself; what Adam lost was not so much the Garden of Eden but Adam.'[25] It is because of this deep sense of shared loss that Old Testament scholar Rachelle Gilmour is able to summarize that the theme of Exodus points to the wider learning function of the Bible more generally as 'transformative, integrative, yet troublesome'.[26]

But the troublesome nature of the biblical narrative is clear not only from a wide-angle view, but also when we consider the details of individual stories, chapters, moments and responses. The most basic observation is that disruptive circumstances occur throughout the Bible. God intervenes when and how people least expect. People fail and die, famine hits, ships are wrecked, God does not act when (seemingly) most needed or does so in completely unexpected ways, wars are lost, victories are won. Importantly, all of these scenarios share a sense of unexpectedness (almost always for the characters in the story and sometimes for readers/listeners too) that skews the anticipated direction of both individual stories and, in some cases, the overall story. David is set up (and remembered!) as Israel's giant-killing golden boy, but even the life of the king destined to restore Israel's fortunes does not proceed without significant obstacles and challenges (interestingly, relational as well as political). Similarly, when Jesus arrives on earth, many people refuse to receive him as the fulfilment of the promise they have been told to watch out for, because he is not what they expected! In the face of wide-ranging disruptions, the Bible also demonstrates a range of responses. Some people grumble and despair, some give up on God and actively rebel, on some occasions the response is sheer confusion, anger and/ or violence. But by far the most praiseworthy initial response to disruption in the Bible is variously referred to as amazement or, perhaps more generally, awe and wonder. Usually, when a character's initial response to unforeseen or challenging circumstances takes the form of awe, wonder or amazement, it leads to obedience, praise and other positive transformations.

I must admit that until recently I had associated awe and wonder with giving up on learning rather than an active sign of it. However, I now understand awe and wonder as a catalyst to transformed thoughts and actions. Here are just a few examples: Moses had no idea what to make of being spoken to from a bush and so the best action seemed to be to drop to the ground in awe (Ex. 3.6). From this position Moses was able to hear from, converse with and receive instruction from God. In the New Testament, Jesus heals a lame man (Luke 5) and

as the people glorify God for the 'remarkable things' they had
seen (5.26, NASB) they assume a posture of awe and wonder.
Neither Moses nor the crowd are exactly sure what is happening, but in response to God's unexpected intervention their
initial response was to marvel. Throughout the Bible, from
the Psalmist to the writer to the Hebrews and from Israel's
prophets to those gathered around the throne in John's vision
of the new heavens and the new earth, awe and wonder are
regularly presented as a deeply appropriate way to respond
and witness to God's extraordinary (and deeply disruptive)
presence and action, but what does it have to do with learning?

A first hint is offered by Christian educationalist John
Westerhoff:

> The Christian is called to feel and act as a whole person.
> Christian education which does not take a [person's] total
> behaviour–lifestyle seriously is simply not Christian. For
> too long we have neglected the realm of the affections. For
> example, one important theme in the Bible is wonder or awe.
> I would argue that when people experience wonder or are
> in a state of awe they are very close to a biblical view of life,
> very close to understanding our world and ourselves through
> the eyes of faith.[27]

Westerhoff claims that awe and wonder cannot be categorized
as either entirely rational/logical or entirely emotional, but are
a response that encompasses both, pointing to 'a biblical view
of life' that is deeply holistic. Digging deeper into this, Hebrew
Bible scholar William P. Brown explains that, although 'wonder
is undoubtedly an emotional response, it also has another side:
far from ignorance, blissful or otherwise ... [it is] the very basis
of deep inquiry.'[28] Brown goes further in explaining the different elements of a response of awe and wonder as:

> a potent mix of curiosity and perplexity. On the one hand,
> wonder carries the unsettling element of bewilderment. On
> the other hand, there is the element of insatiable curiosity

or passionate desire to know. Wonder, thus, bears an inner tension.[29]

Simultaneously, wonder gives access to 'experiences of disorientation in which the unknown rudely backs into the world of the familiar' and 'a sense of order that invites enthusiastic affirmation, a "yes!" alongside the "wow!".'[30] In short, 'Wonder, thus, freely traverses between experience of order and disorientation, self-critique and celebration, fear and fascination.'[31]

Returning to Moses and the crowd in Luke 5, what they witnessed left them both flummoxed and interested. They were aware that 'working out' what had just happened was probably beyond them but still wanted to investigate, all the same. They were emotionally moved by what had happened but not quite sure how to begin articulating or understanding it. Westerhoff argues that, for Christians, awe and wonder hold together the order and the disorder, allowing learners to celebrate progress without encouraging complacency and dulling the drive to continually press on. Awe and wonder, which naturally hold seeming opposite extremes together, represent an invitation offered to learners by the Christian God. To relate this back to disruptive inclusion, wonder is perhaps the best gateway for learners to experience optimum distance: making space for tension but not providing the motivation to linger there any longer than necessary.

As our direct focus on the biblical basis for disruptive inclusion comes to a close, it may be helpful to imagine the different arguments presented as the different layers of scenery used in a theatre. The furthermost backdrop is the fact that, before reading a word, the multi-layered diversity of the biblical library models participation in specific kinds of disruptive conversations. Just in front of that is the overall trajectory of the biblical narrative that Hull argues should be thought of as a learning journey beginning and ending in *shalom* but with an intervening story shaped by confusion and disruption. Then, the next level forward, in centre stage we find some disruptive themes from within the biblical narrative, such as Exodus and the role of awe and wonder. Finally, downstage (right where the stage ends and the audience begins) we find multiple characters whose individual encounters with God and Jesus are punctuated with moments of awe and wonder. Each layer of the scenery works with the others to present an overall impression to the audience that consistently expects and makes space for disruption. The audience is invited to learn from the Bible, '*in* the differences and not in spite of them.'[32] Christian learners are invited not only to observe the consequences of disruption for the biblical characters but also to join them in the perpetual struggle and find empathy and security in their company. As Hull states, in this way the Bible functions as both a worked demonstration and the source text of CAL – it informs its disruptive shape, function and overall aims, providing 'not only part of but ... *the* integrating pattern for meaning.'[33]

Including disruption in learning: the nature and character of the Christian God

For many of us, the blurring of lines between truth and fiction, between fake and real, has come into its own in the twenty-first century: there is a growing nostalgia for simpler times, a world before the internet, AI and deepfakes. There is no longer clear water between what is invented by someone's (or something's!) imagination for entertainment, manipulation, or maybe both, and what is real. However, I would argue that all that recent advances in technology have achieved is to highlight the messy relationship between 'real' and 'fake' that has always been lurking in the background. As Mark Twain recognized at the turn of the twentieth century: 'Truth is stranger than fiction, but it is because Fiction is obliged to stick to possibilities; Truth isn't.'[34] Or Lord Byron, much earlier: ''Tis strange – but true; for truth is always strange, Stranger than fiction: if it could be told, How much would novels gain by the exchange! How differently the world would men behold!'[35]

Actually, in many areas, fully extrapolating truth from

fiction is rarely considered the most effective path to getting a better handle on what is *really* true or real. In fact, humans have repeatedly turned to fiction as the only realistic way of getting a handle on the truth! At the intersection of truth and fiction is the symbolic, a kind of language that attempts to give access to otherwise impenetrable ideas and concepts. Even the most literal interpreters of the Bible recognize that it heavily employs symbol to convey its message. As biblical scholar Ellen Davis recognizes:

> The most difficult aspect of the Bible's literary complexity is its use of symbols. The Bible speaks often in symbolic, or imaginative, language for the simple reason that the realities of which it speaks exceed the capacity of ordinary, 'common-sense' discourse.[36]

Davis argues here that, on multiple occasions, biblical truth (and, I would add, Christian truth more broadly) is just too deep, too massive, too immense for everyday language to convey and so the closest humans can get to expressing it is to use symbol. Nowhere else in the Bible is this more prominent than the multiple images used to explain who God is and what God is like, both before and since Jesus. In the Bible, God is described as taking on the form of a burning bush (Ex. 3.3), a wind (Gen. 1.2), a cloud (Ex. 13.21), a dove (Matt. 3.12), a shepherd (Gen. 48.15), an angel (Gen. 16.7), a rock (Gen. 49.24), light (1 John 1.5), reason (John 1.1), Father, Son, Spirit (for example, Matt. 3), gardener and vine (John 15.1), among a range of other images. However, it does not necessarily follow that in being revealed via these objects God is reduced to any particular form or substance. Humans are compelled to use symbolic language in an attempt to stretch as far as possible in understanding the divine nature and character, while simultaneously recognizing that God is beyond the ability of any word, idea or image to describe.

Our exploration of this topic could focus on any one of these images. However, throughout the centuries two particularly mind-bending concepts have shaped Christian belief about God more than the others: the incarnation and the Trinity. What can we understand about the processes of CAL from the Church's continuing insistence that God is indivisibly One, but in fully representing God on earth Jesus had two natures: human and divine; and that God's oneness is also best represented in three persons: Father, Son and Spirit?

Incarnational/trinitarian tension and CAL

Growing up, I was encouraged to memorize passages from the Bible. If you ever meet me in person, you have my permission (should the mood take you) to ask me to prove it by reciting the Bible alphabet! However, the most meaningful portion of the Bible I committed to memory was the first chapter of the fourth Gospel. As an eight-year-old, I am pretty sure that the mind-boggling claims of John 1.1 went over my head (and to be honest, they still do). Who truly understands how God has been and continues to be the same since the beginning but at one point also moved in down the road? It just makes no sense that humanity can now fully know God because God had the audacity to take on human flesh. For disruption, we need look no further.

Even all these years later, I am not too critical of myself for finding the depths of John 1.1 tricky to fully process. Especially for those who have been familiar with the Jesus story for a long time, it can be difficult to take a step back and fully appreciate the bizarreness of the Word made flesh – what theologians refer to as the incarnation. The claim that Jesus, born of a human mother, inhabited a fully human body while somehow retaining full divine status (that is, in no way compromising his god-ness) has boggled every generation since (and even arguably before) it happened. Many who met Jesus could not fathom it; the early Church wrestled hard with how to explain it; the Church throughout the ages, right up to today, has argued over what kind of words and images best express it; and many still struggle with what was achieved by the life, death and resurrection of Jesus, the God-man.

It is important to recognize, however, that these questions about the nature and character of God, as represented by Jesus, have remained critically important not just because their potential answers are interesting to know. As Jesus instructed his first followers, Christians are not only called to know about him but to become like him, sharing his message, doing the kinds of things he did and even going beyond what he achieved while on earth (John 12.12). And so we reach the key issue that arises where questions of the nature and character of God and CAL meet. If Jesus came to earth so that Christians could know what God is like and become more like God by following Jesus' example, then what example of learning does Jesus set? Did Jesus learn? If yes, then does this mean that God is also a learner? If yes, what implications does this have for CAL and what does this potentially mean for the Christianness of disruptive inclusion?

Hull had some strong opinions on this topic, recognizing that 'Jesus as the Teacher rather than Jesus as the Learner [has] made the greatest impression upon the Christian mind',[37] but that the Gospels contain examples of both. He highlights how, on the one hand, Jesus demonstrates supernatural knowledge in exchanges such as the one with a Samaritan woman (John 4.9) but, in contrast, is surprised and challenged by a Syro-Phoenician woman's comments (Mark 15.34). Similarly, 'the Markan Christ dies with a question on his lips' while the Johannine Christ dies with a sense of 'finality and composure'.[38] In the wider New Testament, Hull highlights how Jesus is also recognized as causing widespread bafflement (1 Cor. 1.23). However, despite being only one element of how Jesus is presented by the Gospel writers and the early Church, his identity as the 'authoritative and all-knowing teacher' has swallowed up Jesus the humble, lowly 'questioning learner'.[39]

Fundamentally, Hull was deeply concerned that if Christian adult learners aspire to the character of 'a God-man who was himself not a learner', then it is likely to lead to a 'theology of ineducability'.[40] To counter this, he makes the (for some, somewhat controversial) claim that Jesus Christ, God and humanity partner together in learning; that is, Christian adults do not just learn *for* God or *from* God but *with* God.[41] It follows not only that learning is an appropriate action and character trait for the divine, but that, as a result, CAL should not be understood as a necessary evil due to human fallenness but as a pivotal component of how Christians bear witness to God's nature and character in the world. Theologian and educator Mark Chater acknowledges how many find it challenging to imagine Jesus as a learner because it conflicts with the belief that, as God, Jesus did not lack in knowledge or insight: 'In the case of Christology, the assumptions about Jesus as a master teacher or omniscient being will need to be re-evaluated, while for pedagogy, superficial parallels between teachers and Christ need to be left behind.'[42] How could Jesus learn without undermining his divine power, immutability (unchangingness) and omniscience (all-knowingness)? Whether you find Hull's claims convincing or deeply troubling (or, more than likely, a bit of both!), they expand our attention beyond what Jesus teaches to what can be potentially learned from Jesus about learning.

Hull's basis for understanding Jesus as a learner is the idea explained in Chapter 1, that learning is concerned with quality of engagement and connection, not only recall or retention of information. Another key cornerstone of his argument is an epistemology (a way of knowing – more on this in Selah 4) in which the total of all that can possibly be known is not static or fixed. Put simply, there is always newness to be discovered even for God, and therefore CAL must be an ongoing, dynamic process with no definitive end point.

> The world which is there available for knowledge, is continually expanding, and God, whose omniscience continually embraces and perfectly keeps pace with this expanding and continually more detailed universe, is continually learning from it.[43]

The key word to highlight in this sentence is 'perfectly'. Most contemporary uses of perfect refer to something complete and static that has nowhere else to go and is impossible to improve. Hull's claim that God learns perfectly is different, based in the idea that God repeatedly and flawlessly responds to creation in its continual unfolding. In this case, perfection is dynamic. Hull continues to explain that neither the Church, nor the divinely designed and created Universe, nor the God they represent can be 'timeless and unchangeable'[44] because they possess 'a potential for genuine novelty and exhibit ... real creativity' in their evolving relationships.[45] Nothing can be truly relational and perfect because relationality requires the ability to respond and grow in connectedness to others. Relationships cannot develop if the parties have nothing to discover about each other. As feminist theologian Carter Heyward explains, 'God is *in* the dynamic, sparking movement among and between us, within and beyond us, beneath and above us.'[46] For Hull, this does not call into question the reliability or loyalty of God's character but suggests that those traits are expressed in God's willingness and determination to be relationally responsive to creation. He uses Matthew 5.48 to summarize the dynamically perfect learning pattern into which Christian learners are invited:

> When we seek to be perfect as our Heavenly Father is perfect, we do not seek less change but more, so that we may become more receptive towards the creative freedom of the world.[47]

For many, the idea of Jesus as a model of dynamically perfect, divine learning in which 'God is fully open because [God] perfectly loves and perfectly knows'[48] is difficult to accept (or even imagine) because it goes directly against the idea of the all-knowing, all-seeing God that is regularly taught. Much of this, however, and particularly the idea of perfection being closely aligned with completion, is not necessarily originally derived from the Bible or ancient Christian tradition but from the work of the Ancient Greek philosopher, Plato.[49] Hull muses on how different perceptions of God might be more prominent in contemporary Christianity had other views gained as much traction as Plato's. For example, in stark contrast to Plato, fellow Greek philosopher Heraclitus suggested that creation is not a fixed reality but its true identity is found and expressed in developing connectivity and constant change. Heraclitus 'finds permanence in the negation of permanence; being of reality consists in never "being" but always "becoming", not in stability but change.'[50] Brueggemann's view of God aligns far more with this dynamic worldview in which the universe reflects the nature of its creator in its state of constant change and flux: 'The God of the Bible is endlessly ... capable of coming and going, judging and forgiving, speaking and remaining silent – in ways that make the next time endlessly uncertain.'[51] Like Brueggemann, Hull believes it is entirely possible for God to be faithful, trustworthy *and* endlessly changing in response to creation. In fact, he argues that God's ongoing responsiveness to creation is a demonstration of divine faithfulness and trustworthiness but perhaps more than both of these, of joy and delight.

However, Hull does not claim that Christians learn exactly as God does. To understand the differences that he identifies, we need to consider a concept called *emergence*. At its most basic, emergence is the idea that a whole can be greater than the sum of its parts. In the natural world, it means that 'complex entities (like organisms) can have properties that do not exist within the elements (such as molecules) that make up the complex entity.'[52] In terms of learning, emergence describes how the outcomes of learning can be vastly different in quality and quantity from what was input. In other words, learning often bestows characteristics that are greater than the sum of the pre-existing knowledge, personality, skills and information 'deposited' into learners. When emergent learning happens repeatedly, it makes genuinely 'new' or transcendent learning possible,[53] and it is at this point that Hull imagines the paths of human and divine learning diverging.

Human learning cannot escape being, at least partially, motivated by lack, need, insecurity and selfishness. It will always 'fill gaps' in partial knowledge or skills, meaning that once any particular need is fulfilled, learners must search for fresh inspiration or motivation. However, God's learning does not address lack or need. God learns as an expression of perfectly dynamic character and consequently does not need to search for fresh learning motivation or fuel. Put simply, whereas human learning might be described as a process of change 'from darkness to light', on the other hand ' God changes from light to greater light.'[54] Therefore divine learning is perfectly emergent because its source is its own perfect, joy-fuelled momentum. Perhaps this kind of perfect emergence was what the Apostle Paul imagined when he urged the Corinthian Church in 2 Corinthians 3.18 to allow the Spirit to transform them 'from one degree of glory to another'?

> God learns without ever having to overcome ignorance. *God's* learning is never frustrated by distraction or apathy, never imperfect because of inadequate intelligence or insufficient sympathy, never spoiled by failing to remember, never fractured by isolation from the rest of knowledge. *God* expresses *God's* perfect wisdom by being the perfect learner just as *God* expresses *God's* perfect love by being the perfect friend ... *God* is continually renewed through learning, and so is both the ancient of days and the eternal child.[55]

In a theme explored further in the next chapter, the most significant implication of this is that it suggests a different underlying motivation for CAL. Jesus does not learn because he needs to, and therefore the model of learning to which Christians aspire is not a necessary means to an end but an experience of joy and delight, the ultimate expression of being alive. Hull describes divine learning in terms of love and intimate relationship; a two-way relationship beautifully outlined in the following example: '"The morning stars sang together for joy." And God, who made it possible for them to sing but did not write the score, is delighted.'[56] So then, just as 'human beings are not merely capable of remarkable learning, they are dependent upon this learning for the effective living of their lives,'[57] so too God's learning is an essential expression of a core element of God's relational character and identity.

Therefore, if Jesus is a learner and invites others to follow his example, it is an invitation to join God in the enjoyment of spontaneous novelty, surprise freedom – and dare I suggest, disruption? – in responding to creation as it is continually revealed. In the developing nature of creation itself and God's ongoing engagement with it, Hull perceives a creative and participative learning model for Christian adults:

> So, God, being surprised, learns from ... creation, and this is a feature of *God's* perfection, for surprise is a feature of the relationship between free entities, and the absence of surprise is a feature of the relationship between ... a master and ... slaves, between a performer and ... puppets.[58]

Why is this important? In learning in and from creation, the incarnate Christian God simultaneously models the best of the divine *and* human natures, not one at the expense of the other. Divine learning demonstrates that Jesus' divinity and humanity are, in fact, not in conflict at all but in perfect, dynamic synergy. In this way, Jesus' human nature was not just a necessary (but inconvenient) limitation that God embraced to sort out humanity's mess, but a means of more fully expressing divine relationality and connectedness. Therefore the example set for those who would become more like Jesus is that embracing and expressing the fullness of God does not require escaping the quirks of human form but leveraging all of its opportunities to become the best version of grounded, relational and responsively connected humanity possible. And to try to learn to delight in the twists and turns of the ride!

The deeply relational character of divine learning requires a brief closing note about the second image I mentioned earlier – the Trinity. We will return to the practicalities of trinitarian learning in Chapter 6, but there are a few fundamental implications of the Christian Trinity that must be acknowledged

here. Franciscan priest and author Richard Rohr highlights
many of them in his book *The Divine Dance*:

> History has so long operated with a static and imperial
> image of God – as a Supreme Monarch who is mostly living
> in splendid isolation from what he – and God is always and
> exclusively envisioned as male in this model – created. This
> God is seen largely as a Critical Spectator (and his followers
> do their level best to imitate their Creator in this regard).[59]

For Rohr, at the most fundamental level, the Trinity makes a
statement about how Christianity is both constant *and* ever
changing – God's persistent reliability is not compromised by,
but requires, dynamic movement and exchange. God cannot
be an isolated observer, because God is engaged and involved,
at the very least, with the other members of the Trinity. But
more than this, the Trinity adopts an outward-facing posture
in a dance that has space for others to join in. Whatever God
is like, whatever relational engagement happens within the
Trinity, whatever learning dance is taking place, there is no
room for observers. Christian learners are offered a hand and
invited onto the dance floor!

Selah 4: How do we know anything anyway?

In several places our discussions have touched upon a discipline that academics call epistemology (eh-pist-eh-mol-oh-gee).
Epistemology is the study of how knowledge works. What can
be known? Are there differences between facts, beliefs and
opinions and if so, what are they? There are lots of different
claims about how knowledge works, but two views in particular are important to our discussion: apophatic (a-poh-fa-tick)
and cataphatic (cat-a-fa-tick) knowing. When we apply these
to knowledge of God, the first – apophatic – says that a human
being is 'incapable to employ either her natural faculties or her
senses in her effort to achieving knowledge of the divine,'[60]

and that the only way to learn is by entering 'the cloud of unknowing' and thereby 'gaining the wisdom that the divine is beyond comprehension.'[61] An extreme version of this says that it is a complete waste of time trying to work God out, because God is beyond human understanding. At the other end of the scale, a cataphatic approach to knowing God says that 'using the natural faculties such as the five senses and reason ... it is possible to achieve a partial understanding and knowledge of the divine.'[62]

It is reasonably clear that neither of these extremes is workable, if only because what humans already know, can know and can never know, and how all these things shape us, are not easy to identify.

> Ideological commitment is a mixture of conscious and unconscious elements. A person knows that [s]he is a Christian, but [s]he does not necessarily realize all of the subtle and profound ways in which that commitment has shaped the whole of the way in which [s]he experiences her/his life.[63]

In other words, humans do not realize what we do and do not know (even about ourselves), never mind have enough of a handle on it to work out how it impacts practical living. We are partially aware of self and surroundings but never completely. An extreme apophatic approach (throwing proverbial hands in the air, because trying to understand God is a waste of time) usually results in disengagement from CAL or, at the very least, passive, disconnected, instructional types of learning that conflict with disruptive inclusion. However, a fully cataphatic approach is equally unhelpful and unrealistic because the limits of the human condition make it impossible to perceive everything clearly, all the time. Perhaps unsurprisingly, we arrive at a further example of how a both-and framework provides an effective foundation for CAL. Knowing God is achieved both in and beyond human perception.

This image is powerfully embodied in Hull's experience of physical sight loss. For sighted people, Hull argued, the world was split into dark and light – night and day – what can be seen and what is beyond physical sight. However, shortly after his physical eyes failed, he also lost access to visual memories, or the mode of engaging the world in which things 'looked like' anything at all. So Hull began a phase of life in which he began perceiving reality on entirely different terms. In 2001, he explained how, 'When one is beyond darkness and light ... the distinction between the conscious and unconscious life becomes vague'[64] but if 'this is a characteristic of God, to whom darkness and light are both alike ... without blind people, the religious experience of sighted people is not complete.'[65] In 1991 Hull went further in declaring, 'I believe that I now see more clearly than before.'[66] Thus emerges the deep sense in which Hull did not consider an inability to perceive as an automatic barrier to learning but an invitation to name and embrace human limits. Once a learner comes to terms with the fact that the best learning brings together the knowable *and* the realization that much is (and some will remain) unknown, it is accompanied with a freedom to build connections, explore and engage without fear. Hull's daughter, Imogen, summed this up beautifully in her recollection of her father's growing confidence in navigating the world with his cane. She explains how he moved around with an assuredness based on the realization that 'there's only so lost you can get.'[67]

Jesus as teacher and learning how to be wrong

Finally, although Jesus has featured throughout this chapter, we now reach the discussion about Jesus and learning that you may have been expecting. Unlike the lack of focus on learner-Jesus, much has been said and written about Jesus' teaching methods. He preached sermons and told stories with multiple levels of meaning. He was notorious for answering questions with questions. He performed miraculous acts and signs, many of which seem to be designed to convey truths about his identity and mission. However, it is important to acknowledge that, by many prevailing contemporary standards, Jesus was not a very effective teacher, given the basic fact that so many people seemed to leave his presence either more confused than before or just plain terrified.[68] From experience, that is the kind of learning outcome that school inspectors are more than happy to classify as unsatisfactory! So was Jesus a successful teacher? If yes, according to what definition of learning? Among the many ways that this question can be explored, Hull repeatedly came back to the idea of being right and wrong.

Most contemporary learners quickly understand that 'to be right is not only to be sane but to be good and to be entitled to reward'.[69] On the other hand, being wrong, ignorant or inaccurate is to be avoided. Therefore, it is unsurprising that aspiring learners invest as much time and energy as possible in being right. In turn, this means that more experienced learners have more at stake, having invested more time and energy in being right. A psychological framework called Personal Construct Theory explains how this works.[70] It suggests that, as humans go about their everyday lives, they create multiple personal constructs. These are best imagined as a set of commitments about the world and how it works. For example, one day you show a kindness to a stranger and then later the same day, someone else shows you a similar kindness. These incidents are completely unrelated, but you interpret them in a connected way. Over time you develop a belief that if you are kind to others it will generally find its way back to you. Personal Construct Theory says that we are forming constructs like this in all areas of life, all the time. These constructs then act as filters through which we make meaning in and from the world and on which we base future decisions.

Another good example of this is the connections made between geographic locations and holidays. If you enjoy a particularly special holiday somewhere, that place becomes associated with all the happy memories and emotions that you felt at that time. However, if you go somewhere and have a less than happy time, a negative construct is formed that is equally difficult to undo and reform. In my case, there was an incident with a flat tyre, some lost luggage and a goat that forever taints Strasbourg in my imagination (again, feel free to ask me more about this over coffee!). Even though the experience may have nothing to do with where it happened, the place and the experience become deeply linked in your worldview. Similarly, I know lots of people who have not pursued certain topics (particularly studying other languages, for some reason!) because of bad experiences with specific teachers of those subjects at school. Personal constructs are difficult (but not impossible) to break and rebuild. They form in clusters and act powerfully in our lives to direct our views, preferences and choices.

Although the above examples are reasonably innocuous, personal constructs help us to gauge what we think and decide to do by drawing connection between ideas, times, feelings, perspectives, opinions, values and beliefs in all areas of life. As life progresses, these form into increasingly interconnected systems or webs which, at any point, represent the 'sum total of everything a person has learned so far'.[71] By adulthood, learners make decisions and form opinions based on elaborate, multi-layered systems comprising 'subordinate' (lower level) and 'superordinate' (higher and top level) constructs.[72] These web-like hierarchies bring the challenges associated with being proved wrong into finer focus. Connections between different areas and levels within these webs are necessary for humans to navigate the world successfully, but they can also cause problems. For example, when higher-level commitments in our personal construct webs are challenged, it has a knock-on effect on multiple areas and the whole system can find the potential changes difficult to bear: it is 'painful and unsettling to question the things which are the source and ground for the rest of our life and its activities.'[73] Constructs relating to religious thinking and experience usually influence the entire system! For many Christians, a central, superordinate construct that governs much of how meaning is constructed is 'the belief in a merciful and forgiving God'.[74] If a new experience or piece of information challenges or displaces this, everything connected to and dependent on it (that is, potentially everything!)

is threatened and the overall integrity of the construct system is undermined. Thus 'there may well be times when a person cannot afford to be wrong, for the damage to the system as a whole would be unacceptable.'[75]

Personal construct theory demonstrates how, particularly as life progresses, learners will need to work harder to remain aware of existing views and convictions (and their rationale) and open to new information and experiences. In fact, it is very common (and not entirely unreasonable) for learners to close themselves off because the risk of the potential damage to the system in being wrong simply becomes too great. It is very common to find that 'the area open to enquiry and playful curiosity steadily diminishes' and learners undergo the process of 'crystallisation ... ossification ...' and 'sedimentation'.[76] For an example of this, we return to the idea of holidays. When my Mum was a child she was taken to Scotland on holiday. In her memory, it rained the entire time and they had a thoroughly miserable time because of it (I do not doubt this is accurate but highlight the fact that this is what she remembers). Therefore, throughout my childhood, my parents refused to take us to Scotland, citing my Mum's single poor experience as the reason. Every time Scotland was mentioned, we were reminded that it was wet, sad and not worth going! By my teenage years my Mum had reinforced her dislike of Scotland so many times that, even if she did change her mind or even somehow forget why she held anything against it in the first place, we would never have known. She had reached a point where she could no longer risk the consequences of admitting that she might have been wrong all this time – she had too much to lose! Fast forward several years and, now retired, Dad somehow convinced Mum to take a trip to Edinburgh for the weekend (I have no idea how) and a thoroughly lovely time was had by all!

This now poses a significant problem for Mum, and her solution is common to many in later life – she 'uncoupled' or disconnected her Edinburgh trip from the rest of Scotland. My Mum's response to, 'I'm so glad you had such a good time in Edinburgh, Mum. Does this mean you have changed your mind on Scotland?' is, 'Oh no, Edinburgh isn't *proper* Scotland, it's a big city.' With my sincerest apologies to any Scottish readers, do you see the move my Mum made here? So that she was not forced to disrupt her longstanding construct and admit she may have been wrong, she created a new construct (or at least a new branch of an existing construct) that does not conflict with the existing one(s). In my Mum's view of the world, Scotland can remain wet and miserable and therefore not worth visiting, while Edinburgh can remain lovely, and never the twain shall meet! She just keeps them in different psychological boxes in her mind.

Many people do exactly this with their Christian beliefs. They uncouple many of the most important areas of their lives, separating what they believe about God and what they believe about creation care (to choose just one example) because there is a deep sense that if the two areas were allowed to inter-inform, it might reveal some significant errors (or at the very least, need for reconfiguration) in one, or both, of the areas in question. Disruptions can only make demands on areas that are connected. If spiritual things have nothing to do with earthly things, then how can Christian faith make any claims on how we treat the planet? By keeping certain views and beliefs entirely isolated, the chances of them undergoing change or being disrupted in any way are significantly reduced.

So what does any of this have to do with Jesus' teaching style? There is a familiar pattern in many of Jesus' engagements with those he encounters, whether with his own disciples, Jewish religious leaders or diverse other individuals and groups that come across his path. It takes many forms, but the core peda-gogical mechanism is simple: You think that the world works like this; in fact, it is more like this. Famously, the sermon on the mount expresses it as: 'You have heard it said ... now I say' (Matt. 5.21–44), but the same pattern appears throughout the Gospels and beyond. From a learning perspective, this offers several options, with many of those Jesus meets falling into one of two categories: they either dare to imagine that they may have been wrong, even if they do not know exactly how, and this process has a transformative effect. Or, faced with the potential cost of even investigating whether they might have been wrong, they 'double down' or separate out particular ideas so that the threat of damage from Jesus' challenge is either entirely eliminated or significantly limited.

As mentioned in Selah 2, Hull understands that Jesus' teaching and learning interactions actively create opportunities for 'direct cognitive conflict' and 'cognitive dissonance', rather than providing coping mechanisms that insulate learners from potential disruption, or the skills to avoid or deny them.[77]

> Jesus used stories to undermine the limited images of those who heard him. The Unjust Judge and the Good Samaritan are classical examples of images involving direct cognitive conflict and indeed, in the image of divine man and a crucified God Christianity presents cognitive dissonance at the very heart of its self-understanding.[78]

Hull's example of the Good Samaritan is a helpful one. Jesus tells a story in response to a lawyer's question, 'And who is my neighbour?' (Luke 10.29). In earlier verses, readers are given a sense of the lawyer's highly connected personal constructs between eternal life, the law, loving God and loving others. Jesus does not throw these concepts out – his suggestion is not that the lawyer needs to reject all existing ideas and replace them with new ones. In personal construct terms, Jesus does not require the lawyer to completely destroy his existing construct network, but his response to the lawyer's question provides the resources to both deconstruct and reconstruct what it means to be a neighbour.[79] In other words, Jesus does not say that the lawyer's understanding of neighbourliness is completely wrong and leave him to work out where to go from there; he provides a reconfiguration of how it works and challenges him (and therefore also us) to investigate what influence this may have on his overall worldview.

Jesus' teaching does not ask his listeners to give up on everything that they think they know, all at once, and it is probably more disruptive because of it! It recognizes that the best learning happens when new ideas are introduced alongside existing ones and allowed to interact. Jesus does not ask the lawyer to give up on many of the ideas and categories with which he was comfortable; rather he models the kind of shift he is suggesting by telling a familiar story but with a signifcant twist (see Chapter 6 for a detailed discussion of this). Even in one of the most dramatic encounters in Luke's Gospel, where 'a certain ruler' (18.18) approaches Jesus and tells him everything that he has done to keep the commandments since his youth, Jesus does not 'pull the rug' and suggest that there is no value to his entire existing worldview. Instead, he suggests just one addition. Admittedly, it is a significant addition, and one that ultimately was unacceptable to the ruler, but Jesus' suggestion is that 'there is still one thing lacking' (Luke 18.22), challenging him to explore how Jesus' suggestion interacts with his existing understanding. More often than not, Jesus' teaching technique is to throw one new idea into the mix and ask whether learners will allow it to reorder their construct system. The underlying challenge is: How does this learning disruption sit with your other convictions and beliefs? Will you allow the disruption to have a knock-on influence throughout your life or have you invested so much in being right, that you dare not even explore whether you might have been wrong?

Overall, Jesus' teaching demonstrates that learners should not aim to have a construct system 'so loose as to be virtually meaningless and useless [nor] ... so tight as to be unable to tolerate ambiguity at all.'[80] 'Room should be left for a commitment which is sincere and deep but at the same time sufficiently exploratory and tentative.'[81] Simply put, this means that strong opinions are good – having key ideas that run deep and shape your life are to be encouraged because they make learning possible. However, if those views and commitments either become disconnected from other parts of life or are so concretely set that they are not even open to tweaking, then they become deeply problematic and make CAL difficult. Equally, if a learner has no strong views or values to the point where almost everything is as unimportant as everything else, this is just as problematic because all sense of how to make meaning and connection is lost. Again, learning becomes very difficult, if not impossible. In summary, Hull suggests that 'oscillation between tight and loose ... is necessary if the construct system as a whole is to be flexible enough and yet relevant enough to undergo development.'[82] This need for a combination of grounded centredness and openness is so critical to Hull that he presents it as akin to a form of rebirth or resurrection which will 'free the believer from naïve absolutist assumptions and will enable him to live again.'[83]

One of my favourite passages in the Bible is Jesus' interaction with Nicodemus in John 3. For many years I was drawn to it because I was convinced that Nicodemus went away from their conversation more confused than when it began (as evidence for this, many scholars point out that the narrator of the fourth Gospel mentions in 19.39 that Nicodemus had come to Jesus 'by night': a symbol of ignorance and confusion). But as time has progressed, my views have changed. Now, my fascination with John 3 focuses on Nicodemus' question in verse 9: 'How can these things be?' and the fact that this can be read in multiple ways. I used to interpret this as Nicodemus shutting down, refusing to contemplate some of the (frankly) crazy ideas that Jesus spouts about life, death, birth, knowledge, spirit, wind, etc. But now, in Nicodemus' words, I hear something more like a first attempt at wondering how Jesus' suggestions might fit with his existing personal constructs. We are not directly told what difference Nicodemus' interaction with Jesus had on the rest of his life. All the evidence points to the fact that he probably did not leave their first recorded encounter with complete clarity. However, given that the writer of the fourth Gospel records him as one of the few who come to anoint Jesus' body for burial (19.39), I now read Nicodemus' question in 3.9 as the beginning of a process of allowing Jesus to disrupt his worldview, a process that transforms the trajectory of his life and entire perception of reality.

Questions/activities

• Have you ever thought about the Bible as a learning tool?
How do you understand it works? How do you use it?
• How do you respond to the inner diversity of the biblical
learning community? Which of its voices do you find resonate
most closely with yours? Which do you find most different or
difficult to deal with?
• Which frameworks for understanding the overarching
message of the Bible are most familiar to you? What kind of
learning journey do they present the Bible as?
• What are the first words that come to your mind to describe
God? If God is a learner, what kind of a learner do these
words point to?
• Think of a time when you realized (or were even forced to
realize) that you had been wrong. How did you respond?
• Pick a learner from the Gospels that best represents you and
your approach to CAL. What is it about their response that
resonates most strongly?
• What is the biggest potential disruption for you in this
chapter? What are the more significant questions raised for
you? Write them down at this interim stage. You may also
want to return to your opening thoughts about CAL. Is there
anything you would now change?

Notes

1 John Swinton and Harriet Mowat, *Practical Theology and Quali-*
tative Research, 2nd edn (London: SCM Press, 2016), p. 13.
2 Quentin Chandler, 'Cognition or spiritual disposition? Threshold
concepts in theological reflection', *Journal of Adult Theological Educa-*
tion 13:2 (2016), pp. 90–102, pp. 96–7.
3 Karen Kilby, 'Seeking clarity' in M. Higton and J. Fodor (eds),
The Routledge Companion to the Practice of Christian Theology (London: Routledge, 2015), pp. 61–71, pp. 66–7.
4 Kilby, 'Seeking clarity', p. 65.
5 Kwok Pui Lan, *Discovering the Bible in the Non-biblical World*
(Maryknoll, NY: Orbis Books, 1995), p. 13.

6 Kwok, *Discovering the Bible*, p. 12.

7 Elisabeth Schüssler Fiorenza, *But She Said: Feminist practices of biblical interpretation* (Boston, MA: Beacon Press, 1992), p. 149.

8 Gloria Durka, *The Teacher's Calling: A spirituality for those who teach* (New York, NY: Paulist Press, 2002), p. 1.

9 Dale Martin, *Pedagogy of the Bible: An analysis and proposal* (Louisville, KY: WJK Press, 2008), p. 87.

10 Anthony Reddie, 'Telling a new story: reconfiguring Christian Education for the challenges of the twenty-first century' in Dennis Bates, Gloria Durka and Friedrich Schweitzer (eds), *Education, Religion and Society: Essays in honour of John M. Hull* (London: Routledge, 2006), pp. 115–27, p. 122.

11 Reddie, 'Telling a new story', p. 121. Disruptive inclusion turns the traditional interpretational circle inside-out, that is, the disruptive experiences of those often deemed on the peripheries or unimportant in interpretive conversations are placed in the centre of the interpretational framework. Here, the Black jazz community naturally embodies disruptive learning in ways that other groups' identities and experiences cannot.

12 Elinor Evans, 'Ron Chernow on Alexander Hamilton: the man behind the hit musical', *History Extra* (4 January 2018), available at https://www.historyextra.com/period/modern/hamilton-the-man-behind-the-musical/ (accessed 31.07.2023).

13 In contrast to Hull, Kwok Pui Lan perceives the Bible as a 'closed canon' and therefore a pedagogical model that mirrors her own and others' ongoing exclusion from learning, leading her to the conclusion: 'I ... do not think that the Bible provides the norm for interpretation in itself.' Kwok, *Discovering the Bible*, p. 18. As an alternative, she suggests: 'The critical principle lies not in the Bible itself, but in the community of women and men who read the Bible and through their dialogical imagination, appropriate it for their own liberation.' Kwok, *Discovering the Bible*, p. 19.

14 Francis Watson, '"Every perfect gift". James, Paul and the Created Order' in K. Hockey, M. Pierce and F. Watson (eds), *Muted Voice of the New Testament: Readings in the Catholic Epistles and Hebrews* (London: Bloomsbury T&T Clark, 2017), pp. 121–37, p. 137.

15 Watson, 'Every perfect gift', p. 137.

16 Walter Brueggemann, 'Against the stream: Brevard Childs's biblical theology', *Theology Today* 50:2 (1993), pp. 279–84, p. 283.

17 Ellen F. Davis, 'Teaching the Bible confessionally in the Church', *Vision: A Journal for Church and Theology* 22:2 (2021), pp. 77–85, p. 81.

18 For a good introduction to biblical theology as salvation history see chapter 2 in Edward W. Klink and Darian R. Lockett, *Understand-*

ing Biblical Theology: A comparison of theory and practice (Grand Rapids, MI: Zondervan, 2012). The Romans Road is explained here: https://www.gotquestions.org/Romans-road-salvation.html and you can find out more about reading the Bible as a five-act play in N. T. Wright, *Scripture and the Authority of God* (London: SPCK, 2005), pp. 91–3. See also Kevin Vanhoozer, *First Theology: God, scripture & hermeneutics* (Leicester: InterVarsity Press, 2002).

19 Hull, *What Prevents*, p. 160. Hull defines wholeness as representing 'the achievement of equilibrium, a synthesis ... in which a more inclusive balance is struck.' Hull, *What Prevents*, p. 157.

20 Hull, *What Prevents*, pp. 160–1.

21 However, there are also multiple biblical patterns that suggest Christian maturity sometimes takes the form of knowing less or becoming like a child! For example, 1 Corinthians 2.2.

22 Hull, *What Prevents*, p. 82.

23 John M. Hull, 'The Bible in the secular classroom: an approach through the experience of loss' in J. Astley and D. Day (eds), *The Contours of Christian Education* (Great Wakering: McCrimmons, 1992), pp. 197–215, p. 198.

24 Hull, 'The Bible in the secular classroom', p. 197.

25 Hull, 'The Bible in the secular classroom', p. 198.

26 Rachelle Gilmour, 'The Exodus in the Bible's teaching and our teaching of the Bible: helping to reconcile faith and critical study of the Bible through Threshold Concept Theory', *Journal of Adult Theological Education* 13:2 (2016), pp. 116–27, pp. 125–6.

27 John H. Westerhoff III, 'Toward a definition of Christian Education' in J. H. Westerhoff (ed.), *A Colloquy on Christian Education* (Philadelphia, PA: United Church Press, 1972), pp. 60–71, p. 70. I have expanded Westerhoff's language in this quote to be more inclusive.

28 William P. Brown, *Sacred Sense: Discovering the wonder of God's word and world* (Grand Rapids, MI: Wm. B. Eerdmans, 2015), p. 8.

29 Brown, *Sacred Sense*, p. 5.

30 Brown, *Sacred Sense*, p. 6.

31 Brown, *Sacred Sense*, p. 6. This is deeply reminiscent of Hull's description of 'oscillation between tight and loose construing'. Hull, *What Prevents*, p. 108.

32 Francis Watson, 'The four-fold Gospel' in C. Barton (ed.), *The Cambridge Companion to the Gospels* (Cambridge, Cambridge University Press, 2006), p. 50.

33 Hull, *What Prevents*, p. 183. Italics added.

34 Mark Twain, *Following the Equator: A journey around the world* (Waiheke Island, NZ: Floating Press, 2009), p. 140.

35 George Gordon, Lord Byron, *Don Juan* (Auckland, NZ: Floating Press, 2009), p. 605.

36 Davis, 'Teaching the Bible Confessionally', p. 79.

37 Hull, *What Prevents*, p. 204.

38 Hull, *What Prevents*, p. 203.

39 Hull, *What Prevents*, p. 204.

40 Hull, *What Prevents*, p. 205.

41 Hull, *What Prevents*, p. 199.

42 Mark Chater, *Jesus Christ, Learning Teacher: Where theology and pedagogy meet* (London: SCM Press, 2020), p. 23.

43 Hull, *What Prevents*, p. 224.

44 Hull, *What Prevents*, p. 81.

45 Hull, *What Prevents*, p. 221.

46 Carter Heyward, *Saving Jesus from Those Who are Right: Rethinking what it means to be Christian* (Minneapolis, MI: Fortress Press, 1999), p. 61.

47 Hull, *What Prevents*, p. 227.

48 Hull, *What Prevents*, p. 226.

49 You can find a good introduction to Plato here: https://iep.utm.edu/plato/ (accessed 31.07.2023).

50 John Marshall, *A Short History of Greek Philosophy* (Luton: CreateSpace, 2013), p. 8.

51 Walter Brueggemann and Patrick D. Miller, *Deep Memory, Exuberant Hope: Contested truth in a post-Christian world* (Minneapolis, MI: Fortress Press, 2000), p. 4.

52 Malcom A. Jeeves and Warren S. Brown, *Neuroscience, psychology, and religion: Illusions, delusions, and realities about human nature* (West Conshohocken, PA: Templeton Foundation Press, 2009), p. 112.

53 Hull, *What Prevents*, p. 168.

54 Hull, *What Prevents*, p. 226.

55 Hull, *What Prevents*, p. 224. Hull generally uses male pronouns for God. Here, and in subsequent examples, I have replaced them with gender-neutral references to God's self.

56 Hull, *What Prevents*, p. 223.

57 Hull, *What Prevents*, p. 56.

58 Hull, *What Prevents*, pp. 223–4.

59 Richard Rohr, *The Divine Dance* (London: SPCK, 2016), pp. 35–6.

60 Catharina Stenqvist, 'Apophatic and cataphatic' in A. L. C. Runehov and L. Oviedo (eds), *Encyclopedia of Sciences and Religions* (Dordrecht: Springer, 2013), pp. 113–14, p. 114.

61 Stenqvist, 'Apophatic and cataphatic', p. 114.

62 Stenqvist, 'Apophatic and cataphatic', p. 114.c

63 Hull, *What Prevents*, p. 67.

64 John M. Hull, *In the Beginning There was Darkness* (London: SCM Press, 2001), pp. 131–2.

65 Hull, *In the Beginning*, p. 132.

66 Hull, *What Prevents*, p. vii.

67 Arte Creative, *Radio H.*, available here: https://www.johnmhull. co.uk/film-shorts (accessed 31.07.2023).

68 Mark's Gospel is the most well-known for the disciples' confusion and fear, with the original ending concluding with them fleeing in terror (Mark 16.8). However, all of the Gospels contain numerous examples of the disciples not understanding and being afraid. See: Matthew 17, Luke 9, John 8, 10.

69 Hull, *What Prevents*, p. 101.

70 George Kelly, *The Psychology of Personal Constructs* (New York, NY: Norton, 1955).

71 Hull, *What Prevents*, p. 107.

72 Hull, *What Prevents*, p. 107.

73 Hull, *What Prevents*, p. 55. This pattern is similar to how changes in senior management in a company are often felt very quickly right through the culture of an organization, even when the outgoing person(s) had seemingly little or nothing to do with the day-to-day running of the business.

74 Stefan Huber, 'Are religious beliefs relevant in daily life?', *Empirical Studies in Theology, vol. 15* (Leiden: Brill, 2007), p. 213.

75 Hull, *What Prevents*, p. 108. Hull's references to both ideological closure and premature closure resonate strongly with Erik Erikson's work as further developed by James Marcia. 'The foreclosed adult has developed a personality structure that resists disequilibrium. If life events do destabilize the foreclosed adult, identity restructuring is likely to be a shattering experience.' Jane Croger, 'Identity development through adulthood: the move toward "wholeness"' in C. McClean and M. U. Syed (eds), *The Oxford Handbook of Identity Development* (New York, NY: Oxford University Press, 2015), p. 68.

76 Hull, *What Prevents*, pp. 126, 62 and 68.

77 Hull, *What Prevents*, p. 82.

78 Hull, *What Prevents*, p. 101.

79 This is similar to the pattern that Brueggemann identifies in the psalms: from orientation to disorientation and then reorientation. Walter Brueggemann, *Spirituality of the Psalms* (Minneapolis, MI: Fortress Press, 2002), p. 11.

80 Hull, *What Prevents*, p. 108.

81 Hull, *What Prevents*, pp. 155–6. Hull explains this parallel solid commitment and determination to explore as 'introduc[ing] an element of spiritual play'. Just as imaginative play creates opportunities for exercising real-life skills in make-believe settings, learners can try on situations other than their own and use their experiences of this new perspective to further progress.

82 Hull, *What Prevents*, p. 108. This also evokes Erikson's cyclical developmental stages – in particular, stage 7, Generativity Versus Stagnation. You can find more on this here: https://www.simplypsychology.org/erik-erikson.html.

83 Hull, *What Prevents*, p. 81.

4

The Christian Basis for Adult Learning: Practice Theologized

Having analysed the experience of climbing the mountain from one side, we now begin the climb again from another base camp, restarting our exploration of the potential *Christianness* of disruptive inclusion, this time from the lived experience of Christian adult learners. Beginning with the Bible drew attention to how CAL involves straddling simple and complex, then and now, boundaried and free. Considering the nature and character of God took us deep into the relationship between divinity and humanity and being right and wrong. Now we turn to what is highlighted when we begin by recognizing that most CAL does not take the form of abstract theories or well-evidenced arguments, but activities or experiences in which groups of Christian adults participate. This leads us to a pivotal focus of this chapter: groups. When we take CAL seriously as a practical, lived experience, it is difficult to ignore that although learning is increasingly treated as an individual activity, much CAL is experienced in communal settings. Therefore, in the practice of Christian faith, learning disruption often occurs when individual learners' identities, ideas, values, goals and expectations rub up against their communal or community counterparts.

The role of community in facilitating learning disruption has already been well established in several ways. The Bible invites readers to observe and participate in the disruption arising from diverse community dialogue. Also, the in-built relationality of God's character ushers learners to join in with the divine dynamism and emergence that makes transformative Christian learning possible but also surprising at every turn. Now we consider how the identity and purpose of Christian community practically influences CAL. In particular, how the coming together of individual and corporate shapes community identity and practice. Theologian and educationalist Thomas Groome sums up some of the key themes of this chapter:

> If self-identity is shaped by interaction with a collectivity, then to become Christian selves requires that we have socializing interaction with a Christian faith community which is capable of forming us in such faith ... All of our educational efforts will bear little fruit unless they take place within a Christian faith community.[1]

Including disruption in learning: the identity of Christian community

On careful reading, Groome claims that the critical importance of a Christian faith community in CAL is its function as the setting where individual identity meets shared, corporate identity, not where individual concerns are swallowed up in the collective. In other words, Christian community works as a kind of mixing bowl where multiple individual styles and concerns are exposed to community corporate identity, causing potential ongoing disruption to both. This is why, from local village fêtes to national conferences, synods and international symposia, making decisions in Christian community can be a really tricky process. There is a constant tension between creating space for individual contributions and preference while also recognizing that sometimes decisions need to be made with the benefit of the whole in mind.

A helpful way of exploring the kind of influence that the relationship between individual and corporate in CAL may have on learning is via a branch of philosophical theology known as Personalism.[2] It is a complex idea with wide-ranging implications, but at its core it attempts to explain how the learning experience of Christian adults is a process by which individual learners discover and develop their full selves via increasingly deeper and richer connection with others.[3] In other words, it suggests that individual and corporate learning work hand-in-hand, not at odds. The term Personalism was first coined in eighteenth-century Germany,[4] but is most closely associated with a group of twentieth-century French Roman Catholic theologians (most notably Jacques Maritain, Emmanuel Mounier and Teilhard de Chardin). They used it to express concern for: 'The cultivation of the human capacity to love God and other human beings in accordance with their divine nature.'[5]

Theologian and historian James Carroll uses an image from the Bible to illustrate how knowledge of self, others and God come together in Personalism, and it is worth reading slowly and carefully:

> The I AM of God, of Jesus, is the 'I am' of every person, and it consists in every person being aware of herself or himself. And that awareness points beyond itself ... 'I know' leads to 'I know that I know' leads to 'I know that I am known.' Here is what we mean by the images of God in which humans are created.[6]

'I know' leads to 'I know that I know' leads to 'I know that I am known': information, self-awareness and relationality in deeply intertwined combination. At the centre of a Personalist approach to learning (especially that of Maritain and Mounier) is the idea that because learners are made in God's image 'the highest achievement of education is ... the formation of a "true human person" who can exercise moral intelligence and practice self-giving love'[7] and that 'authentic bonds are necessary for growing into one's full personhood, and to live solely for one's self is antithetical to becoming fully human.'[8] In the most basic sense, Personalist learning is about becoming fully yourself and nobody can/is designed to do that alone. Therefore the learning goals of individual and community benefit are not in competition but deeply interlinked. You can only fulfil your potential if I fulfil mine and we work together on the project.

Personalism lines up with Hull's insistence that learning cannot be a purely solo activity: 'Learning is an inter-personal activity. It is something which people do for and with each other ... the best learning, especially in the case of adults, is almost always in groups.'[9] He has little time for an attitude to learning in Christian community that suggests 'You have come to worship God in the privacy of your own heart, and you must be allowed to get on with it.'[10] If learning is essentially a humanizing process, a way that people more fully discover themselves, then it cannot be an optional extra available to, or appropriate for, only the few. Personalism demonstrates that including self and others in learning is so foundational to the process that it could be explained in terms of 'the awakening of a person to living activity'[11] or as Hull puts it, the 'process of becoming'.[12]

Finally, we cannot discuss learning as a process of becoming without recognizing the influence of the twentieth-century Liberation theologian Paulo Freire. Freire's most famous work, *Pedagogy of the Oppressed*, speaks out against learning used as a tool of oppression and dehumanization.[13] He argues that learners are: 'Beings in the process of becoming – as unfinished, uncompleted beings in and with a likewise unfinished reality ... in this incompletion and this awareness lie the very roots of education as an exclusively human manifestation.'[14]

Freire scholar Peter Roberts unpacks how, in particular, Personalism's relationally connected, future-oriented, hopeful view of learning sits within Freire's overall pedagogy:

He is adamant that we cannot think, speak, read, write, learn, or be alone. To be human is to be a social being. Humans are beings of relationships: beings whose very existence cannot be comprehended without reference to others. Freire explicitly rejects the Cartesian notion of self-identical, self-knowing 'I' and replaces it with the dialogical, socially constituted 'we'.[15]

Humans learn, Freire argues, as a way of becoming equipped for further relational connection. For example, Freire famously dismisses defining learning as the depositing of information (what he calls the 'banking' model),[16] suggesting instead that educators' roles are to 'structure the environment in such a way that persons can get in touch with their own resources and the resources around them, toward a future.'[17] Taking this into account, teaching becomes a form of learning-networking, skilling learners to connect with themselves and others. Or, as religious educationalist Maria Harris puts it, as learners we 'must come to know first our primary community, then ourselves, our religious tradition, our "people" and our nation, if we would come to community with our planet, our universe, our God.'[18]

According to Harris, learning does not begin by developing a settled, static sense of self and then move on to navigating how that fixed reality fits into the bigger picture. She begins with community: the disruptive, messy, ever in flux group(s) of people with whom we live, eat, work, play and worship. This is the kind of learning setting, she claims, in which Christian learners learn the fundamental skills necessary to then progress on to greater levels of connection.

Koinonia: the source, aim and principal obstacle of CAL

Several scholars press the relationship between Christian community and learning further still. As part of what he refers to as Relational Learning, priest and educationalist Leon McKenzie suggests that Christian community is both the source and goal of CAL.

The medium *is* the message ... the community of learners *is* the kerygma. The social process *is* the proclamation. The context *is* the communication. We do not acquire meaning, explore and expand meaning structures, and learn how to

express meaning primarily on the basis of the study of religious abstractions ... but rather on the basis of lived experiences in a community of shared values ... delineated by the
New Testament concept *koinonia*.[19]

Breaking this down, McKenzie suggests that communities of
Christian learners are not just people who happen to be in the
same place to hear a sermon, study the Bible or sing a song
together; the learning function of Christian community runs
far deeper. His point is that community is not just the vehicle
for the proclamation of a message; the community of learners *is* the *kerygma* (Greek for proclamation/announcement).
As they seek to know God more and follow Jesus' example,
communities of Christian learners and worshippers do not
just receive the message but embody the message. It is only
in entering into this process together that true Christian community occurs. Christians do not just learn *with* others but
also *from* others, a concept that McKenzie expresses with the
Greek term *koinonia*. Like many ancient words and phrases,
koinonia cannot be directly translated by a single English word.
One of the principal Bible dictionaries explains how *koinonia*
encompasses 'Close association involving mutual interests and
sharing, *association, communion, fellowship, close relationship*
... attitude of good will that manifests an interest in a close
relationship, *generosity, fellow-feeling, altruism*.'[20] Among this
collection of terms, the ideas that seem most prominent are a
sense of reciprocity (give and take) and questions of identity,
as well as the everyday mechanics of life. *Koinonia* is the kind
of community that places demands on those involved but can
also bring significant benefits.

Maria Harris develops the connection between *koinonia*
and learning further than McKenzie. For Harris, the learning
of Christian communities takes places in 'the entire course of
the church's life' and within this, *koinonia* has three specific
functions: governing, convicting and not-yet-realized reality.[21] First, Harris says that *koinonia*'s work as a governing
reality is a specifically Christian concept, distinct from how

others live and learn together. In effect, she says that it holds diverse groups of Christians together. On paper, we may be very different from others in our community, but it is exactly this diversity that makes true Christian unity possible. None of us are fully alike – we are not meant to be; what brings us together are our differences and the task of relating together in various outlooks, skills and talents. Harris adds, 'the truth of the Christian community is that ... we contribute our share to the building up of the present, living body of Christ.'[22] Affinity is found in the posture we adopt in relation to one another, not in any shared, personal characteristic. As the Christian community in Corinth is reminded, 'If the whole body were an eye, where would the hearing be? If the whole body were hearing, where would the sense of smell be?' (1 Cor. 12.17).

One of the specific traits of *koinonia*, Harris claims, is its uniquely outward-facing stance that naturally seeks to both benefit from, and share benefit through, connection with others by reaching across its boundaries. This means that Christian learning communities are not limited by the normally perceived constraints of geography and time. In practical terms, this means that the *koinonia* available for Christian adult learners to draw on (and contribute to) is not limited to those in the same building as them, nor the same country, time zone or even point in history. The 'community of saints'[23] into which contemporary Christian learners can connect includes those who learn on the other side of the world, as well as those who learned in the past and will learn in the future. Harris claims that, at any point in time, Christian communities find their identity in connection with the beliefs, practices and legacy of those who have gone before, as well as being called to continue the trend of 'recognizing our communion with those yet to be born'.[24]

Similar to the earlier argument that the diversity of the biblical library offers readers both the freedom and the stability for bolder and safer exploration, and Hull's argument that the pattern of the overarching biblical narrative offers the same, Harris also describes a partnership in which historical, present and future Christian learning communities work together to 'create an environment where one can first come to know limits and boundaries.'[25] Community provides limits and boundaries that create 'Havens of meaningfulness and safety within the context of a diverse and frequently changing world: to engage with it, interpret it, and transform it otherwise would be difficult, if not impossible.'[26] However, as per our earlier foray into jazz, community-created boundaries are rarely permanently fixed. Therefore, 'in the lifelong enterprise where the boundaries and limits are constantly being widened outward toward all realizable reality',[27] a dynamic relationship exists between the universal Christian community and particular historically and geographically located communities within it.

The second and third connections Harris makes between *koinonia* and CAL are interconnected. Alongside *koinonia* as a governing reality, she argues that it functions as both a convicting and a not-yet-realized reality.[28] In other words, the learning function of Christian community is not as straightforward as we may think. Harris argues that, as a convicting reality, *koinonia* is not only the best response to human loneliness, disconnection and estrangement but also exacerbates them or, at the very least, draws attention to the inability of Christian community to address all the challenges associated with being human. Deeper and richer Christian community is both the aim towards which Christian learning struggles *and* one of the main reasons why achieving it is so difficult. The challenges of living in community are both a symptom of the underlying problem *and* its means of potential resolution. Harris continues: 'In our conviction, we are brought up short. At the same time, we are drawn to community, we find ourselves surrounded by bruised and broken community or by the absence of any community at all.'[29] Basically, learning with others makes CAL a whole lot more complicated (or perhaps, *complexified*, see Selah 3), but at the same time is the primary reason why we bother in the first place, and the only means of progress available.

Including disruption in learning: the practices of Christian community

In all these discussions of Christian community, the elephant in the room is that, for most Christians, the primary source, foundational structure and norming-norm of Christian community, faith and practice is the Church. In the previous section I purposefully avoided using the word because, even though it is one of the few universally acknowledged concepts in Christianity, there is little agreement on what it actually is. I agree with systematic theologian Veli-Matti Kärkkäinen's observation, quoting Hans Küng from 1978:

> Though there is much talk nowadays about the Church in the secular world, there is not a corresponding awareness of what the Church is. Whether outside of church or inside, I fear this lack of awareness is even deeper at the beginning of the third millennium![30]

The identity and purpose of the Christian Church is understood in various ways. For our purposes, it is enough to recognize that there is no single, agreed-upon answer; most bring together various aspects of the Church as an activity, location, identity marker and organization, but exactly how these work in combination is another conversation for a coffee shop date (at this rate, we may need to find somewhere that does free refills). As we have already established, CAL is not limited to formal settings. However, neither are they excluded from our investigations. What Christian learning communities do together in their regular gatherings plays a significant role in modelling how CAL can and should work in the rest of life. So the question becomes: What can we discover about CAL from Christian adults' participation in the activities of gathered worship?

Although not actively known as such in all denominations, the underpinning patterns of gathered worship are generally referred to as liturgy. Whether its cornerstones are set prayers or more spontaneous prophetic expression, silence, or a particular type of biscuit at the end of the service, almost every church community, and groups of church communities organized into networks and denominations, have patterns of practice by which they understand their own identities. For example, part of my church community's practice is to eat together. If, one Sunday, no food was offered it would feel very bizarre indeed, raising deep questions about not only the lack of food but the whole purpose and identity of the community. Food is deeply embedded in our liturgical practice. In your setting(s), if the lack/significant change to something would make waves, consider it part of your liturgy! In most cases, Sunday service liturgies include a sermon/homily (a topic fully unpacked in Chapter 7), prayer, praise (whether sung, said or silent) and what some consider sacramental practices such as Holy Communion.

When my church community began eating together, we did it for clear and specific reasons. We wanted to make a statement about sharing lives together and creating space around our table(s) (both literal and figurative) for others to join us. Even though we talk about tables all the time, I must admit that, on Sundays when we eat together, I rarely consciously think about how the process of eating around a communal table is radically transforming both my life and the life of our community – but I believe, and have witnessed, that it is! Therefore the Christian practice of liturgy introduces a new element into our conversation about the nature of CAL. Is cognizance (knowledge/awareness) necessary for Christian learning to happen? Am I being shaped by the repeated practice of eating with my church community when I do not really think about why we do it, as well as when I am consciously aware that I am participating in a deeply spiritual activity? Do Christian adult learners need to be able to understand and/or articulate learning for it to be effective?

Early in his career, Hull was in no doubt that one of the biggest problems relating to CAL in church settings was that 'an emphasis on liturgy, authority and tradition' leads to a simple moralism and 'seldom any encouragement for the laity to ask fundamental questions.'[31] Ultimately, he believed that many elements of church services were ineffective CAL tools because they did not actively or interactively engage those present, nor support them in growing in awareness of exactly how learning was happening. In the most basic sense, Hull was convinced that some church practices prevented CAL by just going through the motions – they just were not sufficiently disruptive! The connection between consciousness and learning was so key for Hull that he summarized the transformation he underwent in losing his physical sight as discovering 'something solid and permanent on the far side of despair and a change in the character of consciousness.'[32] Not only had Hull's awareness of self and surroundings changed, but even his understanding of what it meant to be conscious had itself been transformed, to the point where he described himself as a 'Whole-Body-Seer'.[33] He further explains that the problem with much CAL is that it 'remains at rather a tacit level of understanding, we cannot speak of it because we are barely aware of it.'[34] Or, more practically, Hull asks:

> Why is it that our churches contain so many adults who show resourcefulness, creativity and flexibility in their ordinary working lives but who, in their church life, seem to be quite unable to express a point of view about their faith?[35]

I agree with Hull that a key part of the CAL process is concerned with bringing (and keeping) the unconscious or the difficult to articulate into places where they can be known and investigated. In some cases, he recognizes that the problem is not a complete lack of awareness but a lack of variety of awareness. It is not that learners do not have opinions, but that they are not able to effectively discuss or explore them because they have no awareness *beyond* their own views. Any part of a learner's reality that has been unchanging and ever-present is not available for critical reflection, or as Hull succinctly puts it, 'fish are not aware of water'.[36]

To address this, Hull calls for an approach to CAL that 'involves ... seeing the world from the point of view of the other ... a temporary suspension of one's own beliefs.'[37] To do this, learners are not asked to entirely abandon existing views but to exercise 'partial, temporary and limited abilities ... to step outside of their experience' sufficiently to experience 'glimpses into another world.'[38] The eventual aim of this is to turn 'passive patient to active participant'.[39] For Hull, the key is to grow learner awareness – make it possible for Christian adults to step outside themselves, if only briefly, to perceive their own views and convictions from optimum distance and be able to critically engage with them. However, later in his career Hull seemed to have a slight change of heart, suggesting that there might be another factor at play: 'in the place of consciousness, let us place desire',[40] demonstrating his wrestling with the role of 'unconscious passion' in CAL.[41] If learning is a whole person activity, does learning require a person to be aware or able to articulate it, to be effective?

In a preview of one of the key themes of Chapter 7, this resonates strongly with philosophical theologian James K. A. Smith's work on 'pedagogies of desire'.[42] As Smith repeatedly claims, rather than increasing in knowledge or understanding in particular areas, CAL is better conceived as learners being moved by, or compelled towards, their greatest love or 'ultimate vision of the good life'.[43] Smith asks whether (and how) particular learning activities and patterns of activity move Christians towards love of God and others. More than this, Smith's pedagogy of desire suggests that 'Habits, dispositions, internal inclinations that ... you acquire through being immersed in rhythm, rituals and routines, over time, train your loves, even at an unconscious or pre-conscious level, to be oriented towards something ultimate.'[44] So patterned behaviour, that is, liturgy (of all types), as practised in gathered worship services, is not a barrier to change but how learning transformation happens!

While Smith does not propose that learners must choose between love, desire and emotion on the one hand and knowledge/understanding on the other, he proposes that learning occurs on unconscious or preconscious levels (unaware or before conscious awareness) and that over time desires are cultivated in a different direction or 'conscripted into a rival gospel' via regular, formative practices.[45] In comparison to Hull, who for most of his career downplayed the importance of repeated practices as *going through the motions*, Smith promotes the value of participating in liturgies that function beyond or outside of understanding and articulation (or at least begin there), highlighting their ability to transform at the level of unconscious desire. Regardless of where you land on Smith's argument (more from him in Chapter 7), his core claim, that liturgical practice reveals that the currency of Christian formation is not knowledge, accurate perception or comprehension but desire, complexifies questions about the relationship between disruptive inclusion and Christian faith. Most importantly, whether (and if so, how) it is possible for learners to participate in disruptive inclusion without consciously opting-in or even being aware of it. And what does love have to do with learning?

Benedictine monk Jean Leclercq's 1961 analysis of monastic culture further develops the potential connections between Christian liturgy, learning and transforming desire. He argues that as Christians practise their faith (in whatever liturgical form that may take), they participate in the repeated demonstration of the coming together of learning and love. In what he refers to as '*le poème de la liturgie*' (the poem of the liturgy),[46] Leclercq describes how, rather than providing learning obstacles to be overcome (as Hull would have it), the structure, words and music of various elements of liturgical practice function as vehicles of mystical, pedagogical participation. He summarizes:

> In the liturgy, grammar was elevated to the rank of eschatological fact. It participated in the eternal praise that the monks, in unison with the angels, began offering to God in the abbey choir and which will be perpetuated in Heaven. In the liturgy, love of learning and desire of God find perfect reconciliation.[47]

Leclercq's basic claim is that, as opposed to distracting from the real learning that Hull identifies as active questioning and clarified understanding, liturgy (which Leclercq defines as 'all activities involved in prayer'[48]) is a vehicle for simultaneous growth in love of God and love of learning – as one develops, it feeds the other and vice versa. In this way, as discussed in relation to divine learning, Christian adults can access divinely sustained passion and momentum in learning. One of the key elements of our earlier discussion was that, unlike human learning, divine learning is not motivated by lack or need but resourced by its own perfectly dynamic character and joy-fuelled momentum. Leclercq understands that the poem of the liturgy functions as a gateway for (at least partial) human participation in divinely sustained learning, allowing love of God to fuel ongoing learning progress. In simple terms, the more a person learns, the more they love God and therefore want to learn and love yet more. Returning to Smith's language, in liturgical learning (in whatever form) 'the conversion of the imagination' occurs on an unconscious level[49] (again, more on this in Chapter 7). As Christian adults worship together, they are not just learning about reality but experiencing a reordering of reality that inspires the love of different things (including learning itself!), even if they may not necessarily be able to identify or articulate what is happening.

At the heart of this understanding of CAL is not the comprehension of new information but the (sometimes unconscious) cultivation of the desire for learning – a process of practising finding life in the interaction between reason and revelation; between that which can be seen and that which, as yet, remains hidden and can only be joyfully anticipated, not understood. The principal success criterion for this kind of learning is simple: more and better learning! Christian liturgical practices help us to understand that learning is not a simple, one-way trajectory away from 'sleeping consciousness … awakened to life',[50] but rather a more fluid and ever-deepening combination of conscious and unconscious love and learning; a dynamic and fluctuating interaction between the known and the unknown;

the knowable and that which best transforms without our knowing or ability to explain.

However, this is not to suggest that learner awareness or agency is unhelpful or unwanted. By 1991 Hull was clearly wrestling with the need for both conscious and unconscious learning. In a passage about dream interpretation (demonstrating the growing influences of Karl Marx and Sigmund Freud at this stage of his career), he claims:

> No consciousness is ever entirely false and no dream is ever entirely unconscious, otherwise it would not be experienced as a dream. In our dreaming state, we Christians toss and turn. I believe in ... a pedagogy based on these factors.[51]

This framing of CAL as a tossing and turning between conscious awareness and unconscious ignorance (and perhaps even unconscious awareness!) demonstrates that Hull is not arguing for a choice between them. This is a key element of disruptive inclusion – learning does not only occur in either a state of cognizance or incognizance but in their varied and repeated connection and crossover. CAL takes place in the repeated back-and-forth between active learner awareness and what lies beyond it. As Jesuit priest and theologian Karl Rahner states, mystery is 'not a regrettable imperfection in theology, but rather that which is most proper to it of its very nature ... Theology, then, is to be understood as the "science" of mystery.'[52] The learning function of the practices of the Christian Church are therefore at their best when they not only clarify issues of faith but also help to facilitate an experience of the mystery of God. On the other hand, neither should they only encourage passive learning that avoids personal responsibility. What we are aiming for is, again, somewhere in-between.

Selah 5: Going deeper? Integrating the conscious and the unconscious

We cannot leave this discussion of the roles of conscious and unconscious CAL without mentioning the significant influence of James Fowler's seminal (but much disputed) work, *Stages of Faith*. Fowler presents a framework for human development with six distinct stages: (1) intuitive-projective, (2) mythic-literal, (3) synthetic-conventional, (4) individuative-reflective, (5) conjunctive (or in some places, paradoxical-consolidative) and (6) universalizing.[53] He also goes further than many others in associating these stages with specific ages. For example, he claims that the conjunctive stage (Stage 5) is 'unusual before mid-life'.[54]

For the purposes of our discussion, and particularly relating to the idea of learning as navigating in-between spaces, Fowler explains the transition between Stages 4 and 5 as

> going beyond the explicit ideological system and clear bound-aries of identity that Stage 4 worked so hard to construct and to adhere to. Whereas Stage 4 could afford to equate self pretty much with its own conscious awareness of self ... Stage 5 recognizes the task of integrating or reconciling conscious and unconscious.[55]

In summary, Stage 4 is defined by clarity and separation and Stage 5 is about allowing the known and the unknown to sit together. Similarly to some of the previous patterns we have considered, in Fowler's Stage 5, learning is understood to happen via the combination of what was deliberately kept separate in earlier stages.

As a way of seeing, of knowing, of committing, Stage 5 moves beyond the dichotomizing logic of Stage 4's 'either/or.' It sees both (or the many) sides of an issue simultaneously. Conjunc-tive faith suspects that things are organically related to each other; it attends to the pattern of interrelatedness in things, trying to avoid force-fitting to its own prior mind set.[56]

For Fowler, mature CAL is not concerned with replacing the mysterious with the rational (or vice versa), but involves the interchange of multiple ways of interpreting reality.[57] He identifies how it calls learners to be 'Alive to paradox and the truth in apparent contradictions' and 'strives to unify opposites in mind and experience.' Ultimately, it requires 'boundaries of self and outlook' that are 'porous and permeable'.[58]

So far, this has a lot in common with disruptive inclusion: the blurring of boundaries, the close interchange between ideas and ways of understanding that do not normally sit together. However, one of the most significant differences is the fact that the ultimate goal in Fowler's framework is Stage 6, which he refers to as universalizing faith.[59] The interesting thing about this is that both Fowler and others have doubted whether 'Stage 6 really describes or requires any basic structural advance beyond Stage 5',[60] or whether it is better understood as a mode where learners are able to enact Stage 5 in a sustained way. For example, religious educationalist Gabriel Moran suggests that 'at Stage 6 one becomes an "activist incarnation" of the values of Stage 5'.[61]

This means that the ultimate goal in Fowler's Stages of Faith is a point at which Christian adults can engage in formational processes so effortlessly that they no longer have to consciously think about them in order to remain there. This aligns with the four-stage description of Hull's own learning journey that we considered earlier. Having navigated the fading of the light, the fading of the memory of light and growth in awareness of darkness, the final phase Hull identifies is a fading awareness of the darkness.[62] Thus Fowler's Stage 6, in which learners exist peaceably with the 'suffering and loss, responsibility and failure, and the grief that is an inevitable part of having made irrevocable commitments of life and energy',[63] lines up with Hull's description of the phase in which his awareness of the darkness had faded. However, there is one pivotal difference. In disruptive-inclusive terms, the problem with landing and staying in Stage 6 (or remaining in a faded awareness of darkness) is that learners become too comfortable and familiar to access optimum distance. New levels and awareness of darkness and disruption are required to access deeper (in Moran's terms) cycles of learning.[64] Therefore, I join Moran in asking whether entering and remaining in something similar to Fowler's Stage 6 is a helpful goal for CAL.

In contrast to Fowler's linear progression through six stages, Moran suggests that the central mechanism of CAL is a repeated loop pattern of *out, over, back* and *down*, in which what he refers to as the *ordinary* and *non-ordinary* (his way of expressing the knowable/unknowable or the rational/mysterious) find points of crossover and connection. The learner begins in an ordinary space with sufficient resources to avoid disruption. Then some form of disruption occurs that forces the learner *out* into the non-ordinary (something that the learner cannot understand or include in their worldview according to their existing framework). As they look for and find ways to incorporate the 'outside' into their ordinary view, they are able to connect the two on increasingly deeper levels. In Moran's words:

> The movement is not simply up and down but rather, out, over, back, down. The movement returns to where one began but at a deeper level. A person doesn't pass once in a lifetime to a *non-ordinary* world; instead the person moves constantly toward some center that always eludes a clear location.[65]

Interestingly, whereas many approaches to learning focus on helping learners transcend difficulties or overcome issues and problems, Hull understood progress as a downwards movement (or underscending). This involved daring to be fully present (no matter how deep learners find themselves) and practising connecting with self, God and others there. For Hull, if CAL was about getting somewhere, it was a path of descent towards 'the one human world which lies beneath all the worlds and ties them all together.'[66] By the final season of his life he understood that including disruption was not a means of rising above the issues he faced but allowed him access to deeper awareness and connection with self, others, the world and God.

Putting these frameworks in conversation, Moran's *out, over, back* and *down* helps to explain why simply remaining in Fowler's Stage 6 may not be a realistic or helpful goal for Christian adult learners. Once learners have moved through the initial, potentially paralysing disruption and found a way to embrace the tension of the interrelatedness of unexpected things (Moran's connection between *ordinary* and *non-ordinary*), they naturally (or may with encouragement) pass back into the critical reflection of Stage 4. As we will explore in more detail in the next chapter, retracing steps is not a worthless learning task because 'pilgrimage ... is a life lesson in revision'[67] and therefore more effectively moving between Stages 4 and 5 might, in fact, be a more realistic and effective goal. In this way, mature Christian adult learners are not those who have reached the end of the line and firmly settled into Stage 6 but those who engage in 'continual cycles of deconstruction and disintegration', making them 'resilient enough to repeat the cycle as many times as necessary.'[68]

Questions/activities

- What are your experiences of CAL in community? Do you resonate with the opportunities and challenges discussed in this chapter?
- Speak to those in your learning community/communities. How do they understand CAL happening in corporate and community spaces? Does this fit or conflict with disruptive inclusion?
- What form does the practice of CAL take in your community? What role do you think conscious awareness plays in individual and community learning?
- What is your initial response to connecting learning and love/desire? Do these two come together naturally for you? What do you want most in/out of life? Does your relationship

to learning (whether good or bad) have anything to do with this?

• Think about some of the ways you have changed the most (ask close friends/family, if you need help). Can you identify what brought about the change in the first place, and then what sustained the transformation in the longer term? Were you aware of the change while it was happening? When? How?

Notes

1 Thomas Groome, *Christian Religious Education: Sharing our story and vision* (San Francisco, CA: Harper & Row, 1981), p. 115.

2 I am greatly indebted to Professor Julian Stern for introducing me to this.

3 Hull does not refer directly to Personalism in *What Prevents*, but he makes frequent references to leading Personalist thinker Teilhard de Chardin: John M. Hull, *What Prevents Christian Adults from Learning?* (London: SCM Press, 1985), pp. 20, 103, 135 and 218.

4 *Personalismus* first appeared in Friedrich Schleiermacher's *Über die Religion: Reden an die Gebildeten unter ihren Verächtern* in 1799.

5 Irwin Leopando, *A Pedagogy of Faith: The theological vision of Paulo Freire* (London: Bloomsbury Academic, 2017), pp. 105–6.

6 James Carroll, *Christ Actually: The son of God for the secular age* (New York, NY: Viking, 2014), p. 273.

7 Leopando, *A Pedagogy of Faith*, p. 106.

8 Leopando, *A Pedagogy of Faith*, p. 109.

9 Hull, *What Prevents*, p. 17.

10 Hull, *What Prevents*, pp. 17–18.

11 Emmanuel Mounier, *A Personalist Manifesto* (London: Longmans, Green & Co., 1938), p. 114.

12 Hull, *What Prevents*, pp. 218–19.

13 Hull acknowledges Freire's influence on his thinking in John M. Hull, 'What is Theology of Education?', *Scottish Journal of Theology* 30:01 (1977), p. 23.

14 Paulo Freire, *Pedagogy of the Oppressed* (New York, NY: Continuum, 1990), p. 72. The language of becoming also resonates with the work of John Dewey who claims: 'The "self" is always a self in the making. It is rooted in a temporally evolving process shaped by stabilized habits, but it is also changing as new habits are formed in response to changes in one's environment.' Mark Johnson, 'Dewey's

radical conception of moral cognition' in C. Fesmire (ed.), *The Oxford Handbook of Dewey* (New York, NY: Oxford University Press, 2020), p. 189. In comparison to Freire, however, Dewey does not draw as clear a link between the developing self and others.

15 Peter Roberts, *Education, Literacy, and Humanization: Exploring the work of Paulo Freire* (Westport, CN: Bergin & Garvey, 2000), p. 151.

16 Freire, *Pedagogy of the Oppressed*, pp. 58–9.

17 Maria Harris, 'Isms and Religious Education' in G. Durka and J. Smith (eds), *Emerging Issues in Religious Education* (New York, NY: Paulist Press, 1976), pp. 46–7.

18 Harris, 'Isms and Religious Education', p. 42 considers the specific challenges raised by virtual or online connectivity.

19 Leon McKenzie, 'The purpose and scope of Adult Religious Education' in N. Foltz (ed.), *Handbook of Adult Religious Education* (Birmingham, AL: Religious Education Press, 1986), p. 15.

20 Walter Bauer, Frederick William Danker, W. F. Arndt and F. W. Gingrich, *A Greek–English Lexicon of the New Testament and Other Early Christian Literature*, 3rd edn (Chicago, IL: University of Chicago Press, 2000).

21 Maria Harris, *Fashion Me a People: Curriculum in the Church*, 1st edn (Louisville, KY: Westminster/John Knox Press, 1989), pp. 63–4.

22 Harris, *Fashion Me a People*, p. 77.

23 Harris, *Fashion Me a People*, p. 77.

24 Harris, *Fashion Me a People*, p. 77. Harris envisages future-oriented connectivity achieved by creating space for subsequent generations to participate in community life and benefit from its heritage. Harris probably had Westerhoff's seminal work on this topic in mind: John H. Westerhoff III and Gwen Kennedy Neville, *Generation to Generation: Conversations on Religious Education and Culture* (Philadelphia, PA: United Church Press, 1974); and John H. Westerhoff III, *Will Our Children have Faith?* (New York, NY: Seabury Press, 1976).

25 Harris, 'Isms and Religious Education', p. 42.

26 Daniel Fleming and Terence Lovat, 'Learning as leaving home: fear, empathy, and hospitality in the theology and religion classroom', *Teaching Theology & Religion* 18:3 (2015), pp. 207–23, p. 211.

27 Harris, 'Isms and Religious Education', p. 42.

28 Harris, *Fashion Me a People*, pp. 79–80.

29 Harris, *Fashion Me a People*, p. 80.

30 Veli-Matti Kärkkäinen, 'Ecclesiology and the Church in Christian tradition and Western theology' in G. Green, S. T. Pardue and K. K. Yeo (eds), *The Church from Every Tribe and Tongue: Ecclesiology in the Majority World*, pp. 15–34, pp. 15–16.

31 Hull, *What Prevents*, p. 16.

32 John M. Hull, *On Sight and Insight: A journey into the world of blindness* (Oxford: Oneworld, 2001), p. 232.

33 John M. Hull, *Notes on Blindness: A journey through the dark* (London: Profile Books, 2017), p. 199.

34 Hull, *What Prevents*, pp. 33–4.

35 John M. Hull, *What Stops Christian Adults from Learning* (Salford: Centre for the Study of Religion and Education in the Inner City. The Sacred Trinity Centre, 1982), p. 2.

36 Hull, *What Prevents*, p. 177. Hull borrows this metaphorical language from Heraclitus, famous for his belief that although humans can only see one perspective at a time, this does not necessitate denial of all others. For example, one can accept that the sea is the perfect living environment for fish and simultaneously a hostile living environment for humans.

37 Hull, *What Prevents*, p. 78. Interestingly, Erik Erikson (whose work Hull greatly admired) calls God the '"Ultimate Other", in relationship to one's vital inner core'. John Snarey and David Bell, 'Erikson, Erik H.' in Elizabeth M. Dowling and W. George Scarlett (eds), *Encyclopedia of Religious and Spiritual Development* (Thousand Oaks, CA: SAGE, 2006), p. 148.

38 Hull, *What Prevents*, p. 78.

39 Hull, *What Prevents*, p. 55.

40 John M. Hull, 'Adult religious faith: some problems of definition, of research and of education', *Modern Believing* 40:4 (1999), pp. 39–48, p. 45.

41 John M. Hull, 'Teaching as a trans-world activity', *Support for Learning* 19:3 (2004), pp. 103–6, p. 103.

42 James K. A. Smith, *Desiring the Kingdom: Worship, worldview, and cultural formation* (Grand Rapids, MI: Baker Academic, 2009), p. 62.

43 Smith, *Desiring the Kingdom*, p. 73.

44 James K. A. Smith, 'Higher Education: What's love got to do with it? Longings, desires and human flourishing', *Christian Heritage College*, 18 July 2016, available from https://youtu.be/TAg6sn4XJMc (accessed 31.07.23).

45 Smith, 'Higher Education'.

46 Jean Leclercq, *The Love of Learning and the Desire for God: A study of monastic culture* (London: SPCK, 1978), pp. 287–308.

47 Leclercq, *The Love of Learning*, p. 308.

48 Leclercq, *The Love of Learning*, p. 287.

49 Smith, *Desiring the Kingdom*, p. 265. He takes the phrase from Richard Hays, *The Conversion of the Imagination: Paul as interpreter of Israel's Scripture* (Grand Rapids, MI: Wm. B. Eerdmans, 2005), and his arguments for Paul's reimagining of Isaiah in 1 Corinthians 14.

50 Hull, *What Prevents*, p. viii. See also John M. Hull, 'The ambiguity of spiritual values' in J. M. Halstead and M. J. Taylor (eds), *Values in Education and Education in Values* (London: Falmer Press, 1996); and John M. Hull, 'Spiritual development: interpretations and applications', *British Journal of Religious Education* 24:3 (2002), pp. 171–82.

51 Hull, *What Prevents*, p. viii.

52 Karl Rahner, *Theological Investigations* vol. xi (Baltimore, MD: Helicon Press, 1974), pp. 101–2.

53 James W. Fowler, *Stages of Faith: The psychology of human development and the quest for meaning*, 1st edn (San Francisco, CA: Harper & Row, 1981), pp. 122–99.

54 Fowler, *Stages of Faith*, p. 198.

55 Fowler, *Stages of Faith*, p. 186.

56 Fowler, *Stages of Faith*, p. 185.

57 Gabriel Moran, *Religious Education Development: Images for the future* (Minneapolis, MI: Winston Press, 1983), p. 57.

58 Fowler, *Stages of Faith*, p. 198.

59 Moran, *Religious Education Development*, p. 118.

60 Moran, *Religious Education Development*, p. 118, quoting James W. Fowler and Sam Keen, *Life Maps: Conversations on the journey of faith* (Waco, TX: Word Books, 1978), p. 90.

61 Moran, *Religious Education Development*, p. 119.

62 Peter Middleton and James Spinney, 'Notes on blindness', *The New York Times* (16 January 2014), available at: https://www.nytimes.com/interactive/2014/01/16/opinion/16OpDoc-NotesOnBlindness.html (accessed 31.07.2023).

63 Fowler and Keen, *Life Maps*, p. 81. Equally important in resisting a mentality of martyrdom is Moran's claim that 'the individual's response to suffering, not the suffering itself, is the reason for development'. Moran, *Religious Education Development*, p. 118.

64 Moran and Fowler are among a larger group who present cyclical approaches to human learning and development. For example, J. E. Marcia represents Erikson's identity development cycles in a cone shape, including a sense in which learners 'might recycle through the statuses' as an integral part of progression but with the aim of resolving each stage, rather than necessarily benefitting from the various tensions of (and between) each. James E. Marcia, 'Identity and psychosocial development in adulthood', *Identity* 2:1 (2002), pp. 7–28, pp. 15–17.

65 Gabriel Moran, *Education Toward Adulthood* (New York, NY: Paulist Press, 1979), pp. 59–60.

66 John M. Hull, 'Blindness and memory: being reborn into a different world', *Memory Marathon: The Space Arts* (12–14 October 2012), available here: https://www.serpentinegalleries.org/whats-on/memory-marathon/ (accessed 31.07.2023).

67 David I. Smith and Susan M. Felch, *Teaching and Christian Imagination* (Grand Rapids, MI: Wm. B. Eerdmans, 2016), p. 56.

68 Daniel Fleming and Peter Mudge, 'Leaving home: A pedagogy for theological education' in L. Ball and J. Harrison (eds), *Learning and Teaching Theology: Some ways ahead* (Eugene, OR: Wipf & Stock, 2015), pp. 71–80, pp. 78–9.

5

The Christian Distinctives of Disruptive Inclusion: New Questions and New Answers to Old Questions

The last chapter began to unpack the nature of the relationship between disruptive inclusion and the Christian faith, based in the Bible, the nature and character of God and the identity and practice of Christian learning communities. Taken together, they lay solid foundations for a Christian basis for including disruption in learning. However, I recognize that anyone can (although few do!) present a diverse collection of ancient documents as a basis for modelling and encouraging conversational learning, or adopt Jesus' example of simultaneous deconstruction and reconstruction of worldviews. Community and ritual practice are key factors in learning in almost all cultures and religions. Despite the fact that each of the above strands of argument contains elements that are unique to Christianity, overall, few of the themes introduced in Chapters 3 and 4 are exclusively accessible to those who profess Christian faith. Importantly, this is not an accident. Hull was deeply convicted that understanding the Christianness of CAL in terms of *how* and not *what* means that his version of CAL could be employed effectively by teachers and learners of all faiths and none. Specifically, he repeatedly makes the case for an approach he called *critical openness*, which he summarized as 'listening, respecting, being independent, being in relation, and it conveys a meaning which is closer to Christian faith [than self-enclosed independence]',[1] or as a process of passing on 'not the painting but the paint box'.[2]

Critical openness is not without its problems and many debate whether it is possible, and if so, how.[3] But Hull was convinced that there is a way to take seriously learners' personal responsibility in making meaning without compromising Christian commitments to biblical authority and other non-negotiable convictions.[4] Equally, I am deeply convicted that there is something inherently Christian about a disruptive-inclusive approach to learning that does not exclude those outside Christianity, but whose particular characteristics come into their own, or can be expressed to the fullest, when understood in light of, and worked out in line with, Christian beliefs, practices and experience. Given my claims in the previous chapter about the importance of both the practical and the theoretical, taking a holistic approach and factoring in love, desire, joy, delight and mystery in learning, it would be hypocritical to suggest that any form of theoretical argument can fully demonstrate this. Therefore, this chapter continues to demonstrate how disruptive inclusion is informed and modelled by Christian faith and practice but from a much more personal and experiential angle. In short, I offer an insight into aspects of my own disruptive-inclusive learning journey.

In the Introduction, I identified one of my defining personal characteristics as a pursuit of better questions. This is not to say that the quality of answers is unimportant to me, but more that even the best answers to poor questions are unlikely to be as good as mediocre answers to great questions. Therefore the focus of this chapter is how the Christianness of disruptive inclusion comes into view most clearly, not necessarily by offering new answers to existing theoretical questions, but by allowing the experience of disruptive inclusion to suggest better, more connected questions than are generally currently asked or considered important. Even more specifically, this chapter explores how my own disruptive-inclusive learning journey inspires different questions about the underlying goals and motivation of CAL: where are learners going and what is the point of trying to get there?

Selah 6: Learning to ride the waves

In the first few years of the work that led to this book, I was part of a group of researchers who would come together periodically to encourage, challenge and update each other on progress. When the Covid-19 pandemic hit the UK in 2020, this (like almost everything else) was no longer possible. By 2022, when in-person meetings were allowed again, my thesis was complete. At the first research gathering after the restrictions were lifted, I was asked to share a brief reflection on the last few years. I share it here as a helpful introduction to the rest of the chapter.

We now have some new words that we didn't have the last time we were in the same room together, and some old words that now mean new things. In 2019 I thought furlough was something to do with farming, Zoom was definitely an ice lolly from the 1980s and lockdowns only happened on game shows. But I think, in years to come, my most potent memories of the pandemic will be best described in terms of waves.

As a girl who grew up in a port city, I have always loved waves. Viciously potent but simultaneously soothing and reassuringly regular. My natural reaction to the sea, whether Bondi beach or Blackpool beach, has always been awe. But again, this most recent season has given me a new perspective on waves and my very brief reflection here on the last 18 months of completing my research focuses on a few different examples.

First, the same tide never comes in twice. From far away it must look to the man in the moon as if the same water is hitting the same beach over and over again, but this is not what is happening. The same water and same beach never meet more than once: each wave moves stuff, repeatedly changing the coastline. One of the reasons why the pandemic was such a discombobulating process for us all was that no two waves of Covid were experienced the same. After lockdown one we thought we'd become experts, but the Zoom quiz didn't feel the same in early 2021 as it had in Spring 2020. The banana bread wasn't quite so satisfying and by the time it finally arrived, the experience of 'freedom day' wasn't quite as powerful as its promise. Things are constantly shifting.

Second, the same wave can hit very differently on different parts of the beach. I remember the powerful cartoon from early in the pandemic: we're all in the same boat. However, it was quickly pointed out that we're not actually all in the same boat, but in different boats on the same sea. Crisis magnifies inequalities and many of the ways that certain groups in our society are disadvantaged have been brought into greater focus by the pandemic. I am aware, more than ever, of the need to avoid assuming that others experience the same events exactly as I do. The wave that causes so much joy for the paddling toddler can also wipe out life and livelihoods further up the coast!

Finally, as I experienced when trying to learn to surf in Australia just before the pandemic, sometimes the only way to 'ride' a wave is to swim into it headfirst. You must respect its superior strength, let it give your nasal passages a salt-water clean out and make peace with taking a hit. Denying or resisting the incoming wave only uses up energy that could be better employed, perhaps even in enjoying the process.

For those of you who know something of my research on disruptive learning, all of the above may be unsurprising to you. In short, my own learning journey these last four years is embedded in the content of my work. The waves of the last season have taught me that being a good learner is not about finding 'solid ground' from which to share wisdom with others still searching for it, but about growing in skill and confidence at working within a situation that is constantly changing and perpetually dynamic. I have learned that those of my siblings who enjoy less privilege than I do, for whatever reasons, have been hit by a few more waves than I have and as a result are models I should take very seriously when I'm trying to understand what good learning practice looks like. Finally, I have been pondering, as is so often the case in the Christian scriptures, whether hidden in all the tragedy and pain and suffering and discontent of the last few years is an opportunity, not to attempt to rush back as soon as possible to a place where I feel as if I am in control, but to make peace with the fact that most control is an illusion and sometimes I would be better served in using my energy to just enjoy the ride.

Where are we going? The Christian direction and destination of learning

So far in this book the imagery of navigating the natural world, and physical movement more generally, has taken numerous forms. From Hull crossing his doorstep to the sheep of John 10 moving in and out of the sheepfold, from weary pilgrims entering the narthex of a French church to the learning journey from Eden to the New Jerusalem. However, I am by no means the first to imagine progress in the Christian life and learning as a journey. The psalms describe God's people as those 'in whose heart are the highways to Zion' (Ps. 84.5), and Jesus' earliest followers were known as those who 'belonged to the Way' (Acts 9.2). Sixth-century pope Gregory the Great described a Christian as 'a wayfarer en route between the city of this world and the celestial city',[5] and John Bunyan's central character (Christian) navigates from the City of Destruction to the Celestial City in his 1678 novel, *The Pilgrim's Progress*. From Søren Kierkegaard's *Stages on Life's Way* (1845)[6] to David Smith and Susan Felch's explanation of learning as 'walking the path' in 2016,[7] the association between learning and journeying has found fresh expression through the centuries. Smith and Felch also draw attention to the many unconscious ways travelling/journey vocabulary is used in everyday learning speech. For example: '"Curriculum" is a Latin reference to either the act of running or a racetrack. More colloquially, we refer to a "course" of study, "covering a lot of ground", and to learners "falling behind".'[8] This connection is so strong that, in her research into the use of metaphor in education, Lynne Cameron found that, 'About 14 percent of ... the classroom set of linguistic metaphors could be seen as relating to the system of journey metaphors.'[9]

As a result, the idea that learning is about getting somewhere or making progress towards a particular destination is deeply (and perhaps even unconsciously) embedded. Learning is regularly explained using terminology associated with physical travelling. Across cultures and educational systems there is a deep assumption that successful learning takes the form of (at least somewhat) direct, efficient and straightforward progress towards a predetermined destination. As my research has progressed, and particularly as I have engaged with Hull's work, I have become increasingly convinced that this is one way in which CAL forges its own path. As before, many have raised similar points, including the suggestion that CAL has 'God as its destination'[10] (although I would hope to find God present at every stage of learning). Equally, some have tried to de-emphasize the overall importance of a final place of arrival by claiming that 'It is the journey, not the destination that matters.'[11] However, by pitting one against the other the distinctions between the two are reinforced and, more importantly, there is nothing uniquely Christian about it. Therefore, our first question must be whether disruptive-inclusive CAL influences the potential destination(s) of CAL. Or is part of its paradigm shifting quality to reject the image of learning destination(s) entirely and suggest measuring successful CAL according to a different standard?

Pilgrimage: from where to who and a new kind of home

Almost all of my responses to the above questions are based on the following quote which, from among all Hull's work, has had the deepest and most enduring influence on both my views and my experiences of CAL:

This is why in learning Christ, one does not simply take on board an orthodoxy of received belief. One becomes a pilgrim on a way. He is the true and living way, and he is always before us, disrupting our present equilibrium, and calling us through the pain and transition into the maturity which is our Christian calling.[12]

Pilgrims are a specific type of traveller. They are not going in a particular direction for work or leisure reasons and tagging on another adventure on the side; they set off purposefully in search of renewed understanding, meaning or connection. Although they may not know exactly how, they journey with the goal of being changed. The enduring challenge of Hull's quote is that it highlights how Christ's influence on CAL does not just add another layer or perspective to a pre-existing product but completely redefines the task. Christian pilgrim learners do not just accept or reject a set of static truths but commit to a process of ongoing discovery about self, others, God and all of reality that invariably takes place on bumpy and unpredictable terrain!

Pilgrims, therefore, do not measure learning in terms of examinations passed or qualifications gained; the success of their journey is quantified on different terms. Learning in, with and from Christ does not just shift the goalposts but completely changes the aim of the game. A vision of CAL whose primary understanding of progress is a single, straightforward line is replaced with a framework in which a learner's 'eventual destination' is less about the where and more about the state of their arrival, that is, 'as a different person from the one who set out'.[13] Where learners find themselves at any given moment is not unimportant, but is far less important than who learners find themselves becoming. As theologian and episcopal priest Mary Foulke reminds us (referring to a set of essays called *The Journey is Home*): 'Journeying does not offer stability or essential truths ... it is who we are and who we are with.'[14]

As yet, I have not completed an actual recognized pilgrim walk but I have come to understand many areas of my life as a learning pilgrimage of sorts: setting off in a particular direction with the aim of growing on the way, but not really knowing what I was signing myself up for. Perhaps the most dramatic season of my learning pilgrimage so far was giving up my job in my late 20s and moving 5,000 miles to pursue further theological training. Pilgrim journeys often feature a series of waypoints that linger in the traveller's spirit; moments on the road that continue to influence and shape beyond their immediate significance. On pilgrim walks, such moments are usually marked in some physical way, either by the leaving of a stone on an altar or a personal note in a church or at a monument.[15] For me, one of the moments that has most shaped my onward journey was the first time I visited the educational institution where I would later study. Jetlagged, culturally baffled and deeply questioning whether I had gone completely mad, I sat in an auditorium, in a green theatre-style chair in the second to back row, for a prospective student information session. The then president of the institution welcomed us by outlining the challenges and opportunities of leading a theologically diverse institution. He explained (to the best of my recollection, something along the lines of), 'Conservative Christians criticize us for being too liberal and liberal Christians criticize us for being too conservative. This makes me think that we must be doing something right.' At exactly that moment, I experienced a feeling I have only known that acutely on a few occasions in my life. I felt at home. The jetlag may have contributed, but I cried quietly in my seat and hoped that nobody would notice. It seems like a ridiculous claim to make, to have felt at home, because I had rarely been geographically, culturally, relationally, or in any other way further from home conditions; but at that moment I somehow knew that I had found a place I could grow into. I was not convinced that the road ahead would be straightforward (this was confirmed when the fees were explained!), but from that moment on my thoughts changed from wondering whether it was the way forward to wondering exactly how it would work out. The feelings were fleeting, but even just a tiny glimpse of home was enough to change everything.

148

However, before learners can even imagine finding a new sense of home, pilgrimage requires that they leave comfort and familiarity and enter unknown environments. Religion and education scholars Daniel Fleming and Terence Lovat provide a good example of the deep connections between leaving home and CAL. They introduce the potential benefits of unfamiliar territory with the following quote from philosopher Albert Camus:

> What gives value to travel is fear. It is the fact that, at a certain moment, when we are so far from our own country ... we are seized by a vague fear, and the instinctive desire to go back to the protection of old habits. This is the most obvious benefit of travel. At that moment we are feverish but also porous, so that the slightest touch makes us quiver to the depths of our being.[16]

In summary, Camus highlights how 'being asked to leave home is no small matter ... and the perception of threat ... is always lurking nearby.'[17] Venturing beyond the boundaries of current knowledge and experience (what many of us would refer to as 'moving out of our comfort zone') is unavoidably fraught with jeopardy. However, after establishing that risk is inevitable, Fleming and Lovat focus on the learning opportunities of journeying in deeply unfamiliar territory. In particular, they focus on Camus's use of the terms 'feverish' and 'porous' to describe the impact of the unknown territory on the traveller. They argue that the combination of a particular nervous energy and openness creates opportunities 'that might stretch consciousness beyond itself'.[18] In other words, leaving home makes different ways of seeing and thinking possible. This resonates strongly with earlier discussions of the role of awe and wonder in the Bible and their ability to bring together an 'unsettling element of bewilderment' and 'an insatiable curiosity to know'.[19] For the pilgrim who leaves the comfort of home (whether literally or metaphorically) and is faced with fear and threat, what they are most in need of is empathy and hospitality.[20]

Although at first glance empathy (a psychological posture) and hospitality (a practical action of welcoming) may be considered to belong to very different categories, they share a common sense of give and take. Both require at least temporarily stepping into someone else's space or shoes (to push the travelling imagery further still). On the one hand, empathy involves temporary self-suspension that cannot be achieved by simply restating existing views. For example, Fleming and Lovat describe empathy as 'an intellectual and affective capacity to "think with/as" an other'.[21] On the other hand, hospitality is the practical outworking of empathy that requires 'welcoming the other *and* being a guest in their presence':[22] it must be both offered and received to be effective. Although somewhat commercialized now, well-known pilgrim routes are lined with family-run hostels and guesthouses offering food and accommodation; traditionally they have understood their role not simply as helping weary passing travellers, but participating in the journeys of those who stay. Hospitality is neither the provision of refuge or sanctuary to an otherwise destitute refugee, nor the process of an insider demonstrating to an outsider how things work differently in an unfamiliar place. Rather, it is an opportunity for both parties to participate in, and contribute to, a 'communal imagination'; an activity that may be perceived as deeply solitary becomes shared and relational.[23] The pilgrim leaves something of their journey wherever they stay, and something of each place where pilgrims stay accompanies them on their onward journey.

Thus communal imagination creates shared access to sufficient disruption and inclusion to create the ideal conditions for CAL.[24] As practical theologian Susanne Johnson explains, 'Hospitality … is a willingness not only to receive the stranger, but also to be changed and affected by the presence of the other.'[25] In this way, true empathy and hospitality require the pooling of resources and experiences: the reciprocal sharing of pain, confusion, excitement, energy, drive as well as knowledge and skills will allow for disruptive-inclusive learning to occur. Educationalist Parker Palmer summarizes:

Hospitality is not an end in itself. It is offered for the sake of what it can allow, permit, encourage and yield. A learning space needs to be hospitable not to make learning painless but to make the painful things possible.[26]

Hospitality makes it possible for home to be not a place or even a feeling but a posture; a way of being fully present in all circumstances and settings.

However, as is almost always true, there are points beyond which metaphorical language can mislead. In the case of home, if the claim is that empathy and hospitality make it possible for home conditions to be recreated regardless of a learner's physical location, we must also ask whether referring to home (in the traditional sense of a permanent location) is worth retaining at all. Specifically, if learner pilgrims find themselves back at the home location where their journey began, the intervening transformations that have occurred on the road mean that it is impossible for the pilgrims to 'go back home' because they discover 'that neither [s]he nor his[/her] home are the same as when [s]he left'.[27] It is also true that given 'the rapidly shifting neighbourhood in which ... students' religious "homes" are built' (again, both literally and metaphorically speaking), reconnecting with what learners once knew as home may be as disorienting an experience as initially leaving.[28] Just as Hull claims in *What Prevents*, things are 'never the same again once one has learned how to go in and out'.[29] Home, as an unchanged, static setting waiting for the proverbial prodigal's return, is revealed as an illusion.

Westerhoff claims that in 'wander[ing] the world as a pilgrim', a learner

has no worldly home and yet is at home in the world, the one whose hope does not reside in her/his own efforts and yet believes her/his efforts can serve her/his God, who acts in the world through women/men. The result of such freedom is the ability to venture in the world as a stranger and alien with a vision of a new world.[30]

In this description of a perpetually homeless yet simultaneously always-at-home pilgrim, the metaphor of home is not completely undermined as a way of describing learner experience, but it is redefined. The conventional sense of a static home that provides a motivating and encouraging destination for learning is replaced with a dynamic, richer and more fluid experience of home that is available in both familiar and unfamiliar settings, in the company of strangers and family alike. Fleming and Mudge describe this reimagining of home as a process in which

> [t]he 'four walls of their house' begin to break down as, at the same time, new worlds begin to open up ... a new house is being rebuilt from the ashes of the old – one more appropriate and sufficiently flexible for the next stage of the journey.[31]

Kwok Pui Lan explains it in these terms:

> Home is not a fixed and stable location but a traveling adventure, which entails seeking refuge in strange lands ... Such a destabilized and contingent construction of home dislodges it from its familiar domestic territory and questions the conditions through which the cozy connotation of home have been made possible and sustained.[32]

Hull's reflections on his early years of blindness reveal how the darkness that once threatened to entirely overwhelm him was not replaced by a more comforting location but actually transformed into the 'safer place' towards which he gravitated for orientation.[33] Similarly, the ongoing transformations of disruptive-inclusive CAL mean that, increasingly, learners no longer yearn to either escape from, or return to, what was. Inversely, their 'hope of returning'[34] morphs into a desire of 'finding one's relationship to home transformed, of finding one's self renewed by the journey, of seeing the familiar with a fresh perspective'.[35] As Smith and Felch summarize:

> To be a pilgrim is not just to move forward in a straight line, but also to enter into a circular motion of journeying forth and returning home, perhaps multiple times ... in a culture deeply permeated with ideals of linear progress ... it is well to remember the contrasting circular rhythm of pilgrim journeying.[36]

Therefore, if pilgrimage is to be a helpful analogy it requires not only leaving home but also leaving behind the idea of home as permanent and static and embracing a new and evolving experience of home conditions, continually rediscovered at every stage of the journey.[37]

Back to me in my green chair in the second to back row of the auditorium. My prospective student status turned into actual student status and my 'at home' feelings quickly melted into homesickness (not only for a particular place, but people and a good cup of tea!). However, in turn, embracing this disruption allowed me to perceive and receive the kindness of strangers in deeper and more moving ways and then to create spaces where others could experience their own version of home when they needed it. At this stage of my learning pilgrimage, I experienced first hand how home is a moveable feast, but also how disruptive-inclusive learning means that such luxuries must be treated as a stepping-off point onto the next stage of unexpected adventure, not a place to put on your slippers and never leave. It is almost impossible to fall back into the idea of static, permanent home and not take it for granted.

During my time at seminary, I had the enormous privilege of learning a lot. Church history classes deepened my skills and understanding of what it means to participate in *koinonia*. I can explain the translation difficulties created in the Bible by subjective and objective genitives (I promise not to foist this upon you during coffee and cake, unless you really are interested). I considered different approaches to preaching and expressions of Christian doctrine and spirituality. I discovered Practical Theology. But when I look back, what about my experience changed me the most? What allows any of this above material to make a difference to the way I live, love and engage in my everyday life? The answer is simple and multiple: the room-mates who joined me for frozen yoghurt on the days when 'at home' feelings were a distant memory. The family who had me round for dinner so often that I had my own, personal napkin. The church small group who kept insisting that I turn up and be myself, whether I felt I had something to contribute or not. Those who made (and continue to make) space for me to keep redefining what it means to be 'at home' and, importantly, to help them do the same, wherever and however we found our-selves on any given day.

Selah 7: '… and I will return into God's house my whole life long'

Psalm 23 is a favourite passage for many and perhaps one of the most recognizable parts of the entire Bible. One of its enduring attractions is its tracing of peace and tranquillity (in the opening verses, at least). In its six short verses, the Psalmist paints a picture of life with God without striving, want, fear or lack. The Psalmist just enjoys their privileged position and looks forward to more of the same. This is particularly striking because it stands in such contrast to the psalm directly before, which offers, in some senses, the polar opposite perspective of life with God, dominated by the experience of pain, restlessness and unanswered prayer. However, on closer reading Psalm 23 is more than the vision of an unachievable utopia where even the deepest difficulties do not faze God's followers. If the pro-gress of the psalm is supposed to represent the journey of life, it outlines a pattern that is far more than an unproblematic pathway from green pastures to effortlessly dwelling in God's house for ever.

This is not a full analysis of Psalm 23; many excellent schol-ars have already undertaken this task.[38] In the light of our discussion about the goals of CAL, my focus is concentrated on one detail at the end of the psalm that provides translators with a particular challenge. Let me explain why I think it is so critical. The Psalms are carefully crafted songs whose lyrics convey deep truths in beautiful ways, following a purposeful order. No word is wasted, no expression thrown away.[39] On this basis, I have always been fascinated by the fact that in Psalm 23 there is a potential repeat of one key verb (or at the very least, a play on words) that draws a connection between what appear as two very different and unrelated concepts in most English translations. The words in question are generally translated as *restores* in verse 3, and *dwell* in verse 6.

It is important to recognize that it is very normal for ancient Hebrew verbs to convey a range of different, but usually related, ideas. Unlike the mechanics of European languages in which words are generally understood as containers of meaning, ancient Hebrew words function more like signposts in a field – pointing to the general area of meaning but not necessarily highlighting a specific spot. The best contemporary comparison is perhaps between photorealist paintings and impressionism. The function of photorealism is to try and convey an image (or arguably even enhance the original) by recreating it as closely as possible. If it is difficult to tell the difference between the real object/person and the created image, then it has been successful. On the other hand, impressionism is still an attempt to convey the original scene, but it goes about it in an entirely different way. Monet's smudges of colour suggest rather than realistically represent the plants, scenery and people they depict. The artist represented something other than he actually saw to try and give a richer (and some would argue, truer) sense of the reality he experienced as he painted than a photograph ever could. For example, people often remark about Monet's representation of water that his techniques allow them to hear and see its movement by using colours and patterns that are not found naturally in water. Ancient Hebrew conveys meaning in a similar way to Monet. Its use of words is designed to paint rich, multi-layered pictures and help the reader draw connections. For those translating ancient Hebrew poetry and song into European languages this creates multiple issues, one of which is the many places where the writers build texture by using repeated or overlapping terms. Fully replicating this effect is almost impossible.

Keeping all of this in mind, we go back to Psalm 23. Without going too deep into the minute technical details of ancient Hebrew, the verb that appears in verse 3 as 'restore' is derived from a root word that means to turn back or return. Although there is no evidence of how biblical Hebrew sounded, it is often pronounced as *shoov/shub*. The verb that appears in verse 6 is almost always translated as 'dwell', from a root word that means to sit, remain or dwell, often pronounced *yashab*. But, and this is where it gets interesting, as John Goldingay highlights, grammatically speaking (that is, just based on the form of the word), this is not the only valid option for translating the verb in verse 6b: 'Both "return to" and "dwell in" make partial sense but also raise problems.'[40] The closest equivalent in English is a sentence like, 'they went to bed tired because they had a long row.' The last word of this sentence has two possible meanings: either a fight or propelling a boat down the river with oars. You may have an opinion about which option makes more sense, but grammatically both options are possible: the verb in verse 6b could either mean return or dwell. Goldingay finishes his comment, 'and it finally makes little difference which we follow'.[41] While I agree that arguments for both translations are not straightforward, I disagree with Goldingay that it makes little difference which option is chosen.

One of the biggest issues I find with the choice of translating Psalm 23.6b as dwell/sit/remain is that these convey fundamentally static concepts. To dwell somewhere suggests remaining in the same place, belonging, bedding down. So ending the psalm with this idea gives the overall impression of arriving into God's house and remaining there as the ultimate aim of the Christian life. According to this pattern, the Psalmist's overall journey goes from relaxing in green fields (v.1) to relaxing in God's house (v.6). The reason I find this problematic is simple: it does not fit with the rest of the closing verse, which reads, 'surely goodness and mercy shall follow (hotly pursue) me all the days of my life' (v.6). The psalm's closing image is of the Psalmist spending the rest of their days being chased down by God's goodness and loving kindness. This is not presented as a problem to be solved, but a blessing to be fully embraced. The setting is almost race-like. God's goodness and mercy are hot on the Psalmist's heels, trying to outrun them. And importantly, this action is time marked. It is not just a one-time occurrence but a process that will endlessly continue. Therefore it makes little sense that whatever state the Psalmist ends in, it is inactive or fixed!

Although it requires a little (Monet-esque) artistic licence (but as I have explained, there is something of that embedded in how the ancient Hebrew language works), I suggest that Psalm 23.6 should read something like: 'Surely goodness and mercy will pursue me all the days of my life and I will return into God's house my whole life long.' For me, the crucial point is that the psalm ends with an ongoing pattern of movement. The journey the Psalmist has been on (through the valley of the shadow of death and paraded in front of enemies) has not led to a place of static rest but to more and better movement. The difficulties and disruptions were not a 'means to an end' to allow the Psalmist to then gaze out at the vista for the rest of eternity, but the means of accessing more of God's enabling love and mercy for the continuing journey.

And where or what is the Psalmist spending their entire life running towards? Where does God live? Way before Jesus appears in the biblical narrative, the people of God were confident in declaring: 'Lord, you have been our dwelling place in all generations' (Ps. 90.1). Later, the Ephesian Church was encouraged that the Holy Spirit was available to them, so that 'Christ may dwell in your hearts by faith' (Eph. 3.17). Finally, when the city of God descends, the opening declaration is 'See, the home of God is among mortals' (Rev. 21.3). So perhaps, then, allowing the goodness and mercy of God to constantly chase us home is not about escaping self and becoming someone else, nor getting to a place where God's followers can finally shake off the difficulties of this life and relax, but a way that we can 'discover the secret of being truly human, of reflecting God's image'.[42] For the Psalmist, God's restoration looks like (or perhaps even sounds like!) getting better at, but never completely mastering, the art of continually running home.

Why? The Christian motivation for learning

If at this point you are questioning whether trying to find a way to allow God's goodness and mercy to keep chasing you back into God's house for the rest of your life is worth the effort, I must admit I do not blame you. The idea of relaxed remaining is clearly far more attractive than being constantly pursued (even if God's goodness is doing the chasing!). My response to this is to suggest that disruptive inclusion reconfigures one final question in relation to CAL, and it is potentially the most difficult of all to pin down. Why do (or should) Christian adults learn? What is the underpinning motivation of CAL and how does that set it apart from other approaches? In this final section, before we unpack some of the practicalities of disruptive inclusion, I offer some further personal insights into my own learning journey and explain how they have for ever changed not only how I learn as a person of Christian faith, but why.

Learning between some lines and dots

I am naturally a very structured personality (an extreme 'J' in Myers-Briggs terms). This means that in my formative years I understood the world very much like Nick Hornby's character Will from *About a Boy* (played by Hugh Grant in the film), who claims that the key to life is thinking about days in terms of units of time.[43] As a teenager, formal education helped me with this and my days often looked something like: 1 unit of Maths and 1 unit of French in the morning. 1 unit of English and 1 unit of hockey in the afternoon. After this, 1 unit of television (maybe more) and 2 units of homework in the evening, followed by multiple units of sleep. Life was easily split into two categories – units of 'learning' and units of 'fun'. The learning units were focused on getting things done – mastering concepts and conquering skills. In technical terms, this part of my life was focused on critical engagement. On the other hand, I understood the 'fun' units as frivolous and reasonably meaningless, apart from their ability to help me forget about the stresses of school or university by the end of them. The function of the 'fun' units of life was as an antidote to learning or a form of anti-learning. Fun basically topped up my tank so I could learn again.

It has taken me a long time to articulate it, but I no longer think that this is how the world works. A significant milestone in my journey towards something different happened one autumn day in Paris, in my student days. I vividly remember standing in the Centre Pompidou (Paris's modern art museum that curiously has its inner workings on the outside) and staring at huge canvases by Spanish painter Joan Miró. I stood in front of a mainly blue painting that consists of a single, vertical red line and a series of black dots (do an internet search for them: Triptych Bleu I, II and III) and I was faced with a challenge. As I tried to formulate a response, I realized that, unlike Maths equations or French grammar, the painting before me could not be mastered or somehow solved. Even if I had access to all the information available about Miró's background and the scholarly views on this painting, I might still be no closer to a satisfactory response. However, at that particular moment, neither could I really find a way to enjoy the image in front of me or, in fact, any other painting in the gallery. Critically engaging with the painting was clearly insufficient, but neither was a purely emotional reaction along the lines of 'I really like it' or even 'I really do not like it'. In other words, the prospect before me would not fit into either of my categories and I remember finding it deeply disconcerting – or, dare I suggest, baffling?

At about the same time as I was being baffled by Miró, I had a friend at university who had a very different upbringing from me. Her father loved art and she told stories of carpets being covered and her and her sisters being stripped down and encouraged to explore paint before they could walk or talk! When she explained her relationship with art, her thoughts were not aimed at mastering the topic but nor were they uninformed. She would critically compare different artists' styles and analyse their techniques but also ask questions like, 'What does it remind you of?', 'How do the colours make you feel?', 'Is the combination of X and X something that you would have expected?', 'Why do you think we both have different reactions to this piece?' As I dared to take her questions seriously, I found responses (and more questions) that I did not know I had. As I asked myself how Miró's red line and black dots made me feel, I found myself explaining a sense of unfinishedness and expressing anxiety connected to this. I found myself recollecting long car journeys as a child and started thinking about the similarities and contrasts between lines and dots. Is it only the horizon that allows us to see trees appearing on it, or the other way around? I found myself wanting to know more about Miró and his interests and influences, and ultimately I became aware that I was operating in another kind of learning space – somewhere between the reality I had previously known and experienced and another reality. I was somewhere I did not recognize and had never visited before.

All the above is to say that I discovered that there is something fundamental about CAL that cannot be reduced to either necessity or escapist fun. There is another motivation for learning that is not primarily concerned with completing tasks more easily or becoming sufficiently qualified to make more money, but is also not a frivolous antidote to these; it is consequential and has real-life, grounded, material implications that need to be taken seriously. Somewhere in between these extremes, there is another motivation for learning that is deeply disruptive because it requires learners to recognize and value a 'kind of strange half world'[44] that opens up a whole new range of responses other than like or dislike, useful or useless. The reason why I now want to wrestle with paintings that I find it difficult to either simply like or dismiss is the same reason why I want to do the hard work of living, learning and worshipping with those who are different from me, and the same reason why I want to get better at being chased by the goodness and mercy of God – it is the best option. In fact, I would go as far as to say that it is my only option. I understand that I cannot afford not to. Maybe the change of question here flips 'Why include disruption in learning?' on its head, to 'Why not?'

Clearly, I am not forced to learn at all, never mind in any specific way. I enjoy the privilege of choice, but I have come to think about learning in a much more vital (that is, indispensable for life) way, similar to Simon Peter's response when Jesus asks the disciples if they are also going to leave him. His answer: 'Lord, to whom can we go?' (John 6.68). Simon Peter has not just settled on remaining with Jesus because he does not have access to better options; it is clear that he has realized that Jesus is his best and only option, 'the holy *one* of God' (6.69). The suggestion that I (or Simon Peter) could somehow return to the way life was before is absurd. So why do I embrace disruption as an embedded part of a life of Christian faith? Because, coming full circle back to John 10, experience tells me that the abundance of God's life is found in the in-between spaces and so, where else would I go?

Finding new motivation in playful poetics

As we discussed at the beginning of Part II, one of the key things about practical theology is that understanding shapes practice and vice versa. Mostly, the pattern of this book follows the first of these options: multiple chapters and sections begin by introducing a key aspect of disruptive inclusion and then identifying the practical consequences. But as we have also experienced, this is only one of two routes up the mountain. Therefore, to balance things out, its discussion on learning motivation began deeply embedded in my own learning journey and now moves to explore the subsequent implications for my understanding and articulation of CAL. In other words, since standing in front of those paintings in Paris for the first time, how have I come to understand and explain this differently-motivated learning? Following the (by now well-established) pattern, the best response I have found to this question brings together two ideas that are rarely associated with CAL: play and poetics.

Let us begin with play or playfulness. Priest and educationalist Jerome Berryman claims that play is 'neither silly nor super-ficial. Adults confuse the entertainment or over-stimulation of children with play.'[45] Rather than a demonstration of immaturity, Berryman understands play as a highly complex process that requires 'deep concentration' and practice in order to improve,[46] meaning that many children are in a far stronger position to engage well in learning than adults. Specifically in relation to Christian learners, he suggests that many of the challenges faced are not due to unsolved, theoretical conun-drums but to a lack of skill 'to deeply play, participate in rituals or be active listeners to stories'.[47] Christian learning has protective and expansive properties (helping learners imagine new possibilities), but where creativity and play are avoided, usually in attempts to 'maintain the greatest control and avoid the most risk',[48] the pendulum has swung so far towards the protective that playful learning's ability to help learners 'cope with trouble' has been almost entirely obscured and become perceived as 'trouble itself'.[49]

For Berryman a key function of play is its natural ability to encourage learners to engage in both the real world and imagined reality. Think about an imaginative play scenario where children re-create scenes from shops, hospitals or police stations. They rely on some knowledge of real-life settings but imaginative play can never be fully accounted for by real-life knowledge or experience. In the same way, CAL is funda-mentally an interpretive process that is grounded in knowledge and experience but also immerses learners in more than just a cognitive exercise. In other words, play provides a cross-over point where learners can explore various realities or the culmination of 'many different narratives'.[50]

To play's ability to act as a bridge between reality and imagination we add poetic learning, which operates at a very similar intersection but approaches it from the opposite direction. Poetics is an ancient concept, first introduced (or at least developed) by Aristotle circa 330 BC, with surviving documents navigating issues such as character, tragedy and poetry.[51] However, poetics and poetry are not the same thing. Poetics is a discipline that extends beyond literary theory into philosophy, anthropology, theology, economics and psychology.[52] At its most basic level, poetics is a mode of perception and expression that draws learners deeper and closer into a particular lived experience and simultaneously into an imaginative experience beyond. It usually employs words, but its function cannot be reduced to them. For example, William Wordsworth's famous poem beginning 'I wandered lonely as a cloud' does not just convey information about clouds. In describing how they move he uses the rhythm and sounds of words to usher the reader into an experience of them. When Wordsworth describes the daffodils as 'fluttering and dancing in the breeze … tossing their heads in sprightly dance',[53] the words point beyond their basic meaning to an experience of what they look, feel and even sound like. However, poetic communication also employs ordering, placement and even silence or absence. Literary theorist Terry Eagleton explains that this happens because in the poetic, 'form and content are intimately interwoven … [it] discloses the secret truth of all literary writing: that form is *constitutive* of content and not just a reflection of it.'[54] Poetics is not just a prettier or more dramatic way of presenting information; it 'does intellectual work … a unique model of investigation that is a legitimate source of knowledge.'[55]

Moving towards the world of CAL, professor of theology and creative practice Heather Walton summarizes poetics as: 'Processes of creative transformation through which human

163

language constructs a "something else," ... or "Somewhere Else," beyond the limits of the matter-of-fact, everyday world.'[56] Bringing together many of the themes already discussed in relation to disruptive inclusion, Walton further explains how a combination of groundedness in present reality and otherworldliness is a key trait of poetics, exemplified in the Bible:

> Poetics is ... interested in how human imagination constructs narratives by winding its way amongst and between the factual and fictive. It explores the capacity of metaphoric utterance to embody the exotic, the beautiful, the tragic, the unknown, and the unnameable. It strays beyond the strict bound of the real to proclaim its own form of truth.[57]

Similar to earlier discussions, while some find that Walton's use of the word fictive suggests an unacceptable level of compromise to biblical truth and authority, I am confident that considering CAL on poetic, artistic, playful terms does not demote the Bible's truth and authority in learning. On the contrary, it brings a fresh depth and seriousness to the Bible's ability to facilitate transformative learning experiences. It moves the Bible from being simply an exercise in cognitive ascent (a technical way of saying 'getting it') to an altogether more holistic and joined up learning experience. In a by now familiar theme, specialist in the relationship between poetics and education Sheila Stewart understands poetics as a meeting point for the knowable and unknowable: 'Poised between the sentient and the social, a moment of dialogue' (sentient means able to sense/physically feel).[58] Thus, in simultaneously insisting upon and exposing the inadequacy of words, a poetic learning posture epitomizes the tension of learning disruption: a grounded and measurable experience that also defies normal patterns:

> [It] is like a holiday which, while it is a date in the calendar, is also a break in the sequence of days ... because it uses the

elements of time, like rhythm and pauses, it gives us a means to reflect on time.'[59]

Stewart concludes that poetics is 'a place of bodily knowing attempting to become words, with both unconscious and conscious aspects of mind engaged'.[60] Therefore poetic CAL is an excellent example of how apophatic and cataphatic knowledge (see Selah 4) need not compete, but require each other to work well. All in all, a poetic approach to learning seeks to recognize that 'cognitions as well as affections are part of the experience of being religious.'[61] Rahner takes this further in claiming: 'The capacity and practice of perceiving the poetic word is a presupposition of hearing the word of God ... In its inmost essence, the poetic is a prerequisite for Christianity.'[62]

However, it is important not to confuse poetics with ease, comfort and a general lack of conflict. One of the reasons why poetic learning is effective for Christian adults is its ability to facilitate effective confrontation. English Literature and Women, Gender and Sexuality scholar Mary DeShazer summarizes the function of poetics as 'refus[ing] the pretense of objectivity, instead asserting polemically the terms of their engagement with the topic at hand', 'invit[ing] conflict and confrontation' and 'engag[ing] our participation'. In doing so, she argues, 'We too join a community of resisters.'[63] Philosopher Alva Noë's summary of the function of art can also be applied to poetic CAL:

[It] isn't a phenomenon to be explained. Not by neuroscience, and not by philosophy ... [but] a research practice, a way of investigating the world and ourselves ... [that] displays us to ourselves, and in a way makes us anew, by disrupting our habitual activities.[64]

Importantly, however, the suggestion is that poetics creates not unlimited, uncontrolled disruption for learners to contend with, but opportunities for various learning postures and actions to be rehearsed with reduced potential consequences.

For example, as Hebrew Bible scholar Anne Stewart comments on the poetics of Proverbs 5, it 'represents an unfolding pattern of pedagogy, alternatively exposing the student to visions of the crooked and the straight course ... allowing the listener of the poem to try on various actions and their consequences.'[65] Stewart's claim is that a poetic approach to CAL offers opportunities for the learning 'dry-runs' that are foundational to disruptive inclusion before the stakes are raised in 'real life' scenarios. Finally, a clear consequence of this is that it not only assumes active learning participation in the *trying-on* process, but also decisions and changed actions as a result. Again, Veling's comments on the Arts in general can be applied to poetics: '[They] bring with them a radical call towards change, towards a new way of dwelling in the world. The awakening, the enrichment, the consternation, the unsettling of sensibility and understanding which follow our experience of art *prompt us to action*.'[66]

So, back to me in front of Miró's Bleu II, or one of the multiple similar invitations to include disruption that have been regularly part of my learning experience ever since. Whether faced with abstract art or the death of a friend, I know that somehow attempting to *master* what is before me is a waste of time. Equally, simple expressions of 'I like it' or 'this hurts' are important, but only the beginning. Playful poetics offered me an alternative way to embrace the disruption, to wind amongst and between in a way that did 'not pull me out of this world to some other world; rather, it changes what it means to be in this world'.[67] Playfulness is not flippant, but allows learners a way to be as present as they dare and engage seriously with disruption without the fear of not finding the single, correct answer on the first try (or ever!). Poetics allows learners to be drawn into the details but also set on a trajectory beyond them. Although my 20-year-old self could not have articulated any of this, I am proud of her willingness to frolic in the edge-places for a while, to imaginatively suspend her existing views of the world and her place in it, if only temporarily. That day, not only did I catch a glimpse of plenty of new learning territory to explore, but also new ways of present, connected human *being*. Why do I learn/why can I not afford not to learn? Because I have found that the best way to discover what it means to be alive.

I think I am overdue a return trip to the Centre Pompidou, but for now, a small version of Miró's Bleu II hangs in my bedroom as a symbol that CAL is an invitation to essential, divine, creative participation, not just for arty people but created people. For Christians, playfully and poetically including disruption in learning is a powerful acknowledgement and expression of participating in the life of God, not only for joy and delight and not only out of necessity, but as a far more holistic and fundamental expression of humanity that includes and stretches beyond both. Practical theologian Daniël Louw suggests that we call this artistic reason: 'The experience of "beauty" … reveals the truth of our existence and the occurrence of identification with a "transcendent dimension" which brings about a bridging of meaning and reality.'[68] As Eugene Peterson's interpretation of Philippians 4.8–9 captures, perhaps the single idea that comes closest to defining disruptive inclusion as a distinctively Christian approach to learning is that its most fundamental drive, and most basic aim, is not towards greater efficacy or efficiency or even depth of engagement, but a greater experience and richer definition of beauty:

> Summing it all up, friends, I'd say you'll do best by filling your minds and meditating on things true, noble, reputable, authentic, compelling, gracious – the best, not the worst; the beautiful, not the ugly; things to praise, not things to curse. Put into practice what you learned from me, what you heard and saw and realized. Do that, and God, who makes everything work together, will work you into his most excellent harmonies.[69]

Questions/activities

- What images and metaphorical language do you use to describe your own and others' learning? What (potentially unconscious) claims are you making about it in doing so?
- When have you most felt *at home* in an unfamiliar/unexpected place? Try to describe the feeling. What was the outcome?
- How do you understand Psalm 23.6? What do you think is the relationship between the psalm and CAL?
- Have you ever thought about why you learn? What are your motivations for learning? Ask some other people and see if their answers are similar to yours.
- What elements of play do you have in your life? Can you create some spaces where you (and others) are able to explore and imagine and create without fear of judgement? What might they be?
- How do you understand the relationship between the Arts and learning? What does beauty have to do with CAL progress?
- At the end of a day, try to write about its events and feelings poetically. Don't worry about what others would think or whether you're doing it correctly; just try to use words to convey how you experienced the events and people you include. Remember, silence and space are powerful tools. When you have finished, reflect on the experience.

Notes

1 John M. Hull, 'Christian nurture and critical openness', *Scottish Journal of Theology* 34:1 (1981), p. 209.

2 Hull, 'Christian nurture', p. 208.

3 For example, see Trevor Cooling, *A Christian Vision for State Education: Reflections on the theology of education* (London: SPCK, 1994), p. 34. This issue is discussed in much more detail in my doctoral thesis.

4 Trevor Cooling, 'Enabling the Bible to control learning' in K.

Goodlet and J. Collier (eds), *Teaching Well: Insights for educators in Christian schools* (Barton ACT: Barton Books, 2014), pp. 53–62, p. 56.

5 Craig G. Bartholomew, *'Behind' the Text: History and biblical interpretation* (Grand Rapids, MI: Zondervan, 2003), p. 376.

6 Søren Kierkegaard, Howard V. Hong and Edna H. Hong, *Stages on Life's Way: Studies by various persons* (Princeton, NJ: Princeton University Press, 1988).

7 David I. Smith and Susan M. Felch, *Teaching and Christian Imagination* (Grand Rapids, MI: Wm. B. Eerdmans, 2016), p. 42.

8 Smith and Felch, *Teaching and Christian Imagination*, p. 17.

9 Lynne Cameron, 'Metaphor in educational discourse' in *Advances in Applied Linguistics* (London: Continuum, 2003), pp. 246–7.

10 Peter Berger and Thomas Luckmann, *The Social Construction of Reality: A treatise in the sociology of knowledge* (London: Penguin Books, 1971), p. 17.

11 The exact attribution of this quote is disputed. Although widely associated with T. S. Eliot, some believe it originally belonged to the sixteenth-century French philosopher Michel de Montaigne.

12 John M. Hull, *What Prevents Christian Adults from Learning?* (London: SCM Press, 1985), p. 195.

13 Gabriel Moran, *Education Toward Adulthood* (New York, NY: Paulist Press, 1979), p. 58.

14 Mary Foulke, 'Coming out as White/becoming White: racial identity development as a spiritual journey', *Theology & Sexuality* 1996:5, pp. 35–6.

15 I thoroughly recommend the 2011 film, *The Way*. Watch the trailer here: https://youtu.be/o5VZKWcgw6c.

16 Albert Camus (Philip Thody, trans.), *Notebooks, 1935–1942* (New York, NY: Paragon House, 1991), p. 13. See also Birgit Phillips, *Learning by Going: Transformative learning through long-term independent travel* (Wiesbaden: Vieweg, 2019), p. 87. Kent Eilers, 'Hermeneutical empathy: receiving global texts in local classrooms', *Teaching Theology & Religion* 17:2 (2014), pp. 165–6. Daniel Fleming and Terence Lovat, 'Learning as leaving home: fear, empathy, and hospitality in the theology and religion classroom', *Teaching Theology & Religion* 18:3 (2015), pp. 207–23, p. 210.

17 Fleming and Lovat, 'Learning as leaving home', p. 216.

18 Fleming and Lovat, 'Learning as leaving home', p. 210.

19 William P. Brown, *Sacred Sense: Discovering the wonder of God's word and world* (Grand Rapids, MI: Wm. B. Eerdmans, 2015), p. 5.

20 The intersection between hospitality and pedagogy is more fully unpacked in David I. Smith and Barbara M. Carvill, *The Gift of the Stranger: Faith, hospitality, and foreign language learning* (Grand Rapids, MI: Wm. B. Eerdmans, 2000).

21 Based on Jean Decety and William John Ickes, 'The social neuroscience of empathy', *Social Neuroscience Series* (Cambridge, MS: MIT Press, 2009).

22 Fleming and Lovat, 'Learning as leaving home', p. 209.

23 Darcia Narvaez, 'Neurobiology and Moral Mindset' in K. Heinrichs, F. Oser and T. Lovat (eds), *Handbook of Moral Motivation: Theories, models, applications* (Rotterdam: Sense, 2013), p. 328.

24 This idea of communal imagination is revisited in Chapter 7, in relation to sermons.

25 Susanne Johnson, 'Reshaping religious and theological education in the '90s: toward a critical pluralism', *Religious Education* 88:3 (1993), pp. 335–49, p. 348.

26 Parker Palmer, *To Know as We are Known: Education as a spiritual journey* (San Francisco, CA: Harper, 1993), p. 74.

27 Smith and Felch, *Teaching and Christian Imagination*, p. 57. Fleming and Mudge draw a parallel here with T. S. Eliot's poem 'Little Gidding', which explains this concept as 'know[ing] the place for the first time'; Daniel Fleming and Peter Mudge, 'Leaving home: a pedagogy for theological education' in L. Ball and J. Harrison (eds), *Learning and Teaching Theology: Some ways ahead* (Eugene, OR: Wipf & Stock, 2015), p. 79.

28 Fleming and Lovat, 'Learning as leaving home', p. 212.

29 Hull, *What Prevents*, p. 66.

30 John H. Westerhoff III, 'Toward a definition of Christian Education' in *A Colloquy on Christian Education* (Philadelphia, PA: United Church Press, 1972), p. 61. Gender inclusive language added.

31 Fleming and Mudge, 'Leaving home', p. 78.

32 Kwok Pui-Lan, *Postcolonial Imagination and Feminist Theology* (Louisville, KY: Westminster John Knox Press, 2005), p. 102. Kwok also references James Clifford's language of 'travelling-in-dwelling' and 'dwelling-in-travelling' to capture this image. See Kwok, *Postcolonial Imagination and Feminist Theology*, p. 44. This definition of home also resonates strongly with Jenny Morgans' use of the term *home-ing* in her research on women's experiences at university: 'Home is neither static nor permanent. Rather, *home-ing* involves the fluid and dynamic processes of both leaving and making home. It includes crafting physical and emotional spaces that are *home enough* and *home-like*. Such homes are temporary, and connected to both past and future homes.' Jenny Morgans, 'Home-ing emerging Christian women's transitions at university' (PhD thesis, 2020), pp. 14–15. Available from: https://research.vu.nl/ws/portalfiles/portal/119639761/286396.pdf (accessed 31.07.2023).

33 John M. Hull, *On Sight and Insight: A journey into the world of blindness* (Oxford: Oneworld, 2001), p. 232.

34 Smith and Felch, *Teaching and Christian Imagination*, p. 57.

35 Smith and Felch, *Teaching and Christian Imagination*, p. 57.

36 Smith and Felch, *Teaching and Christian Imagination*, p. 56.

37 Mike Higton employs a similarly *both-and* approach to home metaphors in his argument that theological education can be deemed simultaneously religious and secular. He imagines theological education as 'on the cusp between tradition and critique, between religion and secularity, between familiarity and exile ... between homecoming and an "ascetic code of willed homelessness"'. Mike Higton, 'Criticism, obedience and exile: theological education as religious and secular', *Theology* 112:869 (2009), pp. 323–32, p. 325.

38 Some of my favourite books on the Psalms include: Margaret Daly-Denton, *Psalm-Shaped Prayerfulness: A guide to the Christian reception of the Psalms* (Blackrock, Dublin: Columba Press, 2010); Walter Brueggemann and Patrick D. Miller, *The Psalms and the Life of Faith* (Minneapolis, MI: Fortress Press, 1995); Rolf A. Jacobson, *Soundings in the Theology of Psalms: Perspectives and methods in contemporary scholarship* (Minneapolis, MI: Fortress Press, 2011).

39 For more on this, see Brueggemann's work on the Psalms.

40 John Goldingay, *Psalms: 1–41* (Grand Rapids, MI: Baker Academic, 2006), p. 353.

41 Goldingay, *Psalms: 1–41*, p. 353.

42 N. T. Wright, 'Jesus and the identity of God', *Ex Auditu* 14 (1998), pp. 42–56, p. 42.

43 Nick Hornby, *About a Boy* (London: Victor Gollancz, 1998).

44 Hull, *What Prevents*, pp. 31–2.

45 Jerome W. Berryman, 'Playful orthodoxy: religious education's solution to pluralism' in Dennis Bates, Gloria Durka and Friedrich Schweitzer (eds), *Education, Religion and Society: Essays in honour of John M. Hull* (London: Routledge, 2006), p. 211.

46 Berryman, 'Playful orthodoxy', p. 211.

47 Berryman, 'Playful orthodoxy', p. 211.

48 Berryman, 'Playful orthodoxy', p. 207.

49 Berryman, 'Playful orthodoxy', p. 438.

50 Kwok Pui Lan, *Discovering the Bible in the Non-biblical World* (Maryknoll, NY: Orbis Books, 1995), p. 38.

51 Aristotle's work on poetics can be read in full here: https://classics.mit.edu/Aristotle/poetics.1.1.html (accessed 31.07.2023).

52 I particularly recommend Callid Keefe-Perry's work on theopoetics. See Callid Keefe-Perry, 'Theopoetics: process and perspective', *Christianity and Literature* 58:4 (2009), pp. 579–601; and Callid Keefe-Perry, Dave Harrity and Terry A. Veling, *Way to Water: A Theopoetics primer* (Eugene, OR: Wipf & Stock, 2014).

53 Available here: https://www.poetryfoundation.org/poems/45521/ i-wandered-lonely-as-a-cloud (accessed 31.07.2023).

54 Terry Eagleton, *How to Read a Poem* (Malden, MA: Blackwell, 2012), p. 67.

55 Elaine T. James, 'Biblical poetry and the art of close reading' in J. B. Couey and E. T. James, *Biblical Poetry and the Art of Close Reading* (Cambridge: Cambridge University Press, 2018), pp. 32–48, p. 32.

56 Heather Walton, 'Poetics' in B. Miller-McLemore (ed.), *The Wiley Blackwell Companion to Practical Theology* (Chichester, West Sussex: Wiley-Blackwell, 2014), p. 173.

57 Walton, 'Poetics', p. 173.

58 Sheila Stewart, 'Poetry: learning through embodied language' in Y-L. R.Wong and S. Batacharya (eds), *Sharing Breath: Embodied learning and decolonization* (Edmonton, Alberta: AU Press, 2018), pp. 380–1.

59 Fred Sedgwick, *Read My Mind: Young children, poetry, and learning* (London: Routledge, 1997), p. 6.

60 Stewart, 'Poetry', p. 381.

61 John M. Hull, 'What is Theology of Education?', *Scottish Journal of Theology* 30:1 (1977), p. 10.

62 Karl Rahner, 'Poetry and the Christian' in *Theological Investigations: volume 4* (Baltimore, MD: Helicon Press, 1961), pp. 357–67, p. 363.

63 Mary DeShazer, *A Poetics of Resistance: Women writing in El Salvador, South Africa, and the United States* (Ann Arbor, MI: University of Michigan Press, 1994), p. 271. This also connects to another theme of Hull's work: resistance. I discuss this further in a 2021 article: Jen Smith, 'A pedagogy of resistance and Scouse other-ness', *Practical Theology* 14:4 (2021), pp. 351–63.

64 Alva Noë, 'Strange tools: art and human nature: a précis', *Philosophy and Phenomenological Research* 94:1 (2017), pp. 211–13, p. 213.

65 Anne W. Stewart, 'Biblical poetry and the art of close reading' in J. B. Couey and E. T. James (eds), *Biblical Poetry and the Art of Close Reading* (Cambridge: Cambridge University Press, 2018), pp. 91–2.

66 Terry A. Veling, *Practical Theology: 'On Earth as it is in Heaven'* (Maryknoll, NY: Orbis Books, 2005), pp. 201–2.

67 Veling, *Practical Theology*, p. 206.

68 Daniel J. Louw, 'Creative hope and imagination in a practical theology of aesthetic (artistic) reason', *Religion & Theology* 8:3/4 (2001), pp. 332–3.

69 Eugene H. Peterson, Philippians 4.4–9 in *The Message: The New Testament in contemporary English* (Colorado Springs, CO: NavPress, 1993).

PART III

Reshaping Practice

In the interview for my PhD, when I still had very little clarity on the potential direction of my research, I was sure of one thing: anything I was going to spend lots of time thinking and writing about had to be more than just a good idea. I wanted to invest myself in something with real, *live-outable* consequences for teachers and learners in different kinds of scenarios. That day I explained to my patient interviewers (soon to become supervisors) that my aim was to produce research that would both influence, and be influenced by, how learning happens, not just sound nice. Therefore, having re-directed the conversation about CAL and redefined the task, in this final part, we turn our attention to reshaping practice. What are the practical implications of some of the claims already made in this book? Which guiding lenses and particular techniques lend themselves more easily to disruptive-inclusive learning in various modes? Specifically, what challenges and opportunities does disruptive inclusion present in (and beyond) the CAL classroom, the pulpit and in online learning settings?

If you are not an educator or a preacher, as you begin the following chapters, your instincts may tell you that you have nothing to learn from, or contribute to, this part of the discussion – I would strongly encourage you to resist them! As I have argued from the beginning, a key component of disruptive inclusion is in encouraging learners to play an active role in understanding and taking responsibility for how learning happens. Therefore, if we want practice to improve, dialogue about how CAL happens in all its various settings must equally include those who learn and listen and those who teach and speak. Even if you have no interest in classroom or online learning or do not regularly hear sermons, you are not off the hook! The following examples are excellent ways of assessing your understanding of, and responses to disruptive inclusion. Therefore, no matter the perspective from which you join this conversation, my encouragement is to continue to take an interactive approach to the upcoming chapters. Keep asking: 'Have I ever experienced something similar to this?' or 'What would I say or do if I were a learner (or educator) in this scenario?' Think of how the various examples and their underpinning ideas are similar to or different from your current experience, and/or might be applied in your context(s). To help everyone think carefully about the practical implications of disruptive inclusion from a learner-centred perspective, in addition to the questions at the end of each section, you will also find learner checklists. These are designed to help you reflect on current learning skills and preferences, and to ponder any changes you may wish to make and the potential benefits those changes may bring to your own and others' CAL practice.

Before we begin, a few caveats and acknowledgements: the following chapters contain worked examples and analysis from my experience as a tutor, preacher and learner. The context for most of them is the role I held while I wrote the thesis on which this book is based, Academic Manager and Tutor at King's School of Theology (an independent centre for theological training primarily serving Charismatic Evangelicals: kingstheology.org). I will mention the contributions of specific colleagues as appropriate, but in general, these examples are inspired by everyone who participated in the KST learning community 2015–2020 and, specifically, the students and fellow tutors who engaged in the sessions and activities mentioned here. As I mention in the acknowledgements, it was during my time at KST that the ideas in this book first began to percolate. I am proud of the multiple examples of embracing disruption in CAL that I observed among learners, and in which I participated during my time at KST. In a deeply significant way, this book is both about and for them.

Because of this, the subject of many of the following examples is Christian theology. However, in theory, it could be anything from science to politics, languages to maths, farming to art history. The following examples have been chosen for a few specific reasons. First, because learning about God is the most common topic around which groups of Christian adults learn and therefore provides a rich pool of examples, in both quality and quantity. Second, because theology is the area in which I am most experienced in the teaching of Christian adults, and it would feel disingenuous to move away from my primary area of expertise. And third, because it provides further evidence for a variety of earlier arguments that disruptive inclusion is embedded in both the method and message of Christianity.

While you may wish to borrow some of the ideas mentioned in the following chapters (and you are very welcome to do so), the chosen examples are not meant to represent a blueprint for good practice that can simply be duplicated in any context. The aim here is to put 'skin on the bones' of earlier arguments and present a range of worked illustrations of possible ways disruptive inclusion can be practised, so that we can all ask better questions of how CAL might happen and begin to imagine if, and how, certain approaches, activities and techniques can be adapted to address the particular needs of our setting(s).

6

Disruptive Inclusion and Classroom Learning

First, it is important to clarify exactly what I mean by class-room learning. I use it to refer to any physically gathered, corporate (preferably interactive) learning scenario that involves Christian adults (whether educator, learners or both). This includes any learning setting within church life where there is the expectation of some dialogue, but also Christian adult education and training settings, variously referred to as Bible colleges and schools, colleges and centres of theology, training institutes and seminaries. In terms of physical set-up, many such classroom settings may include traditional configurations of chairs and tables, but not necessarily. The common factor of the learning settings considered here is a structured opportunity for dialogue – active, multi-way engagement (whether between educator and learners or between learners) around a particular topic. In the simplest terms, I define a CAL classroom setting as a structured opportunity for active exploration of one's own and others' views. A classroom could theoretically, therefore, take the form of an archaeological dig, a science experiment or a nature walk as well as more traditional lecture-style presentations – the key factor being the chance for learners to both listen and respond as part of their learning engagement.

Specific classroom challenges

If classrooms were machines, they would have innumerable handles, cogs, pulleys and wheels, both visible and hidden.

Corporate and individual classroom learning experiences are influenced by a huge number of interconnected factors. Where 'a syllabus is two-dimensional ... a classroom is dynamic, organic and multidimensional', meaning that many factors are out of educators' (and even learners') immediate control.[1] Any aspect of learners' previous assumptions and experiences (religious, cultural, political or otherwise), the mode of learning (online, face-to-face, size of group), neurodiversities, or challenges specific to certain topics can combine in creating an infinitely complex learning landscape; so the list of potential variables influencing where learners may find *optimum distance* (the sweet spot giving access to just enough familiarity and disruption to explore new ideas) is also seemingly endless.

These possibilities mean that the optimum combinations of disruption and comfort created in classroom learning environments are more realistically represented as a *sweet network* rather than a sweet spot. Therefore, classroom environments in which disruptive-inclusive CAL can best happen are not created by attempting to strictly control any single factor, but rather in developing both learners' and educators' awareness of the interplay between 'classroom content, context and community'[2] and the 'pedagogical agility'[3] to influence and respond as nimbly as possible. In my own practice, both as teacher and learner, I have experimented with many ways of achieving these; however, the most successful of my attempts can be split into four categories: first, setting a trajectory towards optimum distance; second, recentring classroom learning on embracing tension; third, making the end a beginning; and finally, providing learners with opportunities to practise moving in and out of disruptive inclusion beyond the classroom.

Setting a trajectory towards optimum distance

Many general classroom teaching textbooks begin with the claim that starter activities play a pivotal role in establishing positive direction, building learner confidence and providing a solid basis for ongoing engagement. However, disruptive inclusion challenges some of these claims by suggesting that too much comfort and familiarity can stifle, rather than encourage, learning engagement and progress. Here, I consider the kinds of starters that can effectively facilitate disruptive-inclusive CAL and are most likely to result in optimum distance.

The setting

The following example is from a course introducing the foundational concepts of biblical interpretation and a variety of approaches to the topic, equipping learners to identify and critically consider their own and others' views and practices. It was originally delivered to a group of adult learners representing a wide range of ages, social locations and academic levels but almost all from Charismatic Evangelical backgrounds. Accordingly, the formation and delivery of the module content was informed by a deep awareness that even its premise (that there is more than one appropriate way to interpret the Bible) would probably be deeply theologically disruptive for many.

The activity

The opening activity focused on an eighteenth-century neoclassical French painting, Jacques-Louis David's 1787 work, *The Death of Socrates*. Offering no information about the painting, the session began with the tutor showing the painting to the group and inviting learners to share their initial responses to the work in pairs. Then, in turn, volunteers were invited to reflect their neighbour's first impressions with the group, noting down some of the key vocabulary used. In my experience, this initial conversation has included general observations and basic opinions on the painting's overall style and, in some cases, a particular focus on the characters depicted. Then learners watched a short video called 'The Death of Socrates:

How to read a painting', in which learners were inducted into a variety of ways in which the painting has been understood (this whole section will make more sense if you are able to watch the 7-minute video).[4] In the video the critic explains the setting of Greek philosophy that informs the work, proposes different techniques for interpreting its colours, shapes and patterns when read from left to right or right to left, and identifies how and where the painting was initially, and has since, been received and influenced other artists.

This was followed by an invitation for learners to discuss with a (preferably different) partner the following carefully worded question: 'In the light of this new information, what does the painting mean?' After several minutes' discussion, a final question was raised: 'What does the painting mean *to you*?' and learners were asked to decide which question is 'correct' (or 'more appropriate', depending on the group's response). The discussion at this stage was generally deeply impassioned and enthusiastic, even (and arguably, perhaps particularly) among those who initially expressed a complete lack of interest or disinclination towards visual art. On many occasions, vociferous debate about the significance of David's double signature on the work and the function of specific characters within the composition continued well into the coffee break.

Analysis

The above exercise was carefully designed to create the optimum conditions for disruptive inclusion. First, by requesting learners to represent their neighbour's opinions (rather than their own), student voices formed a learning environment that was not dominated by a few unqualified opinions but shaped by the accurate and respectful representation of a range of perspectives. The choice of neoclassical art as the opening theme for a session on biblical interpretation made an 'unexpected other' the focus of the conversation. Particularly with the group in question, many learners would have entered the session expecting potentially controversial and defensive discussions from the outset. Engaging learners on a topic on which none (or very few) have strong pre-existing views avoids beginning with emotionally charged postures that can stifle genuine exploration in conversations in which much is deemed at stake. Finally, as a piece of visual art, 'reading' a painting bypasses some of the unnecessary barriers to higher level critical engagement faced by those with dyslexia and other neurodiversities, low literacy or English as an additional language, when reading written texts.

In disruptive-inclusive terms, the activities create various learning opportunities. Building on our earlier discussion concerning the role of unconscious learning, when dealing with potentially highly disruptive learning content, optimum distance is more effectively achieved when learners are unaware of exactly how disruption is occurring, usually because it is presented in an unforeseen way. In the above example, learners benefitted from the fact that an experience of optimum distance preceded (and therefore provided a background and framework for) the potentially paradigm-shifting later discussions concerning biblical interpretation. In other words, learners were given the chance to participate in a discussion about the key components of biblical interpretation before they knew it. When learners know, or are warned to expect, learning disruption, they are more likely to adopt a defensive and self-protective stance rather than an open, engaged posture. In other words, telling students that they are going to find something challenging or controversial very often functions as a kind of self-fulfilling prophecy.

Although learner awareness and agency remain important, there is a significant benefit to learners experiencing disruptive learning first and then being inducted into its understanding and explanation. In this case, the art exercise gives learners a significant opportunity to explore the foundational merits and challenges of 'behind the text', ' in text' and 'in front of the text' interpretational modes without such terms first (or even perhaps ever) being introduced into the wider discourse.[5] If an educator does choose to directly introduce such terms later, the trajectory of meaningful, respectful discussion is already well under way and there is no need for the associated hermeneutical challenges to be passively explained to learners. At this point, learners have not only already begun to explore and understand their implications but also already participated in establishing their importance.

Beyond this, the above exercise leverages the fact that it is easier for class or cohort groups to access optimum distance together. In this case, neoclassical French art functions as a suitable, shared entry point into the discussion because the vast majority of learners are equally ignorant of, and emotionally uninvested, in the topic at the outset. This encourages collective empathy; a sense of exploring together rather than drawing attention to pre-existing differences in learner experience and ability.[6] Where learners might otherwise express their views on biblical interpretation in terms of 'I' versus 'you' or 'us' versus 'them', corporate engagement in a new topic means that ongoing dialogue is often introduced by such phrases as, 'When we were discussing the painting earlier' or, 'I find it interesting that our conclusions about the painting ...'. This does not aim to discourage diversity of opinion but highlights how disruptive learning techniques can be much more openly acknowledged and addressed when groups of learners contribute to, and therefore share ownership over, corporate progress. It makes it far less likely that any individual learner will be easily excluded from, or sidelined in, the discussion.

Evaluation: starting, risking and creating opportunities to rehearse

It is important to recognize that some of the observations in this section are in direct conflict with some generally accepted wider wisdom and practice concerning classroom teaching. Most specifically, many teaching textbooks advise educators to begin sessions at the point of maximum and most intuitive connection between learners and course content, or as Robyn Jackson's 2018 book, *The Principles of Great Teaching*, suggests: 'Start Where Your Students Are'.[7] Jackson claims that learning should begin in a place of comfort for learners because it begins a positive feedback loop between the familiarity of the known, tried, tested and pleasing and the potential risks associated with learning. She argues:

> For many of our students, intrinsic motivation has to be developed. It comes only after they have experienced the pleasure of doing well and know the rewards of success ... it is so important to start with what motivates them and then, as they experience more success, help them transfer or become motivated by that success.[8]

For this reason, many educators choose to begin classroom learning sessions with something easy and intuitive.

At first, Jackson's logic seems to align with Hull's foundational suggestion of CAL as connection. However, disruptive inclusion suggests that reinforcing existing feedback loops between comfort, familiarity and learning success makes breaking out of such cycles increasingly difficult, perhaps even impossible (remember my Mum's fixed views on Scotland!). Provided it is carefully managed, meaningful engagement in unfamiliar (and preferably also emotionally insignificant) topics is an effective way to encourage learners in the direction of optimum distance. Disruptive inclusion suggests that the best way to induct learners into new patterns of connected learning is not to reinforce existing connections but to invite them to explore the creation of new connections in low-risk areas before progressing on to the challenges of more potentially significant disruptions. The reinforcement of existing connections without their interrogation makes effective CAL less, not more, likely. Put another way, although it may seem nonsensical, putting emotional distance between learner and subject material can be far more effective than pedagogical proximity in encouraging long-term learner connection. Therefore the disruptive-inclusive educator's task is to locate particular topics that can function well as entrance points for different topics.

However, in another sense, rather than directly contradicting the claim that learning ought to begin in a familiar place, the above example demonstrates how, over time, the aim of disruptive inclusion is to help learners become acquainted with, and skilled at engaging with, the unknown and uncomfortable. In other words, to help learners practise becoming comfortable with discomfort. As per multiple strands of our discussion to this point, rather than accepting an either-or choice between the familiar and unfamiliar, the comfortable and uncomfortable, disruptive inclusion engages across these categories and suggests that the best learning occurs as previously excluded themes and styles find a place and function in the learning experience. Therefore, in a significant way, disruptive inclusion does not dispute Jackson's insistence on beginning where students are, but suggests that this location is not static, and so meeting learners in the in-between is the most effective way to help them to keep moving!

Finally, the above example of a disruptive-inclusive starter activity demonstrates how the disruption of an emotionally distanced learning activity gives an educator far greater agility in navigating between the extremes that theologian Nancy Howell identifies as 'a pedagogy of natural selection' and 'a pedagogy of protection'.[9] The first idea recalls the sink or swim metaphor noted in the Introduction. Students are dropped in deep water and their drowning or surviving depends solely on individual learners' swimming abilities. Disruptive learning tasks do not need to work on the premise of the survival of the fittest! Howell's second option recognizes the equally unhelpful tendency of some educators to become so involved in their students' learning experience that, rather than facilitating learners' engagement, they engage in the disruption on their behalf. However, in choosing a topic that is equally distanced from as many learners as possible, educators can more easily and accurately adjust levels of disruption and maximize potential engagement as the session progresses.

Relating this theme to earlier discussions of crossing boundaries or moving in and out of known and comfortable learning territories, the most effective disruptive-inclusive starter activities increase learner opportunities to navigate at the 'edge' of their experience or comfort zones. In this case, the lower risk and shared space of the art exercise lay the foundations for subsequent discussions concerning biblical interpretation. The open, respectful, inquisitive and unencumbered tone of the conversation around neoclassical French art spills over into the subsequent topics, diluting any potentially overwhelming disruption and suggesting ways of navigating otherwise impenetrable terrain. The above exercises focus on providing multiple low-risk opportunities from which learners can then practise moving back and forward into potentially more highly disruptive learning spaces.

Learners are presented with the opportunity to rehearse repeatedly crossing in and out of disruptive learning territory: the chance to experiment on multiple learning 'dry-runs' before the stakes are raised. In the language of Personal Construct Theory (see Chapter 3), before the learning risk becomes so fundamental that learners shut down due to potential damage to the overall shape and structure of the network, learners can become acquainted with some of the logical arguments and associated emotions of the path ahead. However, it is equally important to recognize that just as the experience of a dry ski slope can only partially imitate and therefore also prepare the first-time skier for the Alps, a learning dry-run cannot, nor should it, mitigate all potential learning risks. To develop the skiing metaphor one level further, an effective, disruptive-inclusive starter activity should function as a pedagogical nursery slope. By providing safe ways to steadily increase levels of disruption, it should allow learners to become sufficiently proficient (and not overwhelmed) at the various stages and transitions of the disruptive surroundings before the need for such skills and awareness is required on narrower and more demanding pistes.

Summary

The first activity of a CAL classroom session should focus on optimizing opportunities for learners to function at optimum distance by offering a 'way in' to a topic that is unfamiliar or unexpected. This creates opportunities to practise operating at the edges of existing awareness, knowledge and comfort and build confidence and agility before the stakes are raised by a change in either setting or topic. It provides opportunities for learners to engage in disruptive learning together, not just observe each other participating, and creates increased flexibility for educators to adjust levels of disruption according to learner response.

Learner checklist

- Think about times when you have been asked to represent your own and others' opinions. What difference does this make to how you present them?
- What have been your best experiences of discussing potentially difficult or controversial learning topics with others? What were the hallmarks of these experiences?
- How do you respond to the idea of 'rehearsing' ideas in safer spaces before the stakes are raised?

Centring on disruptive inclusion: explaining the inexpressible

Having created the conditions for learners to (at the very least begin to) move towards optimum distance, how can the main body of teaching and learning sessions build on this opening trajectory? Put another way, what is at the core of disruptive-inclusive classroom experience? In particular, this section draws on various themes raised in Chapter 4, discussing potential pathways between apophatic and cataphatic knowledge and (potentially) conscious and unconscious learning. Do disruptive-inclusive classroom experiences need to focus on developing learner awareness and/or articulation? Or can CAL function effectively where learner awareness and agency are not possible or advisable?

The setting

The following series of classroom sessions was designed for, and delivered in, a similar setting to the previous section by my former colleague Lizzie Hollow. Their central topic is God as Trinity. As introduced in our discussion of the nature and character of God (Chapter 3), the Trinity is a crucial idea in Christian theology that provides constant reminders of the importance and challenges of articulating the potentially inexpressable. Like no other topic, trinitarian thought illustrates the insufficiency of a solely apophatic or cataphatic approach to learning (at their extremes, the beliefs that nothing or everything can be known). It also provides a good basis to demonstrate some of the key aspects of a disruptive-inclusive classroom educator's role, in facilitating not just an increase in learners' clarity of understanding but also a growth in confidence at navigating the combination of knowable and unknowable.

The activity

The first phase of engagement with the topic is designed to induct learners into the ancient Christian tradition that consists in 'centuries of human attempt to speak the divine, to say the Unsayable, to name the Unnameable'.[10] After the discovery that the concept of Trinity is not named in the Bible (of itself, deeply disruptive for many), discussion proceeds to early expressions of divine three-in-oneness. In turn, this develops into a compilation of a list of analogies used to explain the divine triune nature: an egg comprising shell, white and yolk;

a woman who is simultaneously mother, wife and sister; a plant as 'a root, a stem, and fruit' and how intellectual activity requires 'memory ... intellect ... and will'.[11] One by one, the strengths and limitations of each metaphor are analysed and aligned with ancient Christian heresies.[12]

When there is a general recognition that full representation of the divine triune nature using words is impossible, the second phase moves on to visual representations of the Trinity. Beginning with symbols such as the Celtic knot, class discussion addresses the differences in attempting to visually represent the divine nature rather than explaining it, and eventually progresses on to consideration of Andrei Rublev's famous fifteenth-century icon of 'three angels, exhibiting a shy tenderness'.[13] Learners are invited to analyse the image, suggesting who and what they think is represented and what they draw from it. It is always striking to me how emotive learners' responses to these questions are. They often speak of how they have been moved, as much as informed, by the image, particularly the angels' posture in relation to each other.[14] The final phase focuses on the role of the Trinity in contemporary Christian worship, particularly in music. The group examines a research project on recently created hymns and worship songs which considers the pronouns, prepositions and verbs in the lyrics and asks questions about the impact of the lack of trinitarian language employed.[15]

Analysis

This (unconsciously threefold) pattern of activities reinforces many of the themes we have already discussed. First, the module does not set out to offer unequivocal responses to questions concerning the divine nature. Rather, learners are invited to engage with both the importance and the ultimate insufficiency of attempts to fully understand the nature of God. Invariably, the learning disruption of the topic for many is that, in place of one easily understandable, evidenced and applicable idea, trinitarian thought presents an opportunity to engage with the necessary insufficiency of words and images as 'an attempt to express what is ultimately inexpressible'.[16]

Specifically in the case of learners from Evangelical backgrounds, disruption occurs on multiple levels. In the first phase, the realization that the basis of such a foundational understanding of God's nature cannot be reduced only to the self-authenticating contents of the Bible, but must also include its wider, ongoing interpretation in and by the Church, is a challenging paradigm shift. Also, engaging with the idea that 'the approach to speaking about God ... entails a moment of affirmation as well as negation',[17] that is, acknowledging the limits of reason, adds more disorientation. Second, the focus on imaging God is rarely entirely unfamiliar to learners, but is sometimes unpalatable to those previously instructed to avoid all visual representations of God (usually based in interpretations of passages from the Hebrew Bible instructing Israel to avoid idolatry). In the final phase, the disruption is flipped: the mode of engagement (worship songs) becomes much more familiar to many learners, but the disruption takes the form of considering the theologically connected nature of such experiences through a new lens.

In disruptive-inclusive terms, this series of activities provides learners with multiple opportunities to practise and observe others' attempts at optimum distance. Whether via the relationship between Bible and Church, words, images and silence, understanding and desire, or theological theory and worship, numerous invitations are offered to learners to suspend their existing views and investigate the potential implications of various connections. This session is also an excellent demonstration of the medium being the message. It does not contain a technical presentation of apophatic versus cataphatic knowledge or really any comprehensive discussion at all of how knowledge of God works. However, as the session progresses and learners move from words to images and eventually to music, without finding a definitive resolution in any mode of expression, they experience something of the journey many have taken before them and unconsciously 'find allies in our neglected past'.[18] Sometimes, with hindsight, learners begin to articulate their changing expectations around expressing and articulating who God is, but the immediate experience of this session tends to be a sense of unity – not only with those present in the room, but in joining with all the Church in awe and wonder at who we can know God to be and how God's fullness will probably always be beyond human understanding and articulation.

Recently, I have considered that an appropriate additional final phase to the above sequence of activities would be to show a clip from the 2005 film *Into Great Silence*, which depicts the everyday life of Carthusian monks. Despite being 162 minutes long, the film has very little dialogue: only a few brief interviews with the monks, who speak of their motivation and views of life in the wider world. Without ever stating it, the film's use of 'scenic transitions, as well as cuts between individual shots ... governed mainly by a firm set of oppositions: still/moving, light/dark, silence/sound, work/prayer, interior/exterior'[19] underlines the mechanism of disruptive mutual reinforcement at the heart of disruptive inclusion. Silence is not just what is left over when what is light, loud and exterior has been proven insufficient, but it actively contributes to our understanding of reality. This would offer a profound way-point in the learning journey that many of the students take during this module without undermining its methodology by attempting to explain it. As preacher and theologian Frederick Büchner artfully expounds:

Before the Gospel is a word, it is a silence, a kind of pre-senting of life itself so that we see it not for what at various times we call it – meaningless or meaningful, absurd, beauti-ful – but for what it truly is in all its complexity, simplicity, mystery.[20]

Learner checklist

- What is your natural response when you cannot understand or explain something clearly?
- How do you respond when others ask questions or offer answers that had not occurred to you?
- How do your current approach to formal CAL and what many call devotional time differ? Do you see silence and mystery as more appropriate in one mode than the other?
- Think about one area of your current CAL practice (in any setting or mode). What positive difference could aiming towards optimum distance and centring on disruptive inclusion make?

Making the end a beginning

Where starters are designed to set a disruptive-inclusive trajectory towards optimum distance, and the heart of learning ought to maintain and consolidate a pattern of crossing between the knowable, unknowable and as-yet-unknown, the ends of learning sessions also require a significant paradigm shift to support a disruptive-inclusive learning posture. In approaches to learning that rely on disruption and disorientation, re-establishing interim points for marking progress becomes intrinsically important. In practical terms, learners need guidance and encouragement in expressing their progress on different terms. For example, encouraging learners to note milestones of new topics engaged or existing topics considered from different perspectives, rather than only celebrating attainment-based landmarks.[21]

Therefore, my practical suggestion for a disruptive-inclusive ending to a classroom session, that undermines the pedagogical value of arriving but also recognizes the need for redefined progress markers, is a closing reflective exercise in which learners are asked to identify:

- One thing that I know now that I didn't know before this session.
- One thing that I don't know now that I did know before this session.
- One thing that this session has taught me that I still need to know.
- One tension I am wrestling with as a result of today's session.
- One opportunity before our next session to consider this tension from another perspective.

Learner checklist

- How do you define 'progress' in learning? What kinds of moments/achievements do you think are worth celebrating/ marking?
- How do you notice and celebrate such moments? Or, how could you in future?
- What is your response to living with ongoing learning tensions? Are you more likely to dig in your heels, give up or another response?

Learning beyond the classroom: noticing and practising the disruption of the text

One of the biggest challenges that comes with understanding CAL as happening in all of life, rather than just in classroom settings, is that its success cannot be measured according to how well (by whatever measure) any particular teaching and learning session may have gone! My aims in using disruptive-inclusive techniques in the classroom are that learners may be skilled and confident enough to recreate how they have learned, as well as what they have learned, in situations where the direct guidance of a tutor or educator, or the support of fellow students, is not available. As discussed from the outset, this can take a variety of forms, but as a follow-up to classroom learning, the most common structured opportunity that learners have to practise their learning is via assignments.

The following example comes from the module that began with the neoclassical art starter activity. Assignments were completed in learners' own time and submitted several months after the classroom sessions. I have chosen to include this example for several reasons: first, the submissions for this assignment offered some interesting (and unexpected) insights into the challenges and opportunities of encouraging learners to navigate disruptive inclusion in environments where educators are not present to proactively guide. Second, the following example resonates with multiple earlier themes and provides the opportunity to demonstrate their practical implications. These include the parable of The Good Samaritan as an example of Jesus' disruptive-inclusive teaching methods (see Chapter 3); learners' experience of *koinonia* with those from other times and places by engaging with historical biblical interpretations (see Chapter 4); and the Bible facilitating playful, poetic, in-between CAL (see Chapter 5).

Introduction

The assignment asked students to compare and contrast various interpretations of the passage generally referred to as The Good Samaritan (Luke 10.29–37). These included an allegorical interpretation by Augustine of Hippo; interpretations from Amy-Jill Levine and Craig Evans strongly influenced by other parts of the Bible; and an interpretation considered through the lens of the Indian caste system by M. Gnanavaram.[22] The primary task was to consider the strengths and weaknesses of each interpretation, identify the bases on which these decisions had been made, and compare others' methods and interpretive decisions with their own. There were multiple aims in setting this task. First, although it did provide learners with perhaps a little more reading than was ideal for some (I guided several learners to only engage with a few of the interpretations), being exposed to a diverse range of interpretations created the opportunity to gain some distance from learners' existing, unquestioned readings of the well-known passage and increased the chances of *multiplicity of vision*. In the first part of the task, by asking students to compare and contrast several unfamiliar views (rather than compare their own to one other), it reduced (although did not entirely prevent!) the potential for a defensive posture in which learners seek to protect their pre-existing views from the potential undermining of others. Second, the cultural, ethnic, gender, theological and historical diversity of the interpreters invited learners into the experience of an unlikely, disruptive learning community; and then, third, it invited them to participate in it. By encouraging learners to introduce their own reading of the passage in the final phase of the task and critically compare their own approach with that of others, the final aim of the task was that learners might look beyond what they think the passage means and assess how those decisions were made. Some of the best responses to the task explored how, despite being based in times and places other than their own, diverse interpretations had helped learners to more fully understand and better interrogate their own reading(s).

Response

The responses were rich and varied. Although none of the interpretations received unquestioned support, Augustine's reading attracted the most criticism and scepticism, with multiple learners referring to his interpretation as 'disturbing' and 'dubious'. This aligns with many contemporary scholars' dismissals of Augustine's allegorical reading (where the key characters/objects stand for something else) as 'extrinsic' and 'far-fetched'[23] due to its 'spiritual interpretation', despite the basis of his interpretational approach being very common in his era.[24] For example, in one of his readings, Augustine identifies the inn where the attacked man recovers as the Church and the innkeeper as the Apostle Paul. Central to many learners' general distaste for Augustine's reading of Luke 10.29–37 is his claim that the Samaritan figure represents Christ restoring humanity from certain death (again, in line with many other early views). In contrast, Levine and Evans' conclusions that the passage's central focus is on 'how enemies can prove to be neighbours' or a wider call to 'reassess [a] narrow view of who qualifies as ... "neighbour"'[25] did not attract similarly strong reactions.

A dominant theme from learners well-drilled in the importance of not taking a passage 'out of context' was to judge the various approaches to Luke 10.29–37 according to their perceived proximity to the author's/original intention. One student expressed the concern that 'The interpreter will seek to make the text support his or her preconceived argument rather than allowing it to speak on its own terms.' Fascinatingly, despite this, and where all but a few completely rejected Augustine's interpretation, learners were generally open to Gnanavaram's contextualized reading drawing out similarities between the perception of the outcast Samaritan in the Ancient Near East and the downtrodden Dalit in contemporary Indian society. No student mentioned that, methodologically speaking, neither Augustine nor Gnanavaram claims that their reading is 'identical to "the meaning" for the original audience'.[26] Gnanavaram unapologetically contextualizes the passage in an Indian cultural setting and Augustine (like many of his contemporaries) sees no conflict in arguing 'that the content of the parable interpreted in the Christological sense is true, even if Luke did not intend that sense.'[27] Regardless, many learners accused Augustine of not adhering to interpretational rules that did not exist during his lifetime, meanwhile praising Gnanavaram for what they considered to be an overall valuable and appropriate contemporary contextualization of the passage.

Analysis

Investigating why so many contemporary learners found Augustine's reading misguided and Gnanavaram's (and others like it) praiseworthy, and what this can teach us about disruptive-inclusive CAL and the Bible, requires a much more in-depth analysis of the learning assumptions at play. A fundamental observation, in line with earlier discussions of the Bible facilitating movement between different, seemingly conflicting ideas (Selah 3), is that both Gnanavaram's and Augustine's readings of Luke 10.29–37 seek to recreate Jesus' aim to disrupt a key strand of existing thinking or belief and, crucially, learners were largely unable to identify this. In the words of Stephen Spear, who specializes in Jesus' teaching methods, Jesus' aim was to 'crack the enculturated consciousness of his listeners, thereby moving them from a conventional to a postconventional consciousness and worldview.'[28] Or, as New Testament scholar William Herzog describes, Jesus' parables 're-present a familiar or typified scene for the purpose of generating conversation about it and stimulating the kinds of reflection that expose contradictions in popularly held beliefs or traditional thinking.'[29]

Using Spear's terms, Gnanavaram's interpretation exchanges a conventional model of neighbourliness (associated with power and privilege) for a post-conventional model in which the Samaritan's identity as a victim of negative and oppressive societal stereotypes is exactly what qualifies him as the ideal neighbour. In doing so, he draws a direct connection between the social exclusion of ancient Samaritans and contemporary Dalits in Indian cultural consciousness. 'Dalits cannot be taken as models' in Indian society but Jesus' story inverts this to suggest that 'Dalit people should no more be ashamed of being Dalits' and can be 'rid of their inferiority complex and slave mentality ... as an integral part of Dalit consciousness'.[30] While Gnanavaram's interpretation does not make identification with the Samaritan neighbour impossible, his primary focus is on how emulating the passage's model of neighbourly actions requires the reversal of traditional definitions of neighbourliness and their links to power and privilege.

In contrast, Augustine's reading traces a similar trajectory from conventional to post-conventional but in a very different way. His identification of the Samaritan as Christ recalibrates the listener's/reader's options for taking up their own role within the story. Although contemporary scholars have a far from comprehensive understanding of how Augustine's readings were received by his contemporaries, there is evidence that the most intuitive identification for the story's earliest Christian audiences would have been as giver, not receiver of help. Basing his argument in the letters of Dionysius, a third-century Alexandrian bishop, historian Rodney Stark claims: 'Christian values of love and charity had, from the beginning, been translated into norms of social service and community solidarity. When disasters struck, the Christians were better able to cope.'[31] Therefore, by the time the biblical Gospels were circulating, Jesus' followers had already become synonymous with practical kindness to the poor and needy, although doubtless they were also counted among the sick and suffering.

From this perspective, Gnanavaram and Augustine's shared interpretational method comes into focus, but differently employed. The first argues for a reading of Luke's story that disrupts readers' self-view of victim. In contrast, Augustine's reading, in which 'the whole human race, after all, is that man who was lying in the road, left half-dead by robbers', is most disruptive for those who do not acknowledge their own brokenness and need.[32] If Stark's claim is valid, and a significant element of the ancient Christian community's self-identity was as saviour of the poor and needy, the strongest post-conventional move of Augustine's reading is not only that Christ takes the protagonist role, but that in doing so his listeners/readers are relegated (or promoted, depending on your perspective!) to the relative anonymity of the victim.

Therefore the learning challenge Augustine presents goes beyond a call for a change of action, or even underlying motivation, to a foundational shift in identity. For those with significant social privilege (that is, almost all of the learners completing this assignment), while Gnanavaram's reading has direct implications for the personal identity of those different from them (that is, those who experience significant social discrimination), the suggestion that neighbourliness begins by acknowledging self-need and welcoming support from unexpected sources is potentially significantly and more directly disruptive.

As we touched on briefly earlier, this process of decentralization is reinforced by Jesus' engagement with the lawyer (Luke 10.25) in a process that Spear summarizes as Jesus leading 'his listeners from a consciousness dominated by culture to an alternative way of life centred on God'.[33] Specifically, 'Jesus does not directly answer the question "Who is my neighbour?" but redirects attention to the slightly different question, "Who proved neighbour to the man?".'[34] In this way 'Jesus has transformed the focus of the original question; in fact, Jesus' apparent attempt to answer the lawyer's question turns out to be a negation of that question's premise.'[35] In presenting the lawyer as the subject of the question in 10.29 (both grammatically and thematically), the lawyer's desire to follow Jesus' suggestion to love his neighbour as himself is revealed (10.27). However, it simultaneously reveals his inability to fulfil his duty and receive his reward without also being willing and able to identify with his neighbour.

In the simplest terms, by asking who proved neighbour to the robbed man, Jesus reveals that Christian neighbourliness does not begin with helping others but in a willingness to be helped. New Testament scholar Riemer Roukema summarizes this idea: 'Before they [Augustine's contemporary Christian audience] were ready to identify themselves with the Samaritan who showed his love towards a wounded man, they first had identified themselves with the wounded man helped by the Samaritan.'[36] The key word in the above quote is 'first'. Similarly, many other ancient voices do not rule out the idea of the Samaritan as a model to follow.[37] Rather, and similarly important to both ancient and contemporary audiences, for those already societally perceived as good neighbours (the lawyer in the passage included) Augustine's interpretation betrays the belief that the message of the passage would not translate into changes of attitude or action without a deeply disruptive experience first taking hold.

> The listener's identification with this generic victim allows Jesus to accomplish the purpose of the parable, which is to enable the listener to experience postconventional compassion. To be told that one should be compassionate is not transforming, but to experience compassion is.[38]

Summary and evaluation

In summary, Augustine's reading of Luke 10.29–37 reveals that the Bible's learning methodology is designed to engage learners in a far more holistic experience than just cognitive awareness of new information. Ultimately, this means that the primary function of Augustine's reading is to recreate the lawyer's disruptive experience for a new audience, even if this results, by contemporary standards, in a different message. Applied more widely, this means that the learning value of engaging with pre-Enlightenment (early seventeenth-century and older) biblical interpretations is in their ability to catalyse and guide disruptive learning experiences that are able to further lead to changes in thought and action.

As tutor of this module, my most interesting learning from this exercise was its demonstration of how social location plays (and has always played) a significant role in disruptive-inclusive learning experiences. Although learners do not leave their 'real' identities behind when they arrive at the classroom, entering a physical classroom does signal a temporary suspension of the conditions and expectations associated with their professional and personal lives. However, when learners return to their 'home' settings and re-engage in learning tasks, it is more difficult for them to take a step back from their immediate environment and work from some form of optimum distance. Therefore learners tend to revert back to comfortable territory and unquestioned, well-practised techniques. In this case, this took the form of learners closely analysing how the content of Jesus' challenge may or may not have disrupted the lawyer's thinking. However, few also considered that the wider and deeper message may be embedded in how Jesus used disruption to invite the lawyer to have his imagination transformed, and then comparing this method with the other readings. Overall, this task offered students a guided opportunity to rehearse the patterns of disruptive-inclusive learning begun in the classroom. To further improve similar exercises in future, I will provide a grid for learners to complete in preparation for their assignments, encouraging them to investigate the potential underpinning reasoning of the interpretations as well as their substance.

Learner checklist

- Do you learn differently on your own than in others' company or in more formal settings? What differences do you notice?
- When was the last time your views on the 'meaning' of a Bible passage changed significantly? What caused those changes?
- Read The Good Samaritan. As which character in the story do you imagine yourself? Which role does God/Jesus take? How is this similar to or different from some of the options discussed here?
- Think of a character that learns or undergoes significant change in the Bible. Do you know how or why that change happens? What evidence could you give? Is it the kind of transformation that contemporary Christians could try to emulate?

Questions/activities

- How do you respond to my claims about using less emotionally demanding topics as gateways into the experience of disruptive inclusion? What are the potential benefits and challenges?
- How aware are you of your own learning processes? How often do you practise articulating what you are learning and how? If you find these questions hard to answer, can you identify why?
- How can disruptive-inclusive educators and learners celebrate their own progress and support others in doing the same? What kind of habits could you and your learning community incorporate into your everyday practice?
- Explain a transformative classroom session you have experienced. What made it compelling? How would you re-create this for others?

Notes

1 Nancy R. Howell, 'Proleptic pedagogy, pluralism and pedagogical agility' in S. Mattaei and N. Howell, *Proleptic Pedagogy: Theological education anticipating the future* (Eugene, OR: Cascade Books, 2014), pp. 8–28, p. 8.

2 Howell, 'Proleptic pedagogy', p. 13.

3 Howell, 'Proleptic pedagogy', p. 10.

4 The Nerdwriter, 'The Death of Socrates: How to read a painting' (2015), https://youtu.be/rKhfFBbVtFg (accessed 31.07.12).

5 For more on this see chapter 1 of Joel B. Green, *Hearing the New Testament: Strategies for interpretation* (Grand Rapids, MI: Wm. B. Eerdmans, 2010).

6 It also minimizes the shame associated with being wrong.

7 Robyn Renee Jackson, *Never Work Harder than Your Students and Other Principles of Great Teaching* (Alexandria, VA: ASCD, 2018), chapter 1.

8 Jackson, *Never Work Harder*, p. 51.

9 Howell, 'Proleptic pedagogy', p. 13.

10 Maria Harris, *Teaching and Religious Imagination: An essay in the theology of teaching* (San Francisco: Harper & Row, 1987), p. 16.

11 Declan Marmion and Rik Van Nieuwenhove, *An Introduction to the Trinity* (Cambridge: Cambridge University Press, 2010), p. 13.

12 In particular, learners enjoy a satirical video, 'St. Patrick's Bad Analogies', in which two pilgrims question Saint Patrick as to the nature of the Trinity and demonstrate the insufficiency of his various arguments. Available here: https://youtu.be/KQLfgaUoQCw (accessed 8.11.2023).

13 Marmion and Van Nieuwenhove, *An Introduction to the Trinity*, p. 24. While probably the most famous image representing Abraham and Sarah's mysterious visitors in Genesis 18, it represents a much wider iconic tradition focused on this scene.

14 For more on this, see Marmion and Van Nieuwenhove, *An Introduction to the Trinity*.

15 Mike Tapper, Britt Terry and Jacob Clapp, 'Painting in full spectrum', *Worship Leader* 29:3 (2020), pp. 32–8. Available from: https://issuu.com/wlmag/docs/wl_vol_29_no_3 (accessed 31.07.23).

16 Paul M. Collins, *The Trinity: A guide for the perplexed* (London: T&T Clark, 2008), p. 53. See Romans 11.33–36.

17 Marmion and Van Nieuwenhove, *An Introduction to the Trinity*, p. 14.

18 John L. Thompson, *Reading the Bible with the Dead: What you can learn from the history of exegesis that you can't learn from exegesis alone* (Grand Rapids, MI: Wm. B. Eerdmans, 2007), p. 6.

19 Paul Arthur, 'Review: Into Great Silence', *Cinéaste* 32:3 (2007), pp. 71–3, p. 72.

20 Frederick Büchner, *Telling the Truth: The Gospel as tragedy, comedy, and fairy tale* (San Francisco, CA: Harper & Row, 1977), p. 25.

21 For an interesting discussion of the theological nature of learning outcomes that recognizes both their limitations and their necessity, see Clive Marsh, '"Learning outcome" as a theological concept', *Journal of Adult Theological Education* 11:2 (2014), pp. 110–22.

22 See Roland Teske, 'The Good Samaritan (Luke 10:29–37) in Augustine's exegesis' in F. Van Fleteren and J. Schnaubelt (eds), *Augustine: Biblical Exegete* (New York, NY: Peter Lang, 2001); Amy-Jill Levine, 'The many faces of the Good Samaritan – most wrong', *Biblical Archaeology* 38:1 (2012), p. 24; Craig A. Evans, 'Luke's Good Samaritan and the Chronicler's Good Samaritan' in T. R. Hatina (ed.), *Biblical Interpretation in Early Christian Gospels. Vol. 3, Gospel of Luke* (London: T&T Clark, 2010) and M. Gnanavaram, '"Dalit Theology" and the Parable of the Good Samaritan', *Journal for the Study of the New Testament* 15:50 (1993), pp. 59–83.

23 Joseph A. Fitzmyer, *The Gospel According to Luke I–IX* (New Haven, CT: Yale University Press, 1995), p. 885.

24 Teske, 'The Good Samaritan', p. 349. For more, see Riemer

Roukema, 'The Good Samaritan in Ancient Christianity', *Vigiliae Christianae* 58:1 (2004), pp. 56–97. Clement and Origen's interpretations of Luke 10.29–37 are also very interesting.

25 Levine, 'The many faces', p. 24 and Evans, 'Luke's Good Samaritan', p. 42.

26 Gnanavaram, 'Dalit Theology', p. 75.

27 Teske, 'The Good Samaritan', p. 356.

28 Stephen Spear, 'The transformation of enculturated consciousness in the teachings of Jesus', *Journal of Transformative Education* 3:4 (2005), pp. 354–73, p. 354.

29 William R. Herzog, *Parables as Subversive Speech: Jesus as pedagogue of the oppressed* (Louisville, KY: Westminster John Knox Press, 1994), p. 26.

30 Gnanavaram, 'Dalit Theology', pp. 81 and 78.

31 Rodney Stark, *The Rise of Christianity: A sociologist reconsiders history* (Princeton, NJ: Princeton University Press, 1996), p. 74.

32 Teske, 'The Good Samaritan', p. 351 quoting *Sermo CLXXI*, 2: PL XXXVIII, p. 933.

33 Spear, 'The transformation', p. 355.

34 Spear, 'The transformation', p. 370, quoting Craig L. Blomberg, *Interpreting the Parables* (Downers Grove, IL: IVP Academic, 2012), p. 231.

35 Joel B. Green, *The Gospel of Luke* (Grand Rapids, MI: Wm. B. Eerdmans, 1997), p. 380.

36 Roukema, 'The Good Samaritan', p. 73.

37 For example, 'Augustine – along with Ambrose, Origen, and Irenaeus – would have us understand the parable of the Good Samaritan as revealing Christ's loving mercy toward our fallen race and as teaching us that his love for us provides the standard and model of how we should love one another.' Teske, 'The Good Samaritan', p. 357.

38 Spear, 'The transformation', p. 371.

7

Disruptive Inclusion from the Pulpit

In the last chapter we began by focusing on the practical out-working of disruptive inclusion in learning settings that include clear opportunities for interactive dialogue. However, for most Christian adults their principal, regular, formal learning occurs in a format that does not traditionally allow for open inter-action. Therefore this chapter explores what Hull referred to as 'the traditional sermon ... sometimes called a "teaching" sermon',[1] addressing his 'gravest doubts about the educational value of the sermon'[2] and demonstrating how a disruptive-inclusive approach to sermonizing addresses his concerns.

Hull's misgivings did not hold him back from preaching. He was a regular (and popular) preacher at Queen's Foundation chapel services during the final part of his career,[3] as well as an invited guest preacher at weddings, academic institutions and the churches he attended throughout his life. His sermon transcripts demonstrate the centrality of the biblical text to his approach, with each message focused on unpacking a Bible passage. His questions concerning the educational value of preaching relate to how the general setting of much teaching and preaching, in 'restrained silence', creates an individualistic and non-participatory learning environment that resists 'any kind of personal exchange or dialogue'.[4] Because of this, Hull summarized teaching sermons as an 'autonomous activity ... a neurotic obsessional substitute for learning ... pietistic prac-tice'[5] in which learners' assumptions are 'taken for granted not realized'[6] because they remain 'unexamined ... they do not attract our attention as being debateable'.[7] As already demon-strated, I am not shy in highlighting where I believe existing ineffective learning modes and methods should not continue.

However, in this case I entirely disagree with Hull's claim that traditional teaching sermons are, by definition, an unsuitable vehicle for effective CAL. Here I will both explain and demonstrate how what Hull perceived as a restrictive and disconnected learning mode can create unique opportunities for communal, interactive and participative CAL.

My counter argument begins in Hull's own work. Although it is fair to say that his comments on the topic are mentioned rather than fully developed, Hull clearly acknowledges the possibility that 'a process of dialogical introspection (exploring one's own Christian memory in company with others)' is not only possible, but key to CAL.[8] In other words, connection within CAL does not always take the form of active group engagement; it can happen introspectively within individual learners. Also, and again despite Hull's consistent criticism of the disconnected and individualistic learning patterns which he claims define the traditional sermon format, he leaves the door slightly ajar to other possibilities: 'One can learn alone, although even with a book one is not entirely alone.'[9] This recognizes that even where live dialogical exchange with others is not possible or is not the aim, the potential for interactive, connected CAL remains. Again, building on previous discussions, this chapter will demonstrate how disruptive-inclusive sermons can achieve this via two principal techniques: story and imagination.

Story and imagination

The function of story in theological views of human understanding and reflection is widely documented.[10] Analysis of particular ways in which 'stories can serve important ... functions in support of learning processes', specifically in CAL as well as more generally, has significantly increased during my lifetime.[11] Stories are recognized as fundamental to human experience: 'We are soaked to the bone in story' ... 'thoroughly desensitized to their weird and witchy power' ... 'chugging away beneath our awareness'.[12] Therefore story has both a levelling and invitational effect on learning. As humans, we are all similarly helpless in resisting being drawn into narrative learning participation.

As noted by literary scholar Jonathan Gottschall, story and disruption are inextricably intertwined. 'Regardless of genre, if there is no knotty problem, there is no story.'[13] By definition, story depends on unexpected twists and turns; it requires disruption to exist. Therefore, as promised in Chapter 4, we return to James K. A. Smith's work in which he understands CAL and formation as 'living into a story'.[14] In line with this, disruptive inclusion can be thought of as a process of pedagogical 'restor(y)ing', displacing learners from the story/ies in which they have participated thus far and inviting them to experiment with alternatives.[15]

The full implications of Smith's idea of 'restorying' become clearer when considered alongside the alternatives. As examined in earlier chapters, instructional and problem-solving models engage learners in a one-way journey towards 'correct' answers and measure progress in terms of proximity to error-free performance. On the other hand, the basic expectation of successful storied learning is that its optimum path is rarely direct and uncomplicated. As with all good story, a bit of drama is par for the course! A good example of this is a classic story such as *The Wizard of Oz*. The success of Dorothy's journey cannot be reduced to arriving back home in Kansas; the signs that she is progressing are embedded in her and her companions' characters. Her learning was facilitated (not diverted) by the unknowns of the Yellow Brick Road and the Emerald City.

From a variety of perspectives, it would be difficult to devise a more effective vehicle for disruptive-inclusive CAL than well-crafted story. One of the reasons for this is that story is not a one-time event; it finds its identity in varied and repeated retelling. In the case of CAL, this is best demonstrated in the relationship between the Church and the biblical story. 'We seek story because we enjoy it. But nature designed us to enjoy stories so we would get the benefit of practice.'[16] Therefore the most effective and enjoyable stories are those most widely practised. Whether folk tale, fable, Gospel, biography, cartoon or advertisement, stories reveal the repetitive, broad and participative nature of learning. Building on the previous chapter's claim that classrooms should function as rehearsal rooms for disruptive inclusion: 'Practice is important. People practice ... in low stakes environments so that they will perform well ... when the stakes are high ... story is where people go to practice the skills of human social life.'[17]

Story is also naturally communal, which begins to address Hull's unease with what he perceived as the unavoidably individualistic learning format of teaching sermons. Although a group of people listening together may appear to be a passive, solo learning activity, when it includes story there is significant opportunity for highly interactive, engaged and corporate learning to take place. Theologians and psychologists Brad Strawn and Warren Brown refer to a collective, narrative Christian identity formed by how 'frequently, others help us narrate our lives and the stories others tell us about ourselves.'[18] Philosopher Paul Fairfield adds how the learning function of story 'provides knowledge of what actions are acceptable and in what circumstances ... In other words, narratives instil norms and shape our understanding of what we and others are doing.'[19]

The key element of these observations is that story is an unavoidably connected activity. Whether directly or indirectly, story always addresses someone rather than presenting as abstract theory. Even if you read a story on your own, it is 'a form of inclusion of what is outside of oneself, and for the sake of something larger ... you are never truly alone.'[20] In summary, the structure and mode of story, and storied learning, is deeply (and almost unavoidably) relational, inviting communal participation and response. Even when considered from a scientific perspective, theologian John Milbank argues that stories and understanding self and wider reality are inseparable:

Science does not rid itself of narrative, and indeed, it is just as possible to tell a story in which the characters are atoms, plants, animals, or quasars, as one where they are human beings. Moreover, these stories are always necessarily – however disguised this may become – stories of our human interrelationships, and our social relationships to the natural world.[21]

The repetitive and collective characteristics of storied learning provide a strong basis for how traditional sermon format can facilitate conversational learning participation, even when actual live conversation is not possible. However, to fully understand how this works we must add another key concept into the relationship between learning and story: imagination. This is not, of course, the first time the theme of imagination has appeared in our discussions – it has played a significant role throughout. In Chapter 1 I claimed that we need to reimagine CAL methodology. In Chapter 3 we considered Kwok's suggestion that two-way biblical interpretation should be referred to as 'dialogical imagination'.[22] In Chapter 4 we explored Smith's argument of how regular Christian practice unconsciously transforms learners via 'the conversion of the imagination' and how hospitality creates the opportunity for 'communal imagination'.[23] In Chapter 5 we saw how playful poetics helps learners weave their way between real and imaginary worlds.[24]

Many people immediately associate imagination with fiction and invention. However, as we saw in the earlier discussion of play, when children take the roles of nurses, police officers and parents, the stories they rehearse are not completely 'made up' but deeply embedded in lived experience. Their playful reimaginings of real-life scenarios such as an arrest, medical appointment or childcare arrangements are undertaken as if they had real consequences. 'Children's play is not escapist … play is deadly serious fun. Every day, children enter a world where they must confront dark forces, fleeing and fighting for their lives.'[25] This connection with reality provides children the opportunity to explore the jeopardy of adult life scenarios without the associated consequences. Similarly, when adults exercise their imaginations there are important, real-life implications.

In addition, imagination is often thought of as an internal, individual activity. 'You can't depend on anyone else for imagination. It is the most private and interior of human faculties.'[26] However, religious educationalist Beth Green, using the work of philosopher Charles Taylor (as is true of much contemporary theological discussion about imagination), demonstrates the external and grounded implications of the relationship between imagination and learning:[27]

> The social imaginary is a concept tied to the question of how Western modernity understands itself. Taylor writes that 'the differences amongst today's multiple modernities need to be understood in terms of the divergent social imaginations involved' (pp. 1–2). Taylor is not using the word 'imagination' here to refer to fiction, fantasy or to the inner world; as in 'she has an active imagination' (Smith and Cooling 2017). Taylor is using it to refer to the way people understand the world they live in, how they fit into that world alongside others and what assumptions inform their expectations about what is normal.[28]

Taylor understands imagination as a task of understanding how to live in and fit into the world alongside others. Although this does not rule out the importance of individual responsibility, it begins to highlight how imagination can facilitate learner connection in the 'real world' even when physical or conversational connection is not possible.

Therefore, returning to Hull's earlier suggestion that interactive CAL can occur via 'dialogical introspection',[29] the combination of story and imagination enables internal conversations within individual learners and across groups of listeners as a whole, providing an alternative mode with similar learning functions to live dialogue. As Strawn and Brown explain:

A critical factor in the power of stories is that, in order to understand the actions in the story, the hearer must create in their imagination a simulation of the actions and interactions described in the narrative. To say within a story, 'he climbed the mountain' is to cause to occur within the hearer's brain systems a quick partial simulation (a mental thumbnail action sketch) of climbing a mountain. Otherwise the hearer cannot adequately appreciate what is being said. Recent brain research has shown activation of the same brain areas in a listener that would be activated if the listener were doing the actions being described in the story.[30]

In terms of brain chemistry, as learners imagine themselves participating in a story, or even consider the personal implications of potential participation,[31] they are actively participating as if they were engaging in the imagined conversation or performing the imagined action – there is no difference in brain activity. Physiologically, humans cannot resist imaginative participation in story and, as Harris summarizes, as we do so 'we can alter our existence'.[32]

While imagination comes in as many forms as there are learners (meaning that how, and what, you imagine is very different from me), Harris's reference to 'we' in the above quote reinforces the collective nature of storied learning. As a group of learners engage in story it is ultimately our collective existence that is altered, and therefore I endorse Harris's claim that CAL is driven by a sense of 'communal imagination'.[33] By participating in imaginative, storied learning, disruption occurs at such a fundamental human level that some form of shared experience is impossible to avoid (even if unconsciously). As Büchner puts it,

The distances between the inner world that each of us is, are greater in their way than the distances between the outer worlds of interstellar space, but in another way, the world of all of us are also the same world.[34]

Büchner's point here is that, even though differences in individuals' internal worlds may seem to separate us from each other, when we realize that our diverse imaginings join us in shared humanity we can begin to find points of connection. Where Hull understands sermons as limiting learners to internal isolation, where learners undergo the 'restor(y)ing of their imagination' participative, shared, communal learning experiences are possible.[35]

Ultimately, this means that *storied imagination* is available to all learners who self-identify as human! Hull argues specifically in relation to CAL: 'Education becomes ecclesial when it is appropriate to the whole body of Christ, when it deals with the solidarity of the Church within the solidarity of humanity.'[36] There is a growing body of evidence about the pedagogical value of story and imagination across the age range, among neurodiverse learners and those with specific neurological disorders.[37] Where learners are unable to recall information, understand and organize concepts or develop problem-solving techniques, participation in disruptive-inclusive CAL is still possible by imagining a different story, a different kind of story or a familiar story retold in a different way or place. Recalling the earlier discussion on playful poetics: 'In genuine works of art, the individual does not feel as an observer of a separate and discrete object; the individual feels a participant within the making of the object itself ... something new is created within the self.'[38] As educationalist Josue Tario recognizes, through imaginative story all learners are presented with active opportunities through which 'Movement, uncertainty, and vulnerability can become tools that generate new meanings, new imaginations, and new forms of becoming human.'[39] In the imagining and reimagining of stories, a learner

> [f]ully embraces feelings like 'I don't completely belong in one or the other' because it embraces the unpredictability of becoming human. It embraces the perpetual suspension between the past (being) and the future (non-being). It thrives

in learning to abide in the present moment, in the possibility of becoming something, someone new.[40]

Over time, whether consciously or otherwise, entering into this practice of imaginative storytelling allows learners not only to get used to the tension of learning at optimum distance, but also to come to associate it with their own identity. To be a storied Christian learner is to be defined by the fact that 'the journey or process of "unfinishedness" is at times contradicting and painful but can also be blissfully peaceful.'[41] The idea that the fundamental function of humanity is to get somewhere effectively is replaced with the task of being here well. As a basic expression of human identity, learning is 'to experience and embrace this dialectical relationship between pain and joy, self-love and love for others, difference and commonality, and as much as we don't like to talk about it, life and death.'[42] Storied imagination provides opportunities for engaging in connected learning (that is, when live dialogue is unavailable) and broader and deeper motivation for participation. Exploring how our own stories interact with those of others and the story of God is not just about achieving short-term, individual goals but a far more fundamental tool by which the people of God navigate who we already are and continually imagine and reimagine who we might wish to become!

Learner checklist

- What are the most common stories that you tell about yourself? What do they reveal about you? What are the most common stories told in your family/community?
- Have you ever thought about the relationship between faith, imagination and learning before? What questions does it raise for you?
- Away from formal learning settings, what kinds of story do you enjoy? Books? Film? Podcasts? Music? How might these help you practise storied learning techniques?

Restor(y)ing the imagination via the biblical teaching sermon

Having laid the foundations for storied imagination, the next step is to begin to tease out ways that it can be used by preachers to create opportunities for disruptive-inclusive CAL. Homiletics (the art form of preaching) is a vast discipline, with multiple different strands with their own aims and structures, requiring a variety of different skills. As with the previous chapter, I have chosen to concentrate my examples in a single area to avoid generalization. In line with Hull's direct criticism of their educational value, the following lenses, observations, suggestions and worked example focus on the exposition of the biblical text in sermons, or what Hull refers to as a Bible teaching sermon.

The first guiding lens for how storied imagination can take shape in teaching sermons comes from the work of Mark Allan Powell, who understands the format as an invitation to 'cast the scriptures'.[43] Powell's strategy proposes that preachers imagine casting a particular biblical text as a theatre production.[44] Who would play the roles? How would lines be delivered? Against what backdrop does the action take place? However, Powell also suggests that a single imagining is insufficient. Rather, in a move that strongly aligns with multiplicity of vision, he suggests that preachers should 'Force yourself to empathize with a different character and to experience the story from that character's point of view.'[45] Although Powell does not specify whether the aim is to empathize with a character from within the story or with a character from the story's potential audience, both can be effective in helping to 'Discern polyvalence, to identify a fuller range of options by which audiences can and do create meaning for themselves out of the raw materials the text provides.'[46]

Via this process of engaging with multiple perspectives, Powell argues that the empathy he seeks to build is best achieved by casting both self in the play (personally engaging in storied imagination) and also an understudy who plays the part very differently. This way, the audience is invited into the repeated and varied performance of the play, not to either passively consume or mimic the version on offer. As Brueggemann says of the prophetic voices of the Hebrew Bible: 'The preacher is deeply embedded in the YHWH narrative'[47] and therefore the message cannot be delivered from *without*, because 'teaching *is* the incarnation of subject matter'.[48]

Second, however, as Ellen Davis recognizes, as preachers deeply embed themselves in the process it is important not to attempt to adorn or obscure the biblical text with self (or anything else!) but to draw attention to its existing, compelling beauty:

> Be careful about using an example that is too good, too 'unforgettable'. If your preaching is doing what it should do, then people probably won't remember what you said, and it doesn't matter. Your goal should be that the next time they turn to that part of the Bible, *it* will say a little more to them. *The purpose of preaching is to give the text a little more room to shine.*[49]

As we explored at the end of Chapter 5, my suggestion here is not that every biblical text is easily appreciated as beautiful but rather that a significant element of CAL via restorying the imagination invites a richer, deeper, more tension-filled definition of beauty. Philosophical theologian Karmen MacKendrick explains this sense of redefined beauty so eloquently that I include her description in full:

> What we hear will be strange, as our words and others' and the world's echo and redouble one another, offering both praise for the world as it is and petition for the world as it ought to be, for beauty mourned ... To attend with care, as if to beauty, is not only to discern strangeness, but also even to *make* strange, to force oneself out of the known and the familiar – even in the face *of* the known and the familiar. This is what art often does, transforming rather ordinary

objects and sounds and movement by the very act of presenting them for our attention. In this, in fact, is some important
part of the long shift of our aesthetic sensibility away from
the classical sense of an ordered and symmetrical beauty and
toward a broader sense of the interesting, the surprising, the
arresting ... To welcome beauty is to welcome that making-
strange, looking again at what was boringly familiar; the
strangeness of art, of philosophy, of madness, of love. Even
what we already saw, already knew, may hold the possibility
of something else, of beginning again in wonder.[50]

MacKendrick's claim is that without denying the pain and
challenge of certain biblical passages, the *beauty* of any given
text or interpretation of it is not solely contained in or defined
by the words on the page, but also in the readers'/listeners'
embrace of the interesting, the surprising, the arresting and the
strange. The very possibility that we may learn to perceive any
given idea or story differently over time (or perhaps that it
might grow in/with us) is, in itself, beautiful. Thus, returning
to Davis's call for the text to be illumined by preachers, even
the most potentially inflammatory words and ideas need not
be apologized for or smoothed over; their evolving strangeness
and enduring challenge can be embraced. In short, Davis presents the teacher's role as facilitator of a (sometimes strange
and tension-filled) conversation between the listener and the
biblical text itself, not an agent who represents the text and
speaks on its behalf.

Third, returning to another issue with which we have
wrestled on several occasions already, storied imagination leads
us to how words are both a necessary but also an insufficient
resource in CAL. In sermons they function as pivotal gateways
to participative learning opportunities: 'In the art of preaching
... language is framed in such a way that the congregation is
allowed to enter into a new experience.'[51] Acknowledging, but
also putting aside, the significant lack of diversity in preachers
in the Church as a whole, we must also recognize that the traditional teaching sermon format only allows for one preacher at

a time (or at most, a very small group). Therefore any preacher should use language carefully to actively invite diverse others into learning, rather than forcing them into passivity. Via both choice of words and how they are delivered, preachers communicate whether they perceive themselves as the first contribution, or as one voice among many in an ongoing conversation, or as delivering a monologue. They have the choice of whether their words will re-enforce *their* rights and privilege to be heard, or speak in a way that acknowledges the gaps in the conversation created by those who cannot, or do not presently, speak.

I appreciate that speaking on others' behalf (especially in relation to underrepresented and discriminated groups) is highly problematic and no substitute for diverse voices being welcomed into full participation (whether in imagined or actual conversations). However, it must also be recognized that, rather than being a limiting factor, teaching sermons offer some reassurance to those for whom openly participating in questioning or dialogue is simply too costly or dangerous in any given setting or moment. While the risk of passive disengagement remains, if learners know they will not be called on for a comment or question, the opportunity for full engagement in the world of storied imagination is arguably significantly increased. Practically, this seems an impossible tightrope to walk. How can preachers be participative cast members who model active participation without crowding the imaginative space, so that those who do not contribute to the conversation out loud are still afforded maximum opportunity to engage in storied imagination? How is it possible to provide sufficient disruption, but not too much? Here are a few suggestions.

First, storied imagination relies on the idea that learning is more 'aesthetic than analytic'[52] and therefore its transformative potential lies in its form as well as its content. Therefore disruptive-inclusive teaching should not shy away from aiming to sound beautiful (as per MacKendrick's previous definition of including the interesting, surprising, arresting and strange). However, this does not mean that the structure of teaching sermons is unimportant. Carefully choosing vocabulary and crafting sentences is a similar process to a jeweller selecting, polishing and setting stones in a necklace. In the finished piece, nobody comments on the symmetry of the angles cut into the stones or the proportions of the claws, but they do appreciate how these allow light to pass through the stones, making them sparkle! Language is capable of painting evocative pictures and transporting listeners to both familiar and unfamiliar experiences. Therefore a 'subversive conversation about the nature of reality'[53] does not need to repeatedly ask, 'And how do you respond to this?' or 'What does this mean for you?' Where language is carefully chosen to restory imagination, it makes participative demands on listeners without the need to repeatedly restate them.

Second, imagined as a circle, a disruptive-inclusive teaching sermon should either take learners far enough around a first learning loop that sets the trajectory but in which, ultimately, learners are given the task of joining the dots on their own; or accompany learners all the way around their first revolution and then a little further. In the first case, learners gain a sense of unfinished story that needs continuing and/or a sense of empowerment from having been drawn into full storied participation. In the second, the first revolution acts as a model; a dry-run on which ongoing learning can be based. This is eloquently demonstrated by U2 frontman Bono who, on the thirtieth anniversary of the album *The Joshua Tree*, made the following comments about one of its most definitive tracks, 'Where The Streets Have No Name':

Musically it's great and the band deserve credit for that, but lyrically it's just a sketch and I was going to go back and write it out ... Half of it is an invocation, where you say to a crowd of people 'Do you want to go to that place? That place of imagination, that place of soul? Do you want to go there, cos right now we can go there?' To this day when I say those words you get hairs on the back of your neck stand up because you're going to that place.

He explains that producer Brian Eno had reassured him that 'incomplete thoughts are generous because they allow the listener to finish them'. Eno's challenge brought Bono to the conclusion that 'as a songwriter I have to realise that the greatest invitation is an invocation'.[54] Not offering all the answers, the deliberate presentation of something open-ended in a way that invites imaginative participation is a pedagogical skill both encouraged and demanded by disruptive inclusion.

My final suggestion about how disruptive-inclusive teaching, particularly in sermon format, can avoid paralysing learners with too much disruption, is via combining the sublime and the ridiculous and creating humour. In speaking about the participative nature of learning games, Anthony Reddie points out: 'The use of laughter and comedy is often deliberate because history has shown us that it is often in times of great distress and emotional turmoil that the sharpest and most incisive forms of humour emerge.'[55]

Reddie highlights the very fine line between the serious and the lighthearted. In fact, there is often significant overlap between the two. However, I am not suggesting that preachers should include more jokes, but that as teachers dare to blur boundaries, disrupt categories, retell stories and include new topics, people and places in the restor(y)ing of the imagination, humour results either from empathy, discomfort or a mixture of both. In the following example, stories of Mr Bean and Star Wars, Tiger Woods and my coffee preferences intermingle with the resurrected, victorious Christ, his bride and the whore of Babylon! The aim of this variation is not to undermine the importance of the issues at play, but a hint of absurdity gives learners permission to explore the potentially left-field ideas that the passage may evoke for them. The comic effect created demonstrates that, although deeply challenging, disruptive-inclusive does not need to be a solemn exercise, and is designed to function best when nothing is excluded. Büchner explains:

Sin and grace, absence and presence, tragedy and comedy, they divide the world between them and where they meet head on, the Gospel happens. Let the preacher preach the Gospel of their preposterous meeting as the high, unbidden, hilarious thing it is.[56]

Learner checklist

* Do you ever think about the techniques storytellers are using? Whether preachers, teachers, advertisers or in films or TV? Next time you encounter story, take a step back and ask who the storyteller is and how the story is designed to engage your imagination.
* Think about your favourite storyteller. Again, they may be a filmmaker, preacher, writer or just a friend. What is it about the kinds of stories they tell and the way they tell them that you find attractive?

A disruptive-inclusive teaching sermon: imagining a different kind of victory (Revelation 19–20)

This sermon was originally designed to be heard, rather than read. If you prefer, you can listen here: https://vimeo. com/589071111.

We have reached the final scene of the film. The audience holds its breath as the hero steps up to take on the villain in the deciding dual. Will good win out or will we be left with a cliff-hanger as she literally teeters on the edge? I hate it when directors force us to wait for the sequel to discover what happens. Well, Revelation doesn't make us wait much longer for answers. Our reward for persevering through 19 chapters of the Bible's final book is a gloriously satisfying ending – but perhaps not in the way we may have been expecting. I'm afraid that by this point, it's too late for a spoiler alert. The author of Revelation isn't holding back any more, this passage is unapologetically saturated in the most convincing victory anyone could imagine – the victory of God the Almighty.

As chapter 19 begins, I am transported back to the famous beach scene in *Chariots of Fire* – where Eric Liddell runs through the surf and the iconic soundtrack kicks in. Every time, I have an emotional reaction. My hope rises at the prospect that this unlikely hero might achieve his goal. Everything about that scene is designed to make me feel that way (or maybe that song makes you think of Mr Bean at the London 2012 Olympic ceremony[57] – as I say, either way, spine-tingling!). Now, given that there is no surviving soundtrack to the book of Revelation, its author has to find an alternative way to point out the significance of the story's progression as we reach chapter 19 verse 11. Unless you read very carefully, it's easy to pass right by: 'Then I saw heaven opened' is as loaded with significance as The Imperial March is to Darth Vader's looming presence in *Star Wars* or how Indiana Jones' theme music announces his impending success. Openings are everywhere in Revelation – angels open seals and scrolls, bottomless pits are opened and temples, and mouths and books open everywhere.

However, the heavens only open twice in Revelation – right at the outset of John's visions in chapter 4 and here. This opening announces the beginning of the end. The author declares as clearly as is possible – pay attention! The God who began all of this, who opened the heavens in the first place, now opens the heavens for a final time to usher in the new heavens and new earth finally revealed in chapter 21. The victory we've all been waiting for is about to be unveiled. We should get the same tingling sensations as we do from *Chariots of Fire* ... or Mr Bean!

Interestingly, however, the fact of Jesus' victory is given short shrift by the author: there is no epic battle sequence or drawn-out description of the enemies' state at the end. Rather, a few short, matter-of-fact statements. 'The beast was captured' and 'the rest were killed' (Rev. 19.20–21). Jesus' victory is not a reality that only becomes apparent at this end point of the story, but it defines its entire shape and understanding. There is no big reveal at the end, but, like those films that begin with the ending and then work back through how the characters arrived to that point, the author of Revelation is far more interested in explaining how Jesus is victorious, rather than merely establishing its fact. The author's central interest is – what does it look like for Jesus to overcome?

I think our first clue comes in the inclusion of the righteous rider on a white horse (19.11). Victory isn't a passive, spectator sport – it is not something done to the people of God. All the parties involved in this passage have agency – their actions produce a specific effect. As we've seen on a few occasions in Revelation, horseback is where the battles are won and lost (which is interesting when we come to Palm Sunday, but that's a different sermon). And so, in chapter 19, it's pivotal to notice who gets to ride. The rider on the white horse strides out first but then in 19.14 the armies of heaven, wearing fine white linen, follow him out on their own white horses. Again, this image may not instantly strike us as particularly sensational, but it conveys an incredible idea – yes, Jesus is lead rider here, but he is no lone ranger, he is flanked by the armies of heaven. It seems that the power, authority and agency we see embodied in the differently coloured horses that appear in the front line of battle in Revelation 6 are now under control of the armies of heaven. As those who ride in victory alongside Jesus, the people of God are co-agents of that victory, not observers. Neither is there room for a hierarchy of participation among the riders. In the curious side-scene in 19.10, the author notes an exchange with an angel who rebuffs attempts to be worshipped. The message is stark – in Jesus-style victory, the only distinction made is between God who is worshipped and those who are gifted the privilege of worshipping. As all creation moves back towards the peace and wholeness of its original design, there is no space for competition any more. As a fellow rider with Jesus, the model set is that of participatory worship.

So, Jesus' victory is not about waiting for something to happen – it requires that we take seriously our agency as those who reign with Jesus and whose lives and actions testify to God. However, it's not just important that God's people participate, but it matters what kind of victory we think we're participating in – and this can be challenging, because the view of victory we're given here is contested by many we see in contemporary culture. An example: in March 2013, Tiger Woods regained his place as the world's number 1 golfer (don't worry – you don't need to know or like golf to follow this story!). He had fallen in the rankings in the preceding years after admitting to a range of affairs that broke up his marriage. His sponsor, Nike (a word that interestingly means victory in Greek) celebrated his return to the top of the game with an advert that had the strapline: winning takes care of everything. Nike thought that a good way to promote their brand was to let Woods' victory put the other recent events of his life back into proper perspective – as unimportant. In other words, Nike promotes the kind of victory that is a distraction from the realities and responsibilities of family life rather than the kind of victory that actually gives access to a better quality of life. If you can win on the golf course, then who cares if you don't win anywhere else. There's no attempt in this slogan to pretend that being successful at golf might address Woods' personal problems but rather, that for a minute or two, going around 18 holes in one stroke fewer than the next guy might distract from the pain, and make his mistakes somehow seem diminished.

In Nike's defence, they're not alone in pushing this concept of victory – on the whole, media culture sells the kind of victory that is exhilarating but also temporary; it guarantees a big adrenaline rush but is ultimately just a distraction from other difficulties, not an answer to them. Recently, in response to the latest US election, social commentator Stephen Colbert said that 'Worrying about winning has become a poison in our society', and I don't think we have to look far to see that he's right.

Revelation 19 paints a vivid picture of the differences between this kind of victory and the way God wins, through two key characters: the whore of Babylon and the bride of Christ. In a quick recap from chapter 17, remember that the whore is described as clothed in purple and scarlet and adorned with gold and jewels and pearls, holding in her hand a golden cup. Her outward appearance is a metaphor for the kind of victory she represents. The whore's victory is opulent and calculated in tangible terms – in the eyes of the world, winning is about what you have to show for your own efforts at the end of the day. This contrasts sharply with the bride of Christ who is simply described as clothed in fine linen, bright and pure (19.8).

However, there is one detail above all the others that John mentions about the bride that gets to the real heart of the difference between these two female characters. In 19.8 the bride's clothes are described as having been 'granted' or given to her. All that the bride has has been gifted her. The difference between victory and defeat is not marked by what the women have but who they understand as the source of what they have.

This distinction is reinforced in the name given to the rider of the white horse – faithful and true. Often, I think, with these 'fruits of the spirit' related words we have a tendency to think of them as abstract spiritual theories, but faithfulness and truth here represent deeply practical ideas. Here, Jesus' faithfulness in victory helps us understand its deeply counter-cultural implications. In practical terms, faithfulness is acting in a consistent way that confers high value on something or someone else. For example, my preference for a certain coffee shop and my repeated patronage of that coffee shop adds value to them on several levels. Apart from the financial profit they make from my purchases, my consistent rejection of all other coffee shops sends a message that I value their product and, over time, they are right to grow in confidence as their reputation builds. Although I obviously benefit from this process, overall the value flows from me ... towards them.

Think back to Nike's version of victory. Others are obstacles to my attempts to hold onto or increase my own value, and ultimately victory is achieved at others' expense. Value is denied others in order to be concentrated in me! In demonstrating true faithfulness, Jesus models a pattern of victory for the people of God that doesn't need to desperately snatch value away from others by stepping on them; Jesus-shaped victory looks like conferring value on others in the consistent process of giving value away! This backwards conception is epitomized in what is probably the most well-known verse in this passage – 20.4. Leaving discussions of the meaning of 1,000 aside for now, those whose testimony had previously seen them lose their lives for God's cause come to life and reign with Christ. Similarly to chapter 12, where those who 'did not cling to life even in the face of death' are those who conquer, these weighty ideas see death and life come together in baffling ways.

Like the disciples in Matthew 16 who struggle to understand what Jesus means when he says that to save your life you must lose it, the resurrection and reigning of the dead in Revelation 19 is difficult for us to understand because we like clear lines between gain and loss, victory and failure, life and death. Jesus, though, doesn't seem to respect our desire for control over these categories. Jesus-style victory came to earth as a refugee baby before it came as a mighty ruler, Jesus rides a donkey before a white horse, victory took the form of a criminal's execution before an empty tomb. It required Jesus to cry, 'It is finished' before the seventh angel could cry, 'It is done' and involved the drinking of the cup of wrath before it could be poured out to end the enemy's existence.

Now, importantly, I'm not saying that Revelation 19 paints a picture in which Jesus-style victory is about grinning and bearing through every awful thing that happens, just hoping that everything will turn out well in the end. When we see evil in the world, often packaged as the kind of victory Nike is selling, as representatives of Christ the Church's role is to provide an alternative witness … to tell a different kind of story. But I do sense that maybe the biggest lesson of Revelation 19 and 20 for us is a reminder that Jesus-style victory is so immense, rich and complete that of course it cannot be constrained by human categories and often breaks into our experience way before we're able to recognize it as anything we might expect. I agree with the analogy that Brian Blount makes in his book, *Can I Get a Witness? Reading Revelation through African-American culture.* He compares the visions and hymns of Revelation with the 'music of the Black Church tradition' – its story is not just 'a mere accompaniment to the liberative history of the Black Church tradition; it is the vital life force that paces the beating of its struggling, idealistic, weary, and yet indefatigable heart.'[58] He's saying that in the example of what he calls the 'spiritual blues', as the songs speak of coming victory they're not just prophetic in foretelling future victory, but in some beautiful, mysterious way, they inaugurate, they usher in, God's victory in their singing.

Let me finish with a personal example. This time last year, I had just started a new job, one that I had felt God had gone to great lengths to prepare me for. On paper, it was miraculous provision – every detail seemed made for me. However, very quickly the reality of the day-to-day situation became unbearable. Unable to cope, I was forced to quit. On the one hand, I could dismiss the whole scenario as a failure and despair at why it wasn't successful. However, I find that Revelation 19 and 20 challenge me to engage with the idea that in God's process of redeeming all things back to their best, sometimes victory comes disguised as weakness and defeat. Maybe this season takes its place as part of God's victory in and through me, in ways I just am not yet able to see. It reminds me of Leonard Cohen's famous lyric – 'there's a crack in everything: it's how the light gets in'.

So, I suppose if we're looking for a bumper sticker version of God's victory in Revelation 19 and 20, it's this: expect the unexpected. Don't write something or someone off because they don't immediately look like what you've been taught to expect. In fact, sometimes the lines between gain and loss, victory and failure, life and death become so intertwined that losing everything as the only way to gain anything at all starts to make a bit more sense. Notice this week the number of times you perceive God's victory breaking through in people and situations that the world dismisses as losers. The hero does win in the end, but in a way that is far better than we could ever imagine.

Learner checklist

- Which part(s) of the sermon did you find most disruptive? How? Why?
- Is this sermon different from or similar to those you have previously heard? If a preacher or teacher took a similar approach in one of your contexts, how would you respond? Would that response be different from or similar to usual?
- What are the biggest questions raised for you from this sermon about interpreting Revelation 19—20 and the Bible more generally?

Analysis

The first important thing to acknowledge about the above sermon is that, even before any particular approach is applied, the text's raw material already provides the basis for significant learner disruption. Revelation's 'misogynist reputation and ... penchant for graphic violence' means that many do not have to dig deep into chapters 19—20 to find a disruptive experience.[59] In fact, many of its aspects sit comfortably in feminist scholar Phyllis Trible's *Texts of Terror* category.[60] However, as Elisabeth Schüssler Fiorenza states, the contemporary interpretational challenges of Revelation are not limited to any particular type of reader: 'The Book of Revelation remains for many Christians a book with "seven seals", seldom read and often relegated to a curiosity in the Bible.'[61] For the vast majority of Christian adult learners, the overarching difficulty of the final book of the Bible is not limited to any one element but well summed-up in the paradox, 'Revelation obscures'.[62]

However, for exactly this reason, Revelation is a deeply intuitive choice to demonstrate the potential of a disruptive-inclusive approach in teaching sermons. Returning to our theme of food metaphors, the first sense is well represented in Michelle Fletcher's description of Revelation as a pastiche because it combines, but does not fully integrate, various ingredients. She explains:

Pastiche derives from two terms for two culinary products: *pasticcio* and *pâté*. The Italian *pasticcio* refers to a pasty or stew, where different ingredients are brought together to create something new, but where each is still recognizable, and *pâté* is French for a mixture of different blended elements such as mushrooms, liver and fat, where their original flavours are mixed with each other, but they retain some of their past guise (think Ardennes, not Brussels).[63]

In presenting Revelation as 'a specific practice of imitation and combination that sits somewhere between original and copy, parody and homage, and collage and mosaic',[64] Fletcher does not apologize for Revelation's complex intertextuality (as if it were a contaminated product) but suggests that it provides an opportunity to participate in an openly 'complex multivocal text'.[65]

This sense is exacerbated by the diversity and volume of interpreters who (for better or worse!) have interpreted the book of Revelation. In particular, those who have been inspired 'to seek freedom for the captive and justice for the oppressed, whether in South Africa, South America, South L.A., or elsewhere'.[66]

From the triumphant 'Hallelujah Chorus' to the gentle strains of 'Jerusalem my Happy Home' ... it has fed social upheaval and sectarian religious movements ... Attempts to control the effects of the book by ignoring it or dismissing it have not been successful.[67]

Finally, as recognized by many, Revelation 'throbs with theopoetic energy',[68] and therefore not only does it easily lend itself to a disruptive-inclusive approach but arguably the extreme otherness of Revelation also expedites the process. When Revelation is approached as a puzzle or problem to be pulled apart, its multiple levels of interwoven complexity mean that the dissected result is a 'cadaver rather than a living text'.[69]

Reflecting on specific ways that the above sermon adopts a disruptive-inclusive approach to the text: first, it opens with the standard narrative formula of a hero and villain scenario. However, it subverts expectations by beginning at the end. Without making a direct methodological claim that the biblical text models a pattern of disruption, the opening paragraphs of the sermon frame the text as exactly that. Listeners experience the text, and not the preacher, as the primary source of the subversion and disruption of expectations, which in turn functions as the beginning and not the end of the learning conversation.

Another key disruptive-inclusive mechanism, used in a variety of ways, is the concept of crossing over or inhabiting edge-places between two concepts or arenas. Throughout the sermon, listeners' imaginations are moved from the 1920s to 2012, from *Star Wars* to Mr Bean, from golf to Indiana Jones, from multi-million-dollar advertising strategies to coffee. As demonstrated in Chapter 3, the Bible's ability to hold together the seemingly contradictory encourages learners to hold diverse perspectives, styles of expression and communication, times and even interpretive approaches in tension. Learners are invited to move between the everyday and the lofty, the individual and the systemic, and between different modes of imagination, sights, sounds and memories. In the language of John 10, rather than asking learners to permanently locate themselves on one side of the gate, they are encouraged to move back and forth between the various images and make connections between ideas that may be more or less familiar and more or less comforting and challenging.

Finally, disruptive inclusion is also worked out through what is absent in the sermon. It resists drawing a clear distinction between the interpretation and application of the text. Rather, at the end it draws attention to how the whole presentation is premised on the crossing back and forth between the two. Therefore no formal invitation to participate is needed; there is no closing question such as, 'So, what does this mean for you and your context?' The assumption is embedded from the outset that there are potential connections to be made and that those listening are engaged, active participants in the connected, interpretative process.

Questions/activities

- How do you understand the relationship between CAL and sermons?
- Next time you hear a sermon (or a lecture-style talk), think about whether (and if so, how) opportunities for storied imagination are created. If not, try to create some for yourself. What kinds of disruptive-inclusive learning are made possible when you engage your imagination? What kinds of ideas and emotions does this raise for you?
- Recount a short Bible story to someone. Try to make its telling as *beautiful* as possible. How did you do it? How did your listener respond?

Notes

1 John M. Hull, *What Prevents Christian Adults from Learning?* (London: SCM Press, 1985), p. 18.

2 Hull, *What Prevents*, p. 18.

3 Many who heard Hull preach live reflected on his incredible ability to hold attention in a room despite being unable to make eye contact with his audience. Much of this ease of delivery is attributed to the fact that Hull wrote and memorized full sermon transcripts.

4 Hull, *What Prevents*, p. 18.

5 Hull, *What Prevents*, p. 134.

6 Hull, *What Prevents*, p. 177.

7 Hull, *What Prevents*, p. 55.

8 Hull, *What Prevents*, p. 82.

9 Hull, *What Prevents*, p. 17.

10 For example, N. T. Wright bases his argument on the claim that 'stories are one of the most basic modes of human life', N. T. Wright, *The New Testament and the People of God: Christian origins and the question of God; vol.1* (London: SPCK, 2013), p. 38. For more on this, see also Hans Frei, *The Eclipse of Biblical Narrative: A study in eighteenth- and nineteenth-century hermeneutics* (New Haven, CT: Yale University Press, 1974); Robert Alter, *The Art of Biblical Narrative* (New York, NY: Basic Books, 2011); Paul Ricœur, *Time and Narrative* (Chicago, IL: University of Chicago Press, 1984); Stanley Hauerwas and L. Gregory Jones, *Why Narrative?: Readings in narrative theology* (Eugene, OR: Wipf & Stock, 1997); Alasdair MacIntyre, *After Virtue:*

A study in moral theory (Notre Dame, IN: University of Notre Dame Press, 2007); John Milbank, *Theology and Social Theory: Beyond secular reason* (Oxford: Blackwell, 2006). In the world of philosophy, see Ludwig Wittgenstein, *Philosophical Investigations/Philosophische Untersuchungen* (New York, NY: Macmillan, 1958).

11 Wayne A. Slabon, Randy L. Richards and Vanessa P. Dennen, 'Learning by restorying', *Instructional Science* 42:4 (2014), pp. 505–21, p. 507. Ruard Ganzevoort notes the wide-ranging theological disciplines shaped by narrative in the late twentieth and early twenty-first centuries. Ruard Ganzevoort, Maaike de Haardt and Michael Scherer-Rath, *Religious Stories We Live By: Narrative approaches in theology and religious studies*, Studies in Theology and Religion (STAR), vol. 19 (Leiden: Brill, 2014).

12 Jonathan Gottschall, *The Storytelling Animal: How stories make us human* (Boston, MA: Houghton Mifflin Harcourt, 2012), pp. 2–18.

13 Gottschall, *The Storytelling Animal*, p. 49.

14 James K. A. Smith, 'Restor(y)ing the imagination: part 1', LICC (26 September 2019). Available from https://youtu.be/9hUtF_68Inw (accessed 31.07.2023).

15 Smith, 'Restor(y)ing the imagination'.

16 Gottschall, *The Storytelling Animal*, p. 59.

17 Gottschall, *The Storytelling Animal*, p. 57. This is interesting to consider in relation to the formation of the biblical canon; where stories had a long and wide heritage of oral retelling and later copying, it was considered to consolidate a particular story's authority.

18 Brad D. Strawn and Warren S. Brown, *Enhancing Christian Life: How extended cognition augments religious community* (Downers Grove, IL: IVP Academic, 2020), p. 139.

19 Paul Fairfield, *Education, Dialogue and Hermeneutics* (London: Continuum, 2011), p. 33.

20 Strawn and Brown, *Enhancing Christian Life*, p. 124.

21 Milbank, *Theology and Social Theory*, p. 269.

22 See Selah 3.

23 See Chapter 5: Pilgrimage: from where to who and a new kind of home.

24 See Chapter 5: Finding new motivation in playful poetics.

25 Gottschall, *The Storytelling Animal*, p. 32.

26 James M. Banner and Harold C. Cannon, *The Elements of Learning* (New Haven, CT: Yale University Press, 1999), p. 69.

27 Charles Taylor, *Modern Social Imaginaries* (Durham, NC: Duke University Press, 2004).

28 Beth Green, 'Present tense. Christian education in secular time' in J. M. Luetz and B. Green, *Innovating Christian Education Research:*

Multidisciplinary perspectives (Singapore: Springer, 2021), p. 22, quoting Taylor, *Modern Social Imaginaries*.

29 Hull, *What Prevents*, p. 82.

30 Strawn and Brown, *Enhancing Christian Life*, pp. 137–8. This research concerns how literary fiction causes readers to 'feel and think along with the characters', see Annabel D. Nijhof and Roel M. Willems, 'Simulating fiction: individual differences in literature comprehension revealed with FMRI', *PloS ONE* 10:2 (2015), p. 1.

31 The key point is that empathy is exercised. As Mark Allan Powell explains in relation to biblical engagement, 'Empathy is a primary mode to connect the meaning of the biblical stories with meaning in their own lives.' Mark Allan Powell, *What Do They Hear?: Bridging the gap between pulpit and pew* (Nashville, TN: Abingdon Press, 2007), p. 64.

32 Maria Harris, *Teaching and Religious Imagination* (San Francisco: Harper & Row, 1987), p. 4.

33 Darcia Narvaez, 'Neurobiology and moral mindset' in K. Heinrichs, F. Oser and T. Lovat (eds), *Handbook of Moral Motivation: Theories, models, applications* (Rotterdam: Sense, 2013), p. 331. This communality works across time and space, as demonstrated in Chapter 4.

34 Frederick Büchner, *Telling the Truth: The Gospel as tragedy, comedy, and fairy tale* (San Francisco, CA: Harper & Row, 1977), pp. 3–4.

35 Smith, 'Restor(y)ing the imagination'.

36 John M. Hull, 'Karl Marx on Capital: Some implications for Christian Adult Education', *Modern Believing* 38:1 (1997), pp. 22–31, p. 26.

37 For example, see Christer Hydén and Lars and Linda Örulv, 'Interation and narrative structure in dementia' in A. Nylund, A. De Fina and D. Schiffrin (eds), *Telling Stories: Language, narrative and social life*, Georgetown University Round Table on Languages and Linguistics Series (Washington DC: Georgetown University Press, 2010). See also Miriam A. Locher and Franziska Gygax, *Narrative Matters in Medical Contexts Across Disciplines*, Studies in Narrative (Amsterdam: John Benjamin's Publishing Company, 2015) on the role of imaginative narrative for those with Dementia and Autism respectively.

38 Nathan Crick, 'Democracy & rhetoric: John Dewey on the arts of becoming', *Studies in rhetoric/communication* (Columbia, SC: University of South Carolina Press, 2010), p. 171.

39 Josue Tario, 'Critical spirituality: decolonizing the self' in Njoki Nathani Wane, Miglena S. Todorova and Kimberly L. Todd (eds), *Decolonizing the Spirit in Education and Beyond: Resistance and solidarity* (Cham: Springer, 2019), pp. 179–93, p. 189.

40 Tario, 'Critical spirituality', p. 189.

41 Tario, 'Critical spirituality', p. 189.

42 Tario, 'Critical spirituality', p. 189.

43 Powell, *What Do They Hear?*

44 The language of stage plays resonates with earlier references to Wright, *Scripture and the Authority of God*. Smith claims: 'We act in the world more as characters in a drama than as soldiers dutifully following a command.' See James K. A. Smith, *Imagining the Kingdom: How worship works* (Grand Rapids, MI: Baker Academic, 2013), p. 127, and Ricœur's suggestion that, 'To participate in the mystery of incarnate existence means to adopt the internal rhythm of drama.' Paul Ricœur, Erazim V. Kohák and Don Ihde, *Freedom and Nature: The voluntary and the involuntary* (Evanston, IL: Northwestern University, 2007), p. 17.

45 Powell, *What Do They Hear?*, p. 61.

46 Powell, *What Do They Hear?*, p. 61.

47 Walter Brueggemann, *The Practice of Prophetic Imagination: Preaching an emancipating word* (Lanham, MD: Fortress Press, 2012), p. 14.

48 Harris, *Teaching and Religious Imagination*, p. 41.

49 Ellen F. Davis and Austin McIver Dennis, *Preaching the Luminous Word: Biblical sermons and homiletical essays* (Grand Rapids, MI: Wm. B. Eerdmans, 2016), p. xxiii.

50 Karmen MacKendrick, 'The hospitality of listening' in R. Kearney and K. Semonovitch (eds), *Phenomenologies of the Stranger: Between hostility and hospitality* (New York, NY: Fordham University Press, 2011), p. 105. MacKendrick's reference to wonder here links to our earlier discussion.

51 Elizabeth Achtemeier, *Preaching as Theology & Art* (Nashville, TN: Abingdon Press, 1984), p. 52.

52 Smith, *Imagining the Kingdom*, p. 174.

53 Brueggemann, *The Practice of Prophetic Imagination*, p. 14.

54 Rhian Daly, 'Bono says "Where the streets have no name" is "unfinished"', *NME* (20 July 2017), available at https://www.nme.com/news/music/bono-unfinished-streets-name-2113648 (accessed 31.07.23).

55 Anthony Reddie, *Theologising Brexit: A liberationist and postcolonial critique* (Abingdon: Routledge, 2019), p. 161.

56 Büchner, *Telling the Truth*, p. 71.

57 If you missed it or just need a smile, you can watch it here: https://youtu.be/CwzjlmBLfrQ (accessed 8.11.2023).

58 Brian K. Blount, *Can I Get a Witness?: Reading Revelation through African American culture* (Louisville, KY: Westminster John Knox Press, 2005), p. 93.

59 Blount, *Can I Get a Witness?*, p. viii.

60 Phyllis Trible, *Texts of Terror: Literary-feminist readings of Biblical narratives* (Philadelphia, PA: Fortress Press, 1984).

61 Elisabeth Schüssler Fiorenza, *The Book of Revelation: Justice and judgment* (Minneapolis, MN: Fortress Press, 1998), p. 13.

62 Blount, *Can I Get a Witness?*, p. 1.

63 Michelle Fletcher, *Reading Revelation as Pastiche: Imitating the past* (London: Bloomsbury T&T Clark, 2017), pp. 49–50.

64 Fletcher, *Reading Revelation*, p. 48.

65 Fletcher, *Reading Revelation*, p. 47.

66 Michael J. Gorman, *Reading Revelation Responsibly: Uncivil worship and witness: following the Lamb into the new creation* (Eugene, OR: Cascade Books, 2011), p. 8.

67 Craig R. Koester, 'On the verge of the millennium: a history of the interpretation of Revelation', *Word & World* 15:2 (1995), pp. 128–36, p. 128.

68 Gorman, *Reading Revelation Responsibly*, p. 35.

69 Mitchell G. Reddish, *Revelation* (Macon, GA: Smyth & Helwys Publishing, 2005), p. 230.

8

Disruptive Inclusion and Online Learning

Since I began researching CAL, its biggest changes have undoubtedly been in the area of online learning. Therefore it is appropriate that this final chapter focuses on the implications of adopting a disruptive-inclusive approach in virtual learning settings. Since the turn of the twenty-first century, online video calls, distance learning programmes and virtual learning environments have gone from niche add-ons to essential but still specialist tools, to almost the only way that formal teaching and learning took place during the Covid-19 pandemic. Since then, educational institutions and churches have been deciding whether and how technology can continue to be used to enhance learning moving forward.

However, the use of technology to enable virtual participation in CAL is far from new, preceding not only the pandemic but even the digital age! In the year that Windows version 1.0 was preparing for release, Hull addressed the particular challenges of creating learning communities in the '"electronic churches" of America which have no congregational or corporate reality, but exist as a network of individuals watching television'.[1] Of course, Hull's comments did not take into account the teleconferencing and broadcasting resources now widely available (or even the internet that makes any of it possible!). Despite this, and whatever your view on Hull's suggestion that watching a service on a screen creates a network of people who lack any congregational and corporate reality, his comments about non-physically gathered CAL offer a very early insight into some of the questions still developing approximately 40 years later: What does it mean to practise Christian faith via video or live streaming? What are the theological and pedagogical implications of online CAL?

Online learning raises questions that have been posed by Christians for millennia and those nobody could have imagined until very recently. On the one hand, the debate around the importance of physical, embodied presence is well-established (for example, the Apostle Paul is deeply bothered about the fact that he is unable to be with the church in Thessalonica; see 1 Thess. 2—3).[2] But on the other, analysis of the possibilities and limitations of virtual/online presence is still in its infancy as technological developments continue to move the debate forward.[3] While few of us would disagree that the processes and experiences of online and physically-gathered learning (whether in classrooms, churches or other settings) are very different, exactly how or why is less well understood. This chapter aims to identify some of the key issues by making practical observations about CAL in online settings and exploring the potential contributions that disruptive inclusion might make to future phases of its understanding and practice.

Blurring the lines between online and offline

One of the repeated patterns of this book is that where questions seem to offer either-or choices, disruptive-inclusive responses come in a both-and format. As a framework for understanding and practising CAL, disruptive inclusion does not aim to promote or undermine any specific mode of learning, but rather to support learners in (critically!) navigating CAL however it presents itself. In line with this, the aim of this chapter is not to promote either online or offline learning as more appropriate than the other; both have aspects that make effective learning both easier and more challenging, depending on multiple factors. It is also common sense that, in many scenarios, decisions regarding learning mode will be based on the particular practical or pedagogical advantages that various options may bring.

As ever, from the perspective of disruptive inclusion, the aim is for learners not to remain in the unquestioned comfort of what they have always done and how they have always done it, but to take advantage of the opportunities for connected learning made available at *optimum distance* and when practising *multiplicity of vision*. Based on my recent experience, for the majority of (but by no means all) Christian adult learners, their 'comfort zone' is physically gathered, instructional learning, meaning that moving into virtual and more participative learning spaces and modes can create significant learning disruption. However, for the generation(s) whose formal education was moved online during the pandemic and are far more likely than their parents to 'self-learn' using online resources,[4] I fully expect the prevailing learning 'comfort zones' to change, for increasing numbers to find physically-gathered settings unfamiliar and challenging, and for online learning engagement to become 'the norm' for many.

As we have also explored in several different ways, regardless of the direction(s) in which learners are moving, the biggest obstacle to disruptive inclusion is when learners will not, or cannot, move at all. Specifically relating to online engagement, practical theologian Angela Williams-Gorrell highlights a particular reason why crossing the boundaries between online and offline may be particularly difficult, going as far as suggesting that the two categories are becoming increasingly defunct, collapsing into a reality she refers to as 'always on'.[5] Her claim is that the accessibility of internet-enabled technology now means that apart from those consciously opting out, most people can receive and send information electronically, regardless of the time of day or proximity to a computer. In the most basic sense, there is no such thing as online or offline any more. Even when I physically arrive at the supermarket, I am still encouraged to use an app on my phone to scan and pay for my shopping. When I arrive at the bus stop, often the only way I (or the electronic sign in the bus stop) know when the next bus is due is by accessing the internet. The collapsing of online and offline was demonstrated in the extreme during the pandemic when, for many, almost all social, learning, economic and religious activity occurred in online spaces. Kitchens served as classrooms, exercise studios and sanctuaries, merging the gaps between breakfast, pilates, assignment writing and worship services. The *in-between* physical spaces bridging the working day's last meeting and making dinner (normally provided by the bus, train or car ride home) no longer existed (and, for many, have not been completely restored in the same way since). As a result, where many learners' normal pattern of life naturally created opportunities to transition between various online and offline spaces, many of these distinctions have been significantly reduced or no longer exist.[6]

Therefore the biggest implication of the growing influence of online CAL is not a lack of disruptive learning opportunities but rather their all-pervasiveness. As the lines between offline and online, home, study and work become increasingly blurred, a key problem is not entering into disruption, but escaping it! The increased overlap between online and offline 'extends suffering that occurs in physical spaces into digital spaces',[7] a pattern that has both individual and systemic consequences. Although online learning can be said to remove some logistical barriers to equality of participation (that is, for those with physical disabilities or unable to travel for other reasons), it must also be acknowledged that it consolidates (and in some significant ways exacerbates) the discrimination and inequalities ingrained in everyday live societal engagement. For example, despite a range of initiatives to address the issue, online racial abuse of minority ethnic groups in the public eye (specifically, but not limited to, professional sportspeople) continues to increase with the popularity of social media. The anonymity and invisibility of online engagement lead to expressions of hatred and discrimination far more rarely (or, at least, less brazenly) expressed in other settings.[8]

Another way in which the blurring of lines between online and offline learning modes has brought disproportionate disruption to a particular group of learners relates to those for whom technology is inaccessible. Although perhaps not instinctively considered as 'suffering', those who do not have the privilege, finance, skills (or a combination of all three) to participate in online learning are at a significant disadvantage to their peers. In early 2021, the British Academy's initial assessment of the impact of the pandemic on education was that it 'will not be felt equally' and will likely 'entrench aspects of existing inequality, impede intergenerational mobility and constrain young people to education and career binary paths, limiting their options and reducing the agility of the labour market.'[9] The comparison between how online learning can lead to entrenchment for some and agility for others is deeply significant. Although beyond the scope of the above report, research into the influence of the pandemic on adult education found similar patterns: those who do not have appropriate equipment or internet connection (or ability to use them) cannot access as many learning opportunities as those who do.[10] Therefore, whether it takes the form of consolidating discrimination in a variety of forms, or the logistical and technical challenges associated with online learning, the blurring of lines between offline and online learning worlds provides extreme (and unequally distributed!) disruption for many learners, even before any learning content has been introduced.

Learner checklist

- Have you noticed the collapsing of 'offline' and 'online' categories? What impact does increasing online engagement have on you personally, professionally, socially, etc.?
- Think back to the height of the pandemic. How did you respond to the increased need to connect in online spaces? What temporary changes did it bring to your life? What permanent changes has it brought since? Do you consider these positive, negative or a combination of both?
- What influence do you think offline or online modes have on how you learn? Think of an example where you have learned/learn well in both modes. What makes it effective/ useful for you?

Some initial observations and first steps

Unlike the examples of classroom activities and the sermon outlined in previous chapters, online learning does not easily lend itself to demonstration in written formats. Therefore, in place of a single worked example I have included some key observations and patterns from my own practice in both live, gathered online learning settings (like virtual classrooms using videoconferencing) and asynchronous online learning (primarily hosted by a virtual learning environment where learners largely work at their own pace). In response to the patterns identified in the previous section, disruptive inclusion has some significant contributions to make, to both a wide-angle, systemic view of online CAL and the practical, everyday details of how it is practised by educators and learners. First, it offers improved awareness of how and why moving in and out of online and offline learning modes is challenging, and guidance on how to keep the disruption at manageable levels. Second, it suggests a way in which the unavoidable disruption and disorientation of online learning can be leveraged towards learner progress as opposed to isolation, discrimination or paralysis.

Helping learners move in and out of online learning spaces

One of the aspects of physically gathered learning that is almost impossible to fully recreate in gathered online learning is the moments immediately before and after a session, and the communal coffee break. In adult learning settings, these in-between spaces provide opportunities for learners and educators alike to segue between various elements of life and responsibility. As they enter the physical classroom, learners discuss the pre-reading or assignment choices and ask questions of their peers' understanding, and educators have one-to-one, informal conversations that meet individual learners' needs: a narthex is created that enables learners to practise coming in and going out. On the other hand, in online settings, learners cross over from one space instantaneously (while actually physically remaining in another!). According to our earlier discussions about disruptive inclusion working best when learners are able to be in two places at once, videoconferencing should be the ideal tool to facilitate this by allowing learners to join others in a classroom *and* remain in the comfort of their own context. However, when the lines are so entirely blurred (or categories entirely collapsed) between home and study, online and offline, and on top of this, entrance and exit to the online space is instantaneously achieved by simply clicking 'join' and 'leave', locating and lingering in optimum distance can be very challenging.

On the surface, the virtual video conference classroom recreates multiple key aspects of a physical classroom setting (and the various features of different companies' software reveal the diversity of views on what this comprises). However, regardless of the format, it is almost impossible for any online 'room' to recreate the porous boundaries of a physical gathering. Thinking back to Chapter 6, online settings make it far more difficult for learners and educators to ease into disruption, or for disruptive CAL to begin before learners are aware of it. In online learning, side conversations, informal chitchat and general relationship building is harder because 'attention online is not elusive; rather, it is conclusive. There is evidence.'[11] In other words, the multi-layered, multi-focal engagement of physically gathered, disruptive-inclusive classroom engagement is much more difficult to achieve in an online setting that only really allows a single voice to speak at once and in which potentially not all participants can always see one another; and there is a far greater awareness of the gathering being dictated by the clock and calendar.

To lessen these effects and help Christian adult learners in improving crossing between offline and online learning modes, more attention needs to be paid to how learners lead into and out of live online learning sessions. In physically gathered learning, most experienced educators have cultivated a liturgy of entrance and exit into the classroom that defines the kind of environment they wish to facilitate. I, for example, try to verbally engage with as many learners as possible while I set up. Particularly, I will make a point of encouraging learners who find formal classrooms challenging and get a sense of how the group are feeling about the course content (and potential preparation activities). By the time the session formally begins, almost everyone has had a chance to warm up to the setting and those they will share it with. Equally, at the end of physically gathered classroom sessions (or even when preaching), there is the opportunity to read the body language of those who gather their effects and leave immediately and those who hang around, looking to engage with others and potentially also the educator/preacher. When entrance and exit to a learning space is controlled by the touch of a button, recreating the functions of these 'warm up' and 'warm down' learning spaces requires lateral thinking and deliberate interventions.

So far, I have trialled the following: replicating opening, informal greetings by addressing each virtual student by name and engaging them in some friendly interaction unrelated to the course. Another option is to begin sessions with a message encouraging learners to ask someone else in the chat about their day so far or represent their week so far with an emoji (although this does have some potential risks!). Practically, this means that educators should encourage students to enter the virtual classroom before the set time of each session, and equally, tutors need to be fully ready to begin in advance of the scheduled start time. Another way to 'warm up' live online sessions is to begin by setting an offline task (using an on-screen timer to keep learners focused) that uses non-digital resources (for example, asking learners to read a particular Bible passage and offer a comment in the chat/on the whiteboard). This eases learners into the online environment a little more gently than asking for verbal participation and unconsciously invites them to practise moving between the physical and virtual environments. Similar activities can be set in between online classroom sessions.

Creating 'third' learning spaces

Throughout this book, disruptive inclusion has repeatedly highlighted the importance of learners being able to access learning spaces that are neither 'here' nor 'there' – not so close to their familiar and unquestioned environment that they are unable to ask new questions, but neither so far out into the unknown that they feel entirely isolated and paralysed by fear. Therefore, where live online gathered sessions make it difficult for learners to either fully enter into, or get any kind of distance from, their physical setting or the virtual classroom, my suggestion is that perhaps the best option is to focus learning activities in a kind of 'third space' that provides some access to both. There are a variety of ways such learning spaces can be created.

First, as per Chapter 7, storied imagination can be used to invite learners to engage in activities focused on a third space: grounding learners in reality by encouraging them to imagine beyond their immediate context(s). The most effective way I have found to achieve this is with the use of case studies and worked examples. For example, rather than asking learners to explore the implications of the session's content for their own contexts, breakout groups explore case studies together. Using detailed, invented scenarios (helps with the imaginative part) gives learners the freedom to safely practise contextualising the course content. It also provides the opportunity to develop empathic connection with others via hospitality (as a side note, does the language of 'host' in video calling set an interesting expectation that learners are 'guests'?) by sharing with and feeding back to others. The effectiveness of these spaces can be further improved when groups regularly return to the same example. Each time, the learners' task is not only to respond in the light of new information, but also to assess whether they still believe their previous responses to be appropriate and why. This creates a connective narrative thread that reproduces some of the relational structure of regular physically gathered learning.[12]

Alternatively, 'third spaces' can be created much more tangibly in hybrid learning settings. The language of hybridity is used in various ways in learning, but here I am referring to a scenario in which a physically gathered group is joined by some online learners via videoconferencing, creating a hybrid classroom. In this learning setting the educator is generally physically present with the gathered group, but not always. As far as possible, hybrid educators should aim to provide equality of access for all. So, for example, if physical objects are demonstrated, educators should carefully consider whether the level of detail can be equally experienced online as in the physical classroom, or if close-up photographs (or equivalent) need to be provided to online students. Similarly with written resources and exercises, the key question becomes whether (and how) all learners can gain access. While equality of access can be achieved in different ways for different learners (for example, providing paper handouts for physically gathered learners and online documents via a virtual learning environment for online learners), sharing resources and centring learning dialogue in a 'third space' that is as equally accessible to all (I generally use virtual whiteboards: see the next section), creates many more opportunities for connection between learners, tutors and the learning content.

In practical terms, educators should think carefully about the arrangement of the physically gathered students and the camera and microphone placement for online learners. What perspective do the online students have? Do all the learners have similar or different views? Where is the tutor in relation to learners? As we noted earlier in relation to the paradigm shift of traditionally discriminated groups taking up a central role in disruptive inclusion, tweaking existing frameworks is likely to result in a swift (and probably unconscious) return to the status quo. Most Christian adult educators are conditioned by the teaching of physically present groups, meaning that unless online learners are prioritized the focus will probably swing back towards those physically gathered, creating a situation in which online learners can be treated as observers watching a session being delivered to others! To address this, wherever possible I deliver hybrid teaching 'in the round', with physically gathered students and tutor in a semi-circle facing the online students and camera on a screen, in effect creating a complete circle. In this sense, the space in the middle of the circle becomes the 'third space' to which all learners have as equal visual and audio access (as far as technology allows). Where this is not possible or appropriate, educators ' should think carefully about how hybrid learning sessions can be designed so as not to relegate online learners to observers or limit their participation.

Balancing structure and disruption

For some learners, even after multiple years' practice, participating in online learning can be an extremely disruptive experience for a variety of reasons. Therefore one of the challenges for educators is to not allow disruptions created by learning mode and content to snowball to overwhelming levels. One practice I have developed to avoid this is to structure online courses in a much more consistent way than their physically gathered equivalents. In physically gathered learning educators may purposefully vary the pattern and structure of delivery to keep it fresh and engaging. However, in online settings the disorientation caused by such variations, coupled with the potential disruption caused by online learning more generally, may simply be too much to allow some to fully engage with the material. To do all I can to ensure that online learners can focus as much of their energy as possible on including the potential disruptions of the course content, I employ a structure that underpins the values I wish to communicate and stick to it religiously! I currently employ the following colour-coded, four-level pattern in all asynchronous online courses:

A. Key questions and introduction
B. Core reading or watching
C. Interactive activities and tasks
D. Further/optional reading

Although by no means pedagogically groundbreaking, my experience is that the predictability and ease of access created by patterns like this allow learners to engage with more of the potential learning disruptions in the course content than otherwise would be the case.

The most basic point revealed by this use of structure is that online educators cannot simply assume that learning sessions originally designed to be delivered in physically gathered settings can be directly transferred to delivery in other modes. Perhaps the most obvious example of this is the difference in human attention span depending on the medium of the message. The recent popularity of podcasts has demonstrated that despite human attention spans generally getting shorter, where content is compelling to listeners (and interestingly, does not involve a screen!), learner focus can differ significantly (in quality and quantity) from live learning situations because learners have greater control over the time and setting in which they engage and can rewind and relisten if necessary.[13] Based on this, I now introduce each unit of online learning content with a short, informal (no more than ten minute) audio introduction. Its aim is to recreate the opening few minutes of scene setting and addressing of practical concerns that would normally be offered in a physically gathered classroom. Before learners engage with any of the content or attempt the activities, it gives me the opportunity to model how the various tasks and resources may connect and make some suggestions about how learners may choose to plot their path through the unit material. Learner feedback has been very positive and the overall quality of engagement has improved.

More generally, I have also found it very fruitful to discuss online learning modes directly with learners. In particular, I openly explain (and include in module information documents) not only what learners are expected to do, but why. For example, I articulate how formative tasks are designed to offer opportunities for learners to practise certain elements of any summative tasks. I also outline various options for accessing module resources and encourage discussion around how learners may benefit from engaging with resources in different ways. For example, where reading is offered in both e-book and paper form, I invite discussion about how 'readers may be more efficient and aware of their performance when reading from paper compared to screens'.[14] Although this raises lots of questions about how 'efficiency' and 'performance' are measured, it acts as a useful entry point for suggesting to learners that how they engage with the course content is just as important as the quality of the resources provided.

Another cause of disruption in online learning is the high level of self-awareness required. In physically gathered learning environments, learners are rarely forced (or even encouraged) to see themselves or relive their contributions to discussions (apart from psychologically!). Where learning happens both in online gathered mode via videoconferencing and asynchronously, it is far more difficult to avoid engaging with self. Whether this takes the form of seeing your own face in a video call, reading your own contributions to online discussion in forums or in chat apps, or just being expected to adopt a more self-directed and reflective approach, invariably the role of self is far more prominent in online than physically gathered learning.[15] Just as the majority of educators would employ in physically gathered classrooms, the extremes of this can be tempered by using a variety of foci in online settings. The most appropriate option for achieving this will depend on content, setting, number of learners, etc., but there are multiple ways to avoid unbroken visual focus on self and others, or even the lecturer's presentation, and offer learners both more variation and autonomous engagement during online learning.

To facilitate many of these, I find online interactive whiteboards (many freely available) an effective central focus for online learning – giving learners a chance to engage with each other's ideas in real time, rather than just stare at each other's faces (although this is not to dismiss the importance of this altogether). The more evolved of these platforms are able to host multiple, different file formats in the same space and facilitate independent movement and interaction, while also providing the tutor with the ability to bring all learners back to a specific location at particular moments. Technological advancements in the areas of both online gathered learning and virtual learning environments are improving all the time via the use of multimedia apps, telestrators, multiple cameras, whiteboard software, etc. As a result, online educators need to consider computer literacy an ongoing, essential component of their core skill development and practice, not just an optional extra.

Learner checklist

- How do you feel and respond at the beginning of online video gatherings (for whatever purpose)?
- What do you find are the biggest challenges of 'hosting' online learning or work conversations in your personal space?
- Have you ever participated in a gathering where some participants are gathered 'in person' and others are online? What are the opportunities and challenges of this mode?
- If you already have some experience, what are the most 'disruptive' elements of online learning for you? If not, what do you imagine would be most challenging?
- Think of one way in which a gathering/event happens in a mode that would not be your first preference. How does this shape your engagement? What practical steps can you take to help you (and others) get the most out of your ongoing participation?

Selah 8: Generative AI and CAL: can machines participate in disruptive inclusion?

As is true of all the issues raised in this chapter, there is insufficient space to offer a thorough analysis of the relationship between AI and CAL. However, as arguably the single most disruptive factor to formal education structures and practice since the printing press,[16] it would have been inappropriate (and hypocritical) to simply ignore it.

Up to this point, I have purposefully avoided references to intelligence (or, more colloquially, *cleverness*). Because many only associate these terms with academic success, they have become a popular way for those who have encountered difficulties learning in formal educational structures to exclude themselves from CAL. A common response from learners encouraged to press on or aspire to new levels of modes of CAL is, 'I don't think I'm intelligent enough to do that.' Recent developments in the use and profile of generative artificial intelligence have brought the question of intelligence front and centre. What really is intelligence? Who or what has it, or can develop it? What is its role in education and learning more broadly? AI algorithms have been working in the background of internet browsing for years, gathering information and using it to make decisions about users' potential interests for targeted advertising. Generative AI uses similar technology in a much more joined-up way (interesting, given disruptive inclusion's focus on connected learning!), consolidating information from vast numbers of sources, developing its ability and learning from its 'mistakes' to offer increasingly more accurate and well-expressed responses. Most recently, several companies have developed AI chat bots that can engage with humans in a conversational way, making it accessible to a much wider audience.

Going right back to the beginning, at the core of a disruptive-inclusive approach to CAL is the idea that 'learning breakthrough happens when someone dares to include something they had formerly considered unable to find God in or through.'[17] Whether they perceive AI as an obstacle or an opportunity, technologists and educationalists are almost unanimous in pointing out that attempts to ignore, avoid or circumvent AI are unrealistic. The proverbial genie is out of the bottle and there is no going back. Therefore many educational establishments and entire pedagogical systems are in the process of rethinking learning policy, curriculum and assessment, based not on whether to take AI into account, but how. This requires an understanding of what AI is good at (and will invariably get better at) and what is beyond its skillset (not just in its infancy, but probably always). In the world of theological education, AI is beginning to fuel an even more multi-layered conversation that involves Christian ethics, the relationship between academic qualification and character formation, as well as practical questions about effective curriculum delivery and assessment. At this early stage, one of disruptive inclusion's most effective contributions to the debate is to influence the fundamental questions being asked about the relationship between CAL and AI moving forward.

AI's primary advantage over the human brain is its ability to process huge quantities of information very quickly. It can locate, summarize and present an overview of information on almost any given topic in seconds. Although it does this without a sense of personal bias, it is important to keep in mind that when generative AI chat bots (such as ChatGPT or Google Bard, among others) are asked a question, the information available for them to draw on is limited (in time and scope) by the companies who run them and the 'training' they have received according to the aims, sometimes the objectives, and the financial goals of the same companies (and their investors!). In short, do not assume that generative AI is as unbiased as it may seem or claim to be. Its other strength is its ability to model how information can be presented in grammatically accurate and well-structured ways. In relation to disruptive inclusion, this means that AI can expose learners to new ideas and ways of expressing them that would potentially otherwise be beyond their scope, or even imagination.

If you ask an AI chat bot whether it has an opinion or can change its mind, it will offer a response similar to this: 'I don't possess consciousness or personal beliefs, so I don't have a mind to change. I operate based on the data and algorithms that were used to train me.'[18] This takes us straight to the elements of disruptive inclusion that will always remain squarely in the category of human learning. Because machines do not have a developing, personal position on any issue, nor personal experience to consolidate or challenge its own or others' views, AI cannot weigh bias or measure the influence of particular social, political or other factors on the information it shares. For example, if you ask an AI chat bot a question about what a particular Bible passage means, it will usually structure an answer like this: first, it will summarize its contents. Second (particularly if it finds information that others have deemed it controversial), it will list some of the most popular questions posed. Finally, it will list some of the interpretations of the passage it was able to find. Crucially, however, regardless of how practised AI becomes at sifting through this kind of information, because it cannot form a personal connection to any of it, nor connections with others who do, it will never be able to understand the importance of various social, ethnic, political and other variables, nor guide learners in recognizing their potential ethical and moral implications.[19]

Ultimately, because AI does not have consciousness or personal beliefs, it cannot experience or respond to disruption. It can highlight minority views and where particular pieces of information conflict with prevailing opinions (it has been told!), but it cannot respond to any question from a nuanced or holistic standpoint. AI cannot extend empathy or hospitality, it cannot express doubt or share information with humility or recognize how particular topics may be sensitive to specific individuals or groups. It cannot knowingly offer responses that go against the grain, actively choose to represent the underdog, or bear the personal cost of maintaining a particular position against the tide of prevailing opinion. In terms of Personal Construct Theory (see Chapter 3), AI bots can be thought of as building and continually adding to a kind of construct network based on the new information they receive, but their decisions on how new information is added, moved and removed from the network cannot take into account its emotional, relational or even physical implications. It cannot factor in the impact of grief, joy, excitement; it cannot weigh questions of life and death or form attachments to other living things. It may be able to describe or draw a sunset, but only based on information provided by others; it cannot be inspired by the feelings of staring at the horizon while holding hands with a friend. Ultimately, AI cannot learn according to disruptive inclusion's definition of connection: it cannot relationally engage with itself, humans, God or the wider universe because it can only collect, store and regurgitate information.

So, then, what are the key uses of generative AI in disruptive-inclusive CAL? Generative AI is an extremely useful tool for learners and educators wrestling with understanding and articulating what it means to be a Christian adult learner: highlighting the importance of reconnecting the *what*, *how* and *who* of learning. If AI can create a passable ten-minute sermon in a matter of seconds, what is the value of a relationally invested human using their time and energy to complete the same task? What is a preacher trying to achieve that cannot be replicated by AI? Or can it? One of the developing aims of my own practice is to use AI-generated responses to skill learners in asking better questions by finding the limits of its answers. For example, in courses with written assignments, AI-generated answers can be used to facilitate conversation about the qualities of strong responses. How did the bot interpret the question? What did it emphasize and leave out? Is all of the information accurate? Appropriate? Helpful? Contextualized? In the longer term, it is my hope that generative AI will force formal education systems to design courses and associated assessments that make it implausible and impossible for learners to directly submit the response of an AI bot as their own work. In the meantime, all of us will need to become more aware of, and more skilled at living in, the disruptive in-between.

The bigger picture: resisting the allure of 'new normal'

To this point it has been appropriate to focus on the practical details of how online learning influences the everyday experience and delivery of CAL in multiple ways. However, my final observation about the relationship between disruptive inclusion and online learning is a reflection on a much bigger picture. With a little hindsight, one of the things that has struck me about the first months of the Covid-19 pandemic is the volume of new vocabulary that was either introduced to the general population by authorities or created as a way of expressing the experience of living through it. From furlough to PPE and PCR tests, language that was previously specialist or restricted became everyday parlance.[20] My closing thoughts are based on a phrase that became extremely popular as the world grappled with the limitations placed on everyday life by Covid restrictions – 'new normal'.

When it became apparent that the pandemic's impact would be wider and longer lasting than many initially hoped, language of 'new normal' was 'deployed almost as a way to quell any uncertainty ushered in by the coronavirus'.[21] The World Economic Forum criticizes the framing of present reality as a progression from one state of familiar stability to another because:

> Far from describing the status quo, evoking the 'new normal' does not allow us to deal with the totality of our present reality. It first impedes personal psychological wellbeing, then ignores the fact that 'normal' is not working for a majority of society.[22]

In relation to disruptive inclusion, the concept of encouraging learners to journey from (presumably) an 'old normal' to a 'new normal' perpetuates the connection between learning progress and locating stability. At all costs, everything will be OK if learners can ignore, avoid or overcome the disruptions of the uncertain *here* and get to *somewhere* (really, anywhere) static and secure, as opposed to learning how to optimally function in unknown and unpredictable conditions. Perhaps, therefore, the most fundamental question raised by the Covid-19 pandemic is not a desperate quest to inaugurate a 'new normal', but whether disruptive inclusion might be a means by which this period of turbulence could invite a much broader valuing of instability in the ongoing development of CAL.

Many attempts to express the way in which people experienced the pandemic take us to the language of abuse and trauma. In her work on the subject, pastoral theologian Barbara Glasson beautifully articulates the paradigm shift I am suggesting here:

> The call to make places of stability in which there is safe enough space for stories to be told, appropriate boundaries negotiated, diversity honoured and creative relationships formed, is not simply so that damaged people can have a chance to flourish but so that the whole of life can be different ... We will be given a clue as to how to transform our society and our earth so that we can all live in a different way.[23]

Glasson argues that the motivation to create safe spaces for stories to be told is not simply so that those involved can find a way back to where they came from (whether physically or figuratively): in many ways, this is impossible. Rather, the suggestion is that the only path to wider and ongoing transformation, the way to any form of 'new', requires completely shedding the idea that any such thing as 'normal' exists. Thinking back to our earlier foray into Greek philosophy, maybe Heraclitus' claim that change is the only constant is the only 'normal' CAL should aim to embrace?

Referring back to Hull's work one final time, he expresses the ultimate goal of CAL as: 'More aware of itself, more coherent, more integrated, more supple, readier for further change and better related to the reality which faith confronts today.'[24] Rather than transferring from one learning approach to another, what if the lessons learned during the height of Covid-19 could function as the basis for a greater natural dynamism and readiness for further change, so that future disruptions can be more easily embraced as integral to pedagogical understanding and practice rather than as momentary obstacles to be overcome? What if the development and acceleration towards online learning during, and as a result of, the pandemic is not just a blip to get over and return to something or somewhere more solidly predictable, but an invitation to recognize that the leaders in CAL are the early adopters; those willing to trial new approaches and ideas before it is even clear whether and how they might be useful? In other words, my challenge to my fellow Christian adult learners and educators is: Can we cultivate the dynamism and agility that will allow us to move from reactive to responsive and be better positioned to model good practice whatever future disruptions present – whether personal, community, societal or global? And can a disruptive-inclusive understanding and techniques help us to do it?

The World Economic Forum's earlier comment argued that stability (or at least the semblance of it) is far more accessible to those with financial, political and social resource. In other words, the poor and disenfranchised (both globally and within individual cultures) feel the greatest negative impact when systems and structures are slow to respond. The demands of anti-racist and anti-sexist campaigners (such as Black Lives Matter and #MeToo) are ultimately about transformative learning and a call for disruptive learning experiences to critically undermine central, underlying structures. Those who demand change recognize that learning according to any 'old normal', or fashioning of a 'new normal' according to the existing rules or frameworks, will be incapable of breaking down the brutal and pervasive inequalities that suppress the voices of those continually pushed to the edges; something entirely different is needed.

Perhaps the most common mistake is thinking that Jesus' sheepfold is static or concretely defined. Do I use my privilege to pin it down (in either my imagination or lived experience) when its constant shifting becomes inconvenient to me? What might it look like for the future of CAL to be shaped by learners and educators whose bodies, or social or geographic locations, do not afford them the opportunity to avoid disruption, the refugees of war and of the Church who are now best practised in navigating disruptive-inclusive theological learning in our communities? What might be the results if we leave the post Covid-19 desire for 'normal' deliberately unsatisfied and instead continually push out further into the life of God only experienced at edge-places? If any of this is possible, even in some small measure, as the closing lines of Hull's final publication suggest, perhaps the potential benefits of disruptive inclusion extend far beyond individual Christian adult learners or even the Church, and might somehow contribute to 'the alleviation of the suffering of the world'?[25]

Questions/activities

- Have a play around with a generative AI chat bot. Ask it some questions. Ask it to improve or define some of its answers. How do you find this experience?
- Do you think there is a limit to how 'online' CAL, and Christian faith more broadly, should become? Are there elements of faith and practice (particularly CAL) that cannot be replicated virtually?
- What kind of 'new normal' do you think CAL should be moving towards? What lessons do we need to learn from the pandemic and its acceleration of online learning and communication?

Notes

1 John M. Hull, *What Prevents Christian Adults from Learning?* (London: SCM Press, 1985), p. 15.

2 For more on the potential relationship between the Apostle Paul and distance learning: https://faithandleadership.com/what-paul-can-teach-us-about-distance-education (accessed 8.11.2023).

3 During the pandemic, University of the Arts, London, shared some of their experience of what they called 'desituated' learning, with access to shared, physical settings: https://teaching.london.edu/exchange/the-importance-of-presence/ (accessed 8.11.2023). Although not from a faith perspective, their thoughts overlap with many themes in Christian theology such as incarnation and transubstantiation. For some interesting discussions of the relationship between CAL and online learning, see: Ros Stuart-Buttle, *Virtual Theology, Faith and Adult Education: An interruptive pedagogy* (Newcastle upon Tyne: Cambridge Scholars Publishing, 2013) and Jennifer J. Roberts, 'Online learning as a form of distance education: linking formation learning in theology to the theories of distance education', *HTS: Theological Studies* 75:1 (2019), pp. 1–9.

4 See YPulse, 'Gen Z & millennials are generations of researchers, and these are their top learning resources', *YPulse* (14 December 2021), https://www.ypulse.com/article/2021/12/14/gen-z-millennials-are-generations-of-researchers-and-these-are-their-top-learning-resources/ (accessed 31.07.2023).

5 Angela Williams Gorrell, *Always On: Practicing faith in a new media landscape* (Grand Rapids, MI: Baker Academic, 2019), pp. 48 and 65.

6 Perhaps, however, it is better understood as the displacement of learning disruption, given that that which formerly defined the familiar and comfortable is now forced into a different function, redefining it as disruptive?

7 Williams Gorrell, *Always On*, p. 3.

8 Daniel Kilvington and John Price, 'Tackling social media abuse? Critically assessing English football's response to online racism', *Communication & Sport* 7:1 (2019), pp. 64–79.

9 The British Academy, 'The COVID decade: Understanding the long-term societal impacts of COVID-19', *The British Academy* (March 2021), available at: https://www.thebritishacademy.ac.uk/documents/3238/COVID-decade-understanding-long-term-societal-impacts-COVID-19.pdf, p. 93 (accessed 31.07.2023).

10 Just one interesting example: Nalita James and Virginie Thériault, 'Adult education in times of the COVID-19 pandemic: Inequalities, changes, and resilience', *Studies in the Education of Adults* 52:2 (2020), pp. 129–33.

11 Williams Gorrell, *Always On*, p. 76.

12 Eugene L. Lowry, *The Homiletical Plot: The sermon as narrative art form* (Louisville, KY: Westminster John Knox Press, 2001).

13 Ranieri & Co., 'Changing Attention Span and What it Means for Content' (19 January 2021), available at: https://www.ranieriand

co.com/post/changing-attention-span-and-what-it-means-for-content-in-2021 (accessed 31.07.2023).

14 Virginia Clinton, 'Reading from paper compared to screens: a systematic review and meta-analysis', *Journal of Research in Reading* 42:2 (2019), pp. 288–325, p. 288.

15 Although certain platforms do allow users to turn off 'self-view'.

16 Rose Luckin, 'Yes, AI could profoundly disrupt education. But maybe that's not a bad thing', *The Guardian* (14 July 2023), available at: https://www.theguardian.com/commentisfree/2023/jul/14/ai-arti ficial-intelligence-disrupt-education-creativity-critical-thinking (accessed 31.07.2023).

17 Hull, *What Prevents*, p. 18.

18 Response from ChatGPT, 3 August 2023.

19 I encourage you to give this a go. Choose a passage and ask several chat bots the same question. You can then ask follow-up questions, asking the bots to develop their answers in particular areas.

20 King's College London, '#CORONASPEAK – the language of Covid-19 goes viral', *King's College London* (16 April 2020), available at: https://www.kcl.ac.uk/news/coronaspeak-the-language-of-covid-19-goes-viral (accessed 31.07.2023).

21 Chime Asonye, 'There's nothing new about the "new normal". Here's why', *World Economic Forum* (5 June 2020), available at: https://www.weforum.org/agenda/2020/06/theres-nothing-new-about-this-new-normal-heres-why/ (accessed 31.07.2023).

22 Asonye, 'There's nothing new'.

23 Barbara Glasson, *A Spirituality of Survival: Enabling a response to trauma and abuse* (London: Continuum, 2009), pp. 110–11.

24 Hull, *What Prevents*, p. 82.

25 John M. Hull, *Towards the Prophetic Church: A Study of Christian Mission* (London: SCM Press, 2014), p. 248.

Epilogue: Always Under Construction?

At the time of writing, Antoni Gaudí's magnum opus, La Sagrada Família in Barcelona, is due to be completed in 2026, 142 years after construction first began. However, its potential completion has sparked a contentious debate that introduces this final part of our explorations in disruptive-inclusive CAL. While some insist that Gaudí always intended the building to be finished, others suggest that its completion would violate the most basic feature of its design. In essence, the argument is whether being constantly 'under construction' has become a fundamental part of the building's architectural identity. As Rowan Moore claimed in 2011, once La Sagrada Família is no longer a 'romantic ruin', it will be, in fact, something else entirely.[1] Without Gaudí available to directly guide development (he was killed by a tram in 1926), is the fullest character of La Sagrada Família maintained by not finishing it and allowing it, purposefully and perpetually, to linger in the in-between?

As unsatisfying as a deliberate sense of unfinishedness may be, it resonates strongly with disruptive inclusion's basic claim that CAL should not be reduced to a single metaphor or practised according to a single set of rules or guidelines. Hull's ultimate pedagogical aim was that learners access a 'trans-ideological' viewpoint[2] or the process of constantly 'plac[ing] a new and self-conscious frame of reference around everything and thus to arrive at a new stage of coherence and control.'[3] Therefore Hull never wanted CAL to hold fast to his (or any other) learning framework, but his work aimed at supporting an ongoing process of transformation that, in turn, makes learners yet 'more vulnerable to further trans-formations'.[4] By Hull's own admission, for his approach to CAL to be proved successful, by definition it must continually transcend any set boundaries or descriptions that attempt to define it. In this way, dynamic and emergent are good descriptions, not only of healthy CAL progress, but also of Hull's and my various attempts to define and explain it. So where does this leave us?

It leaves us in a position where effective disruptive inclusion will keep growing and morphing in response to changing conditions and developing demands. As we considered through the lens of pilgrimage, CAL is about getting better at being underway; recognizing and responding to disruption where it presents itself. Therefore, in closing, to begin the next phase of debate I leave you with some of the remaining questions I have about how various areas of existing or developing disruption (in both the Church and the world more broadly) might benefit from disruptive-inclusive understanding and practice.

Questions/activities

- How might disruptive inclusion influence the kinds of people we trust to fill positions of leadership, both in the Church and in other areas of influence?
- What character traits do disruptive-inclusive leaders display?
- What types of education and training might be needed to grow your answers to the previous question?
- How can we best support and encourage those who have experienced disruption in the form of violence or abuse?
- How does disruptive inclusion influence the potential responses of Christians to the climate crisis?
- What kinds of learning skills and techniques will equip the Church to respond to the deterioration of the planet in transformative and sustained ways?

- Where might disruptive inclusion be most effectively practised in your own learning? What practical steps are you going to take to make this a reality?
- Where might disruptive inclusion be most effectively practised in wider learning contexts in which you participate? What practical steps are you going to take to make this a reality?
- Summarize the potential of disruptive inclusion to (or for!) the following people:
  - Your next door neighbour
  - Your church leader(s)
  - Your small group/prayer group/Bible study
  - Formal theological training

Notes

1 Rowan Moore, 'Sagrada Familia: Gaudí's cathedral is nearly done, but would he have liked it?', *The Guardian* (24 April 2015), available at: https://www.theguardian.com/artanddesign/2011/apr/24/gaudi-sagrada-familia-rowan-moore (accessed 31.07.2023).

2 John M. Hull, *What Prevents Christian Adults from Learning?* (London: SCM Press, 1985), p. 72.

3 Hull, *What Prevents*, p. 34.

4 Hull, *What Prevents*, p. 34.

Index of Biblical References

Old Testament

New Testament

Index of Names and Subjects